PROPHETS AND PROFITS — Architects of New India

Rao Kolluru

PROPHETS AND PROFITS — Architects of New India

Cover and interior illustrations in part by Claire Simon, Chitra Ramcharandas

ISBN 978-0-9749746-9-9

Library of Congress Control Number: 2015904374
Bioxy Source, Montclair, New Jersey

Other Books by Rao Kolluru (partial list)

Business, Science, Spirit — the *Tao of Dow*:

- Creative Minds
  for Innovation and Leadership (upcoming)
- Begin Anew
  Re-setting Your Mind's Odometer [00000]
- Spiritual Entrepreneuring
  Pathway to Lasting Success
- River of a Thousand Tales
  Encounters with Spirit, Reflections from Science

Environment, Health & Safety:

- Risk Assessment and Management Handbook
  for Environmental, Health, and Safety Professionals
  (McGraw-Hill, New York)
- Environmental Strategies Handbook
  A Guide to Effective Policies and Practices
  (McGraw-Hill, New York)

Workshops and Keynotes are shown near the end of the book.

Dedication

This book is dedicated to **YOU**: Architect of New India

Feel free to write your name here:

____

Websites: ProphetsandProfits.com
HimarestGroup.com

Lead me... O God
From the unreal to the Real
From darkness to Light
From death to Immortality

Brihadaranyaka Upanishad

Contents

Acknowledgments

When I sat down to reflect on those who have most influenced my thinking about business and corporate society, it was **Peter Drucker** who came readily to mind. That was no accident. In my first years in America, I took a management course with Professor Drucker and had to write a paper on Tomorrow's Managers. Knowing little about today's managers, let alone tomorrow's, I nevertheless wrote the required mid-term paper: *Demands on Tomorrow's Managers.* I have saved that paper to this day, which reflects not only what the professor thought of the paper but also his sense of humor.

"Dear Mr. Rao: Wonderful!...[but] you lean too heavily on the writings of one dubious authority, and an opinionated one at that [referring to himself]. This is a first rate job... it made me feel very good. A for paper and term."

After I finished writing the manuscript of this book I went back and reread that paper. Many of the ideas in this book were outlined in that paper, written decades ago. A testament, I suppose, to the endurance of fundamental principles even as business climate and practices continue to evolve.

Thanks to Columbia University Business School — Chazen Institute's *India Business Initiative,* and its Global Insights program. Thanks also to New York University Stern School of Business for similar initiatives. Individual speakers are referenced on the following pages.

I learned much from my colleagues at American Cyanamid (now part of Pfizer) and other organizations, big and small. And from my students in business and environment-health risk management courses.

My spiritual roots go back to my legendary grandmother, although she would have been surprised to hear it. In recent times, my spiritual pilgrimage took me to the sages and savants in the Himalayas and elsewhere, including Chinmaya and Ramakrishna-Vivekananda missions. Trekking the banks of the Ganges in the Himalayan foothills, I was fortunate to meet Rishis and Yogis who freely shared their wisdom. They lived simply, eschewing their possessions, even their names. These sources, therefore, must remain nameless.

Many thanks to the following who reviewed one or more incarnations of the manuscript and shared their valuable insights: Tony D. Kamath, Ennala Ramcharandas, Martyn Roetter, Robert Schwartz, Arlene Teck, Montclair Write Group. Ed Charlton of Scribbulations reviewed and speeded up the production of this book to place it in your hands just in time.

Moreover, it is my honor and privilege to receive guidance from the virtual board of directors of this enterprise — Buddha, Krishna, Chanakya — on call 24/7.

****

How to approach this adventure?

You'll no doubt find some of the scenery strange. We jump from theme to theme seemingly at random, sowing confusion. You'll soon discern a method to this madness, though. What is an adventure anyway without detours, surprises, challenges? Yes, this is an eclectic mix of business and purpose, exploring and experimenting, dreaming and doing.

We'll look back in history to see where we're coming from — and look ahead to the history we're now making. We'll peer into the roles and goals of individuals and organizations: business enterprises, educational institutions, governments. You'll encounter bold ideas along the way, including ideas for innovative ventures. And get acquainted with simple yet powerful ***Triple-Pro™*** model, pathway to *Prosperity Summit.*

Please remain open to new signs and symbols — excursions into worldly ideas of business and wealth, as well as other-worldly parables that convey universal messages. This is not only a book to read, but also an adventure of discovery and transformation.

You can choose between two paths to travel: follow the chapters step by step — seeing how India came to be, discerning a vision of New India along the way; or **fly directly to the top of the mountain** and meet with the prophets Buddha, Krishna, Chanakya (toward the end of this book) — and come back to the beginning.

Either way, we'll experience the Prosperity Summit together — our world will never be the same again. This I promise. RK

****

Prologue: the Vision

Rediscovering our roots, Reclaiming our riches

Namaste, Greetings

I am delighted to have your company in this grand adventure. It will change the way we see riches, India, ourselves.

We have the honor of being guided in this quest by three of the greatest prophets, leaders, and mentors of all time: Buddha, Krishna, Chanakya.

We are also privileged to be joined by *entrepreneur-philanthropists* in reinventing a free and prosperous India — and a Peaceful and Prosperous World.

- For entrepreneurs, business students/faculty, industry leaders, government policy makers: You will encounter a bold vision of India — ideas to reinvent an India that once was, and could be again. Here is a springboard to becoming more purposeful and creative — to build shared prosperity
- For those new to India (even if you visited before) this journey will reveal the different depths of a nation at crossroads. Executives of for-profit and nonprofit enterprises: You'll feel the power of Triple-Pro™ in expressing your purpose — what you stand for, what makes you stand out — to build an enduring legacy

  Along the way we will:

1. Discover India's hidden assets, heighten individual performance, conceive ideas for innovative enterprises
2. Guide American/global companies to participate in India's success; help Indian companies connect with global markets — investing in *socially uplifting and economically attractive* ventures
3. Advance strategic partnership between the two largest English-speaking democracies across the planet with complementary interests — and shape the 21st Century with a democratic alternative to China

Foreigners need to learn to navigate the *crowds, chaos, complexity* that is India — a window to the emerging markets and economies. Executives who tackle such challenges are destined to succeed anywhere — perhaps one reason why many Indians coming to America excel.

Since India was in a limbo for a millennium, it faces formidable challenges. But India's renaissance is pivotal to a prosperous and sustainable planet — one in five is from this region. Global companies and executives that help India make the quantum leap into the 21st century with patience and perseverance will make an epic difference.

Just a generation ago, China seemed hopelessly mired in ideology and poverty. And Brazil was struggling with intractable inflation, known as a *country of the future, and always will be.* Now China has the second largest economy, Brazil the seventh largest.

The Good News is, we don't have to wait a generation to see a new India. It is happening NOW — India is already the 10th largest economy with a critical mass of global companies. We can enjoy the power of prosperity and the joy of being part of a *higher purpose* right now, not in some distant future. We'd not only plant the seeds for a better tomorrow, but also get to taste the fruits today.

*

On call 24/7 to guide us are Buddha, Krishna and Chanakya who marry wisdom and wit, vision and values, prosperity and pathways:

> **Buddha** (563-483 BC), the prince who becomes a prophet, sets out on a mission to find the causes of suffering and discovers the path of freedom. Prophet and visionary, Buddha was the first *Global Mind* that foreshadowed the Global Economy more than two thousand years ago. He points the *Way*, sheds light on the path, but doesn't take you there. He lets you work your own way through.
>
> **Krishna** (legendary *avatar)*, illuminates the nature of dharma and karma, victory and defeat, to his protégé poised for a battle. He displays the spirit of performing one's duty with *whole mind* regardless of personal rewards. And reveals the nature of our personas centered in three tendencies: *Sattva* light, *Rajas* action, *Tamas* inaction.
>
> **Chanakya** (350-283 BC), chief architect of a united India under Maurya Dynasty, is called "Indian Machiavelli" although Chanakya preceded Machiavelli by eighteen centuries. World's first political economist and management guru, Chanakya wrote the first book on economics: *Arthashastra,* a treatise on wealth and the art of government (similar in a way to Adam Smith's seminal *Wealth of Nations*).

We'll soon have the great fortune of meeting our prophets for Questions & Answers. Feel free to call on them whenever you want to. If you prefer, fly over and meet the prophets now and participate in the conversations. Why not also invite them to be on your *virtual board of directors*?

Our adventure begins with the *Beginner's Mind* story. You'll learn to *initialize* your mind [00000] and the mindset of your enterprise — and experience the awareness and wonder that come with Beginner's Mind.

Steve Jobs, legendary co-founder of Apple, wandered across India in 1974 as a teenager, becoming a Buddhist. On his return to Silicon Valley in California, he launched a series of innovations, including the highly successful iPhone. (You may even be reading this book on one of his devices.) Jobs credited his leaps of intuition to Beginner's Mind.

*

In the foreword of the highly informative volume, ***REIMAGINING INDIA: Unlocking the Potential of Asia's Next Superpower*** (edited by McKinsey & Company, 2013), Dominic Barton and Noshir Kaka write: "An abundance of life — vibrant, chaotic, and tumultuous — has long been India's foremost asset... the idea of India itself has inherent power."

I couldn't agree more.

Rao Kolluru, Planet Earth 2014

Coincidentally, as this book is going into publication, the 1.2 billion people of the world's largest democracy are enjoying an orderly transition from a dysfunctional government, a rare political triumph indeed. Narendra Modi has become India's new Prime Minister. The people of India, overseas Indian community, and friends around the world are counting on him to perform an economic miracle. This is India's Century, they proclaim — as envisioned in this book. His success will brighten the future of not only India but the whole planet. We wish him well.

00000000000000000000000000000000000

DAY 0. Begin with the *Beginner's Mind*

00000000000000000000000000000000000

The Chairman of *Enlightened Enterprise* in *Rich Land* sensed the need to replenish his spiritual capital and climb new heights. Having heard about a unique retreat, he made arrangements to make the pilgrimage — and invited the President of the company and a Director of the Board to join him. Together they journeyed to the monastery nestled in the foothills of *Himarest™*.

The monk in charge of business education welcomed the executives, who seemed eager to be enlightened at once. Instead, the monk assigned them manual tasks in the garden. This day, ***Day Zero,*** as he called it, would be devoted to emptying the mind. The monk advised them to "*Put your mind where your hand is*. Pay full attention to the plants and the bees and the flowers. Observe total silence for the rest of the day, feel free to share the silence." With these words, he withdrew to his quarters.

The executives felt annoyed at having to wait another day, but went about their duties in silence.

The next morning, the monk greeted the pilgrims: "Namaste, please join me for a cup of tea on the veranda." While they settled on a mat laid out for them, a disciple came out carrying a teapot and three glass cups on a tray.

One cup was turned upside down. The second cup contained some liquid. The third cup was empty. The monk picked up the teapot and, slowly and deliberately, started pouring the tea on to the first upside-down cup. The tea flowed over the cup onto the tray while the pilgrims watched, perplexed. The monk then poured tea into the second cup; the tea became mixed with the liquid already in the cup, changing color, overflowing. Finally, he picked up the empty cup and poured tea into it and started savoring the tea.

The monk then paused a moment, and looked at the pilgrims.

The chairman spoke first, delighted by his epiphany. “I see what you’re doing. The upside-down cup represents a person with closed mind, not willing to listen and learn, not open to new ideas. ‘Don’t confuse me with facts’ kind of guy. I see them all the time.”

“The second cup has liquid in it, so whatever you pour into that cup is modified by what’s already in it,” the President weighed in. “I suppose this means what we already know or believe, our experiences and prejudices, color whatever else we see and hear. Anything new is colored by what we already know and believe.”

“Only because the third cup was empty and open to receive was it able to accept the tea *as is* — presumably a metaphor for someone open to listen and learn, like a child,” the Director added.”Thank you, guruji, for presenting such a profound lesson with such a simple experiment.”

The monk nodded with a grin, pleased with the understanding.

“Yes, the *empty* cup symbolizes what we call the *Beginner’s Mind*.”

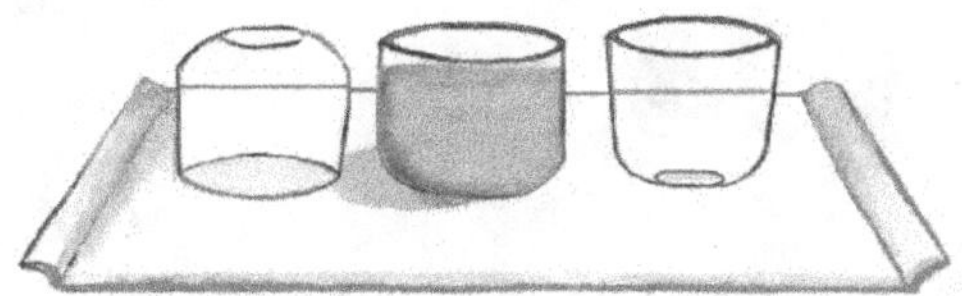

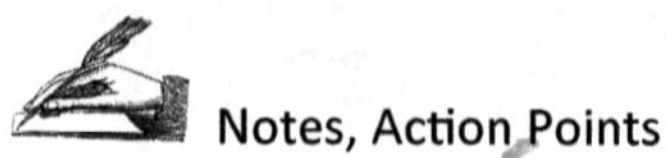

Notes, Action Points

1. Are You Ready?

Once upon a time, a monk by the name of Vivek crossed the oceans from Ancient Land to Rich Land. There he gave a series of lectures on mind and matter, dharma and karma, unity in diversity — and met with leading citizens. One of them, Mr. Richfeller, was reluctant to meet with the monk, but was persuaded by his friends to call on him.

The monk greeted Richfeller warmly with a cup of tea and said: "I understand you have amassed great fortune through your business enterprise. You fulfilled your dharma as a brilliant entrepreneur. Now go forth and share the gifts bestowed on you."

Annoyed by this gratuitous advice, Richfeller walked out. But he returned to the monk a few days later and said, "I've given away most of my wealth to children's health and education. I hope you're happy and grateful."

"On the contrary, it is you who should be grateful for the privilege," the monk responded.

∞

This book is about the privilege and challenge of building a free, fair and prosperous India — to soar again, to become the Everest of the new world.

Once a prosperous and vibrant civilization, India's scientific and spiritual discoveries — zero to infinity, yoga to chess, karate to kamasutra — enrich our lives today, everyday.

As stewards of that great civilization, let us rekindle that spirit. I invite you to join me in this grand adventure — **be the *Architects of a New India*.**

GREAT AGAIN!

How did the richest nation become the poorest? What next?

The other day I was in a meeting at Columbia University in New York on the changing world dynamics and the converging East and West. What a Nobel Prize economist said intrigued me. I had, of course, known that India and China were great ancient civilizations — but didn't fully appreciate that India was the wealthiest nation in the world through much of human history. As I subsequently learned, from around 1000 BC to mid-1700s AD, India accounted for 25% of total world GDP (Gross Domestic Product, proxy of wealth) — and a third of the world's wealth at times, similar to that of America in its heyday over the last half century.

Yes, great once, I thought, but what about now? How is it that the richest nation came to be one of the poorest? Why did India fall into an abyss for so long, despite periods of grandeur as during the reign of Mughal emperor Akbar? What lessons can we glean from the past to guide us now? I posed this question at a Rotary International gathering in Hyderabad and expressed disappointment at India's weak economic growth. A journalist in the audience protested: How can you say that, we achieved 6% growth!

Indeed that was impressive compared to the post-independence *License Raj*. India has made impressive strides in education (Indian Institutes of Technology, IITs), software/information technology (IT), telecom, pharma-medical, atomic energy, aerospace, as well as democratic freedoms. But I was reflecting on the India that once was, and could be, again. Earlier, in 1995, I was a guest speaker at Peking University Center for Sustainable Development and witnessed what China had achieved in just a few years. (That occasion was rendered all the more memorable when my hosts took me in a limo to the newly opened McDonald's.)

Milestones in India's Odyssey

3300 BC-1300 BC Indus Valley and Harappan Civilizations
1700 BC-500 BC Vedic Age, formative period of new Indian civilization
500 BC-700 AD Maurya/Ashoka-Gupta Golden Age (India largely unified)

~1000 BC-1750 AD Wealthiest or near-wealthiest nation

1947: Political independence from Britain, geographic divisions, Jawaharlal Nehru first Prime Minister 1947-64
1950s: Secular Democracy, socialism, *License Raj* taking hold
1960s-70s: First Green Revolution, jump in professional careers in US (Immigration and Nationality Act of 1965 abolished national quotas)

1990s: Economic reforms launched in 1991 triggered by crisis, IT expansion spurred by Y2K *Millennium Bug,* fiber optic networks, globalization
1990-2010: IT/Telecom, pharma/medical, frugal engineering (Mars orbiter) Conspicuous socio-economic transformation
2010-2030: Political freedom to economic and intellectual freedoms, climbing the Prosperity Summit to *Second Golden Age*

Nehru's vision of a democratic, independent nation led to the establishment of IITs and later the Indian Institutes of Management (IIMs). But his "socialist" policies caused economic stagnation giving rise to a sense of cynicism. In the 1990s, thanks to favorable developments in America, Indian entrepreneurs came to see new possibilities, and some have experienced economic prosperity. To let some people get rich first seemed a better idea than keeping everyone poor. Many Indians have come to feel that India should be more like China with its single-minded devotion to development.

Even with the slow start, India has experienced more socio-economic transformation in the past two decades (1990-2010) than in the preceding ten centuries. But most Indians, and foreigners, do not yet see India on top of the prosperity summit.

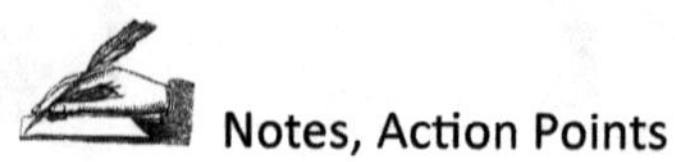

Notes, Action Points

2. My Path of Discovery: Buddha, Krishna, Chanakya

My roots are in India, my branches are spread out in America. My father crossed the oceans to study medicine at Edinburgh University, and worked as a surgeon with the British India medical service. Back in south India, he bicycled to work and practiced integrated medicine (his American car with driver often following him at a discreet distance). My religious grandmother would not let my mother go to English schools — so she studied Sanskrit in ashrams and became a Sanskrit scholar. My mother and father met at a hospital in Madras during the delivery of my aunt's child.

When I was a student in north India many a monsoon ago, I went trekking along the banks of the hallowed Ganges streaming from the Himalayas. I retraced the path of Buddha near Varanasi (Kashi, Banaras) and Sarnath, following in his footsteps — sometimes swimming along with crocodiles that were as ancient as the Ganges itself.

Later I reached the arena of Krishna and *Bhagavad Gita*. The Gita is unique in that it fuses the eternal with the ephemeral, reflection with action — in the middle of a battlefield. It portrays the moral dilemmas of battles between forces of good and evil that inhabit the human mind.

I first encountered Chanakya in history books. The more I got to know him the more fascinating he turned out to be: architect of a unified India under Chandragupta Maurya (340BC-298BC, Ashoka's grandfather) and amazingly versatile — cash streams to poison pills to forest resources. Though not a traditional prophet, his stratagems turned out to be prophetic.

*

I had the privilege of meeting another "prophet" Peter Drucker early in life. Soon after I came to America as a teenager, I had to write a paper as an MBA student for the legendary professor. It was about *Demands on Tomorrow's Managers*. I knew little of yesterday's managers let alone tomorrow's but, as I started writing the paper, dormant ideas bubbled up and — merging with Drucker's ideas on *corporate society* — coalesced bit by bit into my first opus.

I was flattered when I got the paper back with Professor Drucker's comments:

"Dear Mr. Rao: Wonderful... [but] you lean too heavily on the

> writings of one dubious authority, and an opinionated one at that [referring to himself] ... It made me feel very good. 'A' for paper and term"

I revisited that paper, written once upon a time — before the Internet, globalization, smartphones — pondering what we seek today from business enterprises and the people who run them — from you and me?

First, a few words about my predilections.

I didn't know what I wanted to be when I grew up, so ended up studying pre-medicine, science, engineering, business. My graduate education was mostly in New York: MBA at New York University, doctorate in science at Columbia University. I worked with global companies, wrote books, taught part-time — across four decades.

All along there was a nagging feeling that something was missing, I was *not fully present*. I didn't feel the ***power of purpose*** and functioned below my potential with little sense of fulfillment and joy. I received abundant love growing up, but no career guidance except what I observed. Early in life I did have a grand vision of what the world ought to be, but not a clue as to my part in it.

I had my moments — as when one of my handbooks on environmental risks and strategic management turned out to be a best seller in Japan, celebrated at a party in Tokyo's Ginza. The thrill of speaking in Moscow's Red Square is still fresh in my mind. I was apprehensive talking about capitalism in the former Soviet Union, but the Russian audience was curious and extremely friendly — no doubt the first time they heard an Indian visiting from America talk about capitalism in Red Square.

This book grew out of my experiences and aspirations. It is about PROSPERITY, not only money. It reflects what I learned from my successes and, more importantly, from my mistakes. It seems some of life's lessons can only be learned from mistakes, accidents, adversity. In this my *Third Act* (nicknamed *Urban Monk* by a newspaper) — as I turn to Buddha, Krishna, Chanakya consciously — the prophets began to emerge from the shadows and take hold at many levels. I'd ask: What would they see, say, do?

3. The Prophets speak on Profits and Prosperity — The Tao of Dow

Wealth destroys the greedy and the ignorant —
yet not those who seek Prosperity **(Dhammapada)**

From the Krishna avatar we learn that prosperity is inherent in creation, that we need a *prosperous mindset* to enjoy a life of abundance. Chanakya tells us that kings (visionary leaders) are the fountainheads of wealth; it is their duty to engage the earth and foster abundant riches.

What about Buddha, the prince who became a pauper, *bikshu*? Since he chose poverty, what did Buddha have to say about prosperity? He considered wealth a natural byproduct of *Right Intent* and *Right Effort*.

A banker-disciple asked Buddha: Enlightened One, how can I travel the path of dharma, my business itself is money? The Buddha replied in his characteristic tone: Just as a bee takes nectar without harming the flowers while pollinating and benefiting the plant, so should you make a profit without harming the customer. Right purpose points you in the right direction, right effort gets you there.

But *money alone is not prosperity.* The **golden rule of prosperous life** means that you:

....

- ✓ **earn sufficient material wealth to lead a happy, dignified life**
- ✓ **feel that you have *earned* it by doing the right thing, by the sweat of your brow**
- ✓ **enjoy good reputation in the community as an honorable person, and**
- ✓ **know, as you near the exit, that you have lived a good life and are leaving a worthy legacy that will live on.**

....

So *prosperity is not only wealth but a way of life — and death*. We should live well to die well. In some traditions people "die" at age 60, renouncing their physical possessions, even their names. They start anew on *Day Zero* [00000]. (You'll find more on this in conversation with Buddha toward the end of this book.)

Buddha's golden rule of prosperous life implies freedom — freedom to build and enjoy wealth. The business enterprise may well be the most powerful invention for creating material wealth.

But is Buddha still relevant in this *lean and mean* business world? YES. I believe the Buddha was the first to recognize universal kinship: that everything and everyone is connected — people, animals, trees, bees — in an interdependent web of life. His ***Global Mind*** preceded the Global Economy by 25 centuries!

Now that we have Buddha's golden rule of prosperity, what is the **golden rule of profits**? How do you create value for customers and communities to enjoy immediate and lasting competitive edge?

+ **purpose** — what you stand for, what makes you stand out?
+ **novelty** — innovative products, practices
+ **cost —** pricing advantage from efficiency, productivity, speed
+ **quality** — enduring reputation as superior global brand

Let us pause now for a breather

Find a quiet corner. Sit or stand up straight, as if pushing up the sky

Take in a S L O W, D E E P breath through the nose paying attention (breathe deep down to the abdomen like filling a glass with water)

Hold it for 3 or 4 seconds. Let go s l o w l y, consciously (through nose/mouth).

Pause. Resume normal breathing with whole mind-body smile :--)

Art of Quiescence, Observing, Listening

From time to time, intentionally give up talking for an hour or even a day.

Half-second rule: When you are in a conversation, let there be an interlude (half second) after the other person stops talking before you start talking. If there are two people, talk less than half the time.

Invitation to Entrepreneur-Philanthropists to build Buddha World Heritage Center

Imagine with eyes closed. Fly back 25 centuries to the Himalayan foothills. Join the Buddha and his entourage of monks in saffron robes. Walk in Buddha's footsteps along the Ganges, indulging in his folksy tales.

Imagine the greatest cultural and spiritual enterprise rising, shaped by artisans from around the world. Catch a glimpse of the living monument to Buddha — echoing his teachings, his wit and wisdom.

A Million Millionaires Prosperous?

Free markets and global trade have spawned entrepreneurs and economic prosperity across wide swaths of the planet, lifting a billion people from the shackles of poverty, especially in China (600 million) and India (300 million) — a most underreported story. Millions have been catapulted into the ranks of millionaires. By 2010, the number of *dollar millionaires* (individuals with assets of USD one million or more, excluding one's home) reached 11 million. The world is adding a million millionaires a year. (One million USD, or US$, is about six crore Indian Rupees, INR)

The performance of business is usually validated by the profit it generates — money is the thing, any benefits to customers and society are considered incidental byproducts. (Even so, consumers have the ultimate power. When we buy a product, we are indirectly supporting that company and its distributors.) But can the success of a company and its leaders be framed solely in terms of the financial "bottom line"?

I think not. The power of profit in creating material wealth is well proven. But there is more. Corporations wield enormous power to transform society for better or worse. Whether or not we work for them, they touch our lives in myriad ways: the air we breathe, the water we drink, the dreams we dream. Here we see profit as a measure of contribution to society, *value added;* **money is a form of creative energy** like sun's energy stored up in trees. Thus, *profit is necessary for a company to survive and continue its mission, but not its purpose any more than the purpose of humans is to ingest food.*

In other words, what if we started with the idea: this is a good way to help people — and it's also a good way to make money?

This idea is not new. The other day I was at a *Quakers* meeting north of Philadelphia. During the coffee hour, an elderly lady asked what I did, and I said I was writing this book. "Ah, it sounds like what we Quakers have done. We came to Philadelphia to do good and ended up doing well."

In our voyage together, we'll translate these values of science and spirit into a culture of ethical practices: Start with higher PURPOSE, practice INTEGRITY in the workplace, treat workers, customers and investors responsibly — *profit with purpose, doing well by doing good* in enlightened self-interest. This is also reflected in the ***Harvard MBA Oath*** of 2009, adopted by hundreds of business schools around the world.

*

In the Indian tradition, the **underpinnings of a fulfilling life** are: Dharma (sense of duty to divine order), Artha (wealth, power), Kama (guilt-free pleasures), Moksha/Nirvana (liberation after dharma and karma are fulfilled).

Focusing on Artha here on earth, how do we make plenty of profits heeding the advice of our prophets? The Triple-Pro™ model of Prosperity (wealth), Progress (evolution), Progeny (legacy) — embodies those principles (details of the model in just a minute). Consider these investment guidelines:

- ✓ Strong balance sheet based on Triple-Pro practices; managements that do not usurp large shares of short-term profits with *financial engineering*
- ✓ Attractive Price-Earnings (P/E) ratios for 5+ year projected earnings covering more than one market cycle
- ✓ Long investment horizons — owning companies, not only renting shares

In the words of Warren Buffett of Berkshire Hathaway, one of the world's most successful investors, called the Oracle of Omaha: *Be fearful when others are greedy, and be greedy when others are fearful.*

Most Indians do not invest or trade in company stock now but, with rising middle class, there is increasing awareness of such possibilities. The two major stock exchanges are headquartered in Mumbai: the Bombay Stock Exchange (BSE, SENSEX index) and the National Stock Exchange (NSE). Founded in 1992, NSE has proven to be quite innovative, introducing Interest Rate Futures in 2009. The number of companies listed on these exchanges was consolidated from around 5000 to less than 2000 in 2013-14. The OTCEI (Over-The-Counter Exchange of India) is an electronic stock exchange of small and medium-size firms, somewhat similar to the American NASDAQ.

Staying in Business

There once was a popular monk who expounded eloquently about rights and wrongs, riches and rags, and the virtues of renunciation. People visited him day and night to clarify all sorts of doubts. The only requirement to see him was to bring a piece of fruit and a silver coin.

This went on for months. One day a village skeptic approached the monk: "Namaste guruji. You've resolved all my doubts except one. You spoke persuasively about renunciation and non-attachment to fruits of labor, yet insist on a fruit and silver coin from each visitor?"

"Ah, that's because I have to survive long enough to go to the next village and secure a place to spread the message," the monk replied.

The tenacious villager called on the monk again the next day along with fellow farmers. They complained about receiving barely enough to survive even after breaking their backs from dawn to dusk.

The monk explained: I know you receive very little money even though you are the pillars of our society. But think of work and rewards in three different ways: physical, mental, spiritual.

At the **physical level** *you reap what you sow* — apply knowledge and skills to produce a variety of wholesome foods — plant good seeds to get bountiful harvest; sell food grains and other produce at the right time in the right market to fetch the highest prices — sell directly to neighbors and travelers interested in fresh *local* food so the money circulates within the community. I, too, benefited from roadside hospitality during my travels.

Mentally you learn from your own experiences, and from others, on how to plant on small plots using as little water and other resources as possible. Through work you learn and grow, adapting innovative practices, getting better season by season. And celebrate the harvest inviting the poor and the rich alike.

Spiritually you fulfill dharma through your work, doing your best each day as if working for god — respecting your heritage and the gifts of nature, honoring your ancestors and descendants by leaving the land better than you found it. Your legacy will live on in the health of the land and the health of our children and grandchildren.

*

Business is a balancing act to balance the interests of employees, customers, shareholders, and society at large. We all play multiple roles as workers, consumers, investors, environmentalists:

As **workers** we want jobs with good pay, good working conditions, fulfilling work
As **consumers** we want a wide choice of good products at low prices
As **investors** we want high returns on our money with minimal risk
As **environmentalists** we want to preserve the quality of our life-support systems: clean water, air, soil, oceans — for ourselves and generations to come.

....

Coca Cola "Coke" illustrates the many dilemmas faced by a global company. Probably the most well-known brand in the world, valued in excess of US$70 billion, it has been in and out of India since 1950 and is now back in. Both Coke and Pepsi sell beverages in just about every country. The main ingredients are water and sugar. Their arrival in a community is often greeted with protests because they compete for scarce groundwater. Such soft drink companies also face criticism for crowding out traditional healthy drinks (water, buttermilk, coconut water) with sugar drinks and diet sodas that contribute to obesity and diabetes.

On the positive side, both companies are working to make their bottling *water-neutral*, returning to the environment water equal in quantity to that used in their beverages. Coke is also working to preserve river basins — and would earn eternal gratitude if it helped restore the iconic **Ganges**. Coke has mentored would-be entrepreneurs, created jobs, introduced solar-powered mobile coolers and rechargers for phones and electric lanterns. According to Muhtar Kent, chairman of Coca-Cola, its "5by20" initiative aims to train and mentor 5 million women entrepreneurs by 2020. Coke is collaborating with Dean Kamen, inventor of portable water purifiers (1000 liters/day), to distribute the water through kiosks, which will also have portals to charge cellphones.

PepsiCo, led by Indian American Indra Nooyi, has embarked on similar initiatives, including vitamin-mineral enriched nutritious beverage marketed in collaboration with Tata Global Beverages. PepsiCo is in a massive expansion mode in China and India. In its China push, Pepsi ran a highly successful publicity campaign; millions competed in a contest to put their pictures (also voting on others' pictures) to appear on Pepsi can.

4. The Triple-Pro™ Paradigm: Prosperity + Progress + Progeny New Model with Ancient Roots

The Triple-Pro paradigm and model embodies the teachings of Buddha, Krishna, and Chanakya. It is about wealth and a way of life: purpose and profit, process and product, journey and destination. It can serve as a mission for individuals as well as companies and countries. By engaging the *Triple-Pro* every step of the way: we can create and enjoy wealth now; evolve through knowledge and experience getting better day by day; and build an inspiring legacy for children and grandchildren everywhere to go further. Imagine it if you like as the *union of body-mind-spirit* in fulfillment of a noble mission.

....

Prosperity (wealth) + **Progress** (evolution) + **Progeny** (legacy)
Ask: Creating wealth NOW? Learning EVERYDAY? Investing in the FUTURE?

> **Prosperity** is about living an abundant life: creating profits/ wealth by doing the right thing the right way, enjoying *shared prosperity*, good reputation.
>
> Bottom line: HAPPINESS AND WELL-BEING NOW (experiencing prosperity mindset)
>
> **Progress** is about *evolving* consciously: learning/improving continually, *breaking out* to excel, helping colleagues succeed, building a greener planet.
>
> Bottom line: TODAY BETTER THAN YESTERDAY (this generation better off than previous)
>
> **Progeny** is about exiting with dignity: investing in sustainable future mindful of three or more degrees of intergenerational connectivity (grandchildren) — leaving the world a better place.
>
> Bottom line: TOMORROW BETTER THAN TODAY (next generation better off than this one)

....

We can play the Triple-Pro "game" individually or in triangles of three players with a bit of role-playing. It'll help us connect in a practical way with the deeper meaning and purpose of life: Why are we here?

ppp

"How are we doing?" Playing the Triple-Pro game

Triple-Pro Reference Points	Individual	Organization	Outsider View
Prosperity			
Elements of economic prosperity			
e.g. revenues, profits (surpluses)			
Progress			
Elements of evolutionary progress			
e.g. innovations, intellectual capital			
Progeny			
Elements of enduring legacy			
e.g. contribution to a sustainable world			

I believe you'll find the Triple-Pro game challenging and fun. For example, in a triangle of three players: one could play the role of himself/herself, another role of enterprise executive, third role of a country (governments, institutions). Each triangle member presents her ideas and proposed actions with respect to Prosperity, Progress, Progeny. Each triangle can network with any other triangle from the same or different organizations in the spirit of cooperation as well as competition.

For Economic Prosperity, think of your role in adding value and generating profits. Evolutionary Progress is made possible by learning from experiences and mistakes, learning/doing something new, climbing to new levels, *getting ahead of the curve* — reflected in innovative products and processes. As an example of Progeny, you may reflect on the legacy of, say, Mahatma Gandhi, Abraham Lincoln or the Gates Foundation/Buffett-Gates philanthropic initiatives.

Use a scale of 1 to 10 to characterize performance in each area (ten is the highest, world class). To be *world-class,* identify the current best products/practices of the best companies — and improve upon them. You can also get an outsider perspective — customer, supplier, shareholder, independent consultant not obliged to agree with you (perhaps invite an alien from outer space) — and compare it with yours as a reality check. This will give you a baseline picture to track progress over time as a *Triple-Pro enterprise*.

Please note any ideas and *action items* below. Later return here and play the game again. Look for progress.

Notes 

The Wobbly Tripod — the three legs of a viable enterprise

To celebrate the opening of a new wing, the Himarest Monks sponsored *Triple-Pro@Work*™ Business Conference. They invited the chief executive of *Do-Good-Do-Well* Company to be the keynote speaker.

Following the meeting, the monk in charge of executive education invited the chief executive to a cup of tea on the veranda. An apprentice brought out a teapot and two cups and placed them on a tripod.

After a pause, the monk turned to the executive, "What's on your mind?"

Startled at first, but no stranger to the subtle ways of the monks, the executive replied: "As I said in the keynote, we feel proud to be inspired by a noble purpose. It is our CALLING, not just a job. Our company won numerous awards for family-friendly and earth-friendly policies. But we are being penalized by *Money Street* for not making more money."

After a second's silence, the monk put his tea cup back on the tripod, which wobbled a little. "Ah, a lack of balance can be a problem. Your first duty is to generate **surpluses** or profits to enable your enterprise to continue on its mission. The second is to continually **evolve** through experiments, mistakes, successes — build beneficent products in a wholesome workplace and offer them to customers at fair prices. The third is to share surplus wealth with present and future generations, leaving a worthy **legacy**.

"A business is not unlike this tripod. One leg is short and it could topple over any time. I've taken the liberty of asking one of my colleagues to meet with you — he was the CEO of a company that nearly went bankrupt. I see you have an Apple iPhone. You may know the story of Steve Jobs visiting these foothills and later introducing the iPhone with Beginner's Mind — linking computer, phone, music and movies with mobility — making Apple the most valued company financially and culturally."

Be-Know-Do paradigm — Know thyself

Let's take a little detour to get to know ourselves better.

The Be-Know-Do paradigm complements the Triple-Pro. Be who you are, yourSelf; Know what you really want; Do express yourSelf.

What does it mean to be yourSelf? What really defines your identity? What makes you, YOU?

The DNA you inherit? The things you possess? The titles you bear? The roles you play? The masks you wear?

In order to understand who you are — get to know your ***Sattva-Rajas--Tamas* persona**. Bhagavad Gita sheds light on this: Our birth and nature predispose us toward three *gunas* or qualities called Sattva, Rajas, Tamas. Although all of us have a mix of these, we are centered in one quality at a time in each stage of life.

Sattva: light, knowledge, goodness — centered in higher purpose

Rajas: energy, action, control — focused on money

Tamas: inertia, rest, apathy — no purpose, no focus

Sattva is enlightenment, magnanimity, harmony. Sattva-centered people are tranquil and balanced, in touch with higher Self, guided by a sense of duty. They share light and help others climb the mountain.

Rajas-centered are action-oriented, motivated by wealth and power, seeking control and external validation. Their passion and self-interest in pursuit of wealth and power benefit society at large — as in Free Markets (suggestive of Adam Smith's proposition in the Wealth of Nations).

Tamas-centered are lethargic, lacking in purpose and social consciousness, unaware of the effects of their behavior on others. They tend to procrastinate and seek instant gratification.

It is through the Sattva spirit that the higher Self (*Atma*) is expressed. That is when we feel fulfilled — being mySelf, being yourSelf. We can develop an awareness of the higher Self by associating with spiritual fellowship, practicing mindfulness and meditation, doing good and doing well.

Rajas and Tamas qualities are also essential. What we need is the right balance. We cannot sleep without Tamas, for instance. Sometimes the best thing we can do is do nothing. Some of the best deals we make turn out to be the ones we didn't. In the can-do, must-do, world — what you don't do, what doesn't happen, what you don't see — can be as important as what you do. (In a Sherlock Holmes story of a missing racehorse and the dog that didn't bark — Holmes' naïve assistant says: What good is the dog, it did nothing? The astute detective points out: Precisely, since the dog didn't bark, it must have known the culprit.)

Young people are Rajasic by nature. It is the Rajas energy and passion that drive the world. Older civilizations tend to become Tamasic over time — India was once a center of creativity. We can break out of the Tamas slumber by becoming more active — not just engaging activity but ACTION that moves us closer to our goals. We need to work with our hands and minds, cultivating new *mindware*.

Sattva spirit offers a portal, gateway, to your Self. The true Self is your moral compass, like an internal GPS. It can guide your decisions on what is right:

- Do I feel like myself or like an imposter? (Sattvic or selfish?)
- How do I feel before, during, and after? (Gut feel?)
- How do I feel at the end of the day? (Peace at heart?)

*

Organizations, too, have distinct Sattva-Rajas-Tamas personas and operating styles:

Sattva vision **Triple-Pro capitalism**	**Rajas action** **Stock market capitalism**	**Tamas inaction** **Archaic**
Guided by Triple-Pro Focus on society Wholesome products	Profit, growth Revenues, bonuses High-margin products	Survival Fixed assets Old products
Decentralized	Centralized	Disorganized
Transparent mode	Need-to-know basis	Secretive
Means as important as ends	End justifies means	Risk-averse
"Co-optive"	Competitive	Reactive
Mindful action	Quick action	Slow/no action

Not Your True Self

The President of Grand Corporation sought out a Monk well known for his connections to the cosmic Self and requested an introduction. The Monk asked her who she was so he could introduce her to the Self. The president gave her name but the Monk pointed out that the name was given to her and she wasn't born with it.

Then she said she had been the president of Grand Corporation for 3 months. The Monk asked who she was before becoming the president. A doctor by training, she said. The Monk again pointed out that since her occupation or position had changed, that wasn't who she truly was. Truth never changes.

The perplexed president started to reflect on who she was NOT, in order to find out who she really was. It dawned on her that it's really a matter of un-covering, removing covers, to see who is underneath. Thus came about the introduction to her true Self.

*

How does the law of **Karma** help me write my life story?

The beginning of your story has been written. You get to write the middle and an ending.

You and I embody our inheritance as well as our legacy. We reap what we sow, and what others sow, over three or more generations — deposited in a sort of *universal bank account* that encompasses the past, the present, the future.

We have the power to alter our karmic trajectory by our deeds in the present, now, which is in our control. *Karma yoga* is pure action, acting with the Whole Mind, regardless of personal gain. (*Attachment to outcomes weakens incomes.*) Help others succeed, and shine light on their good deeds as well — we all hold *joint accounts* in the *universal karmic bank*.

In a sense, karma is a pilgrimage from the selfish self — transient, finite, mortal — to the transcendent SELF — experiencing its constancy, infinity, immortality.

Any good deeds to deposit today?

Is the world a better place because of you/me?

What story will you tell the teller?

The Power of Prosperity Mindset — how to grow a new future?

The popular saying, *I'll believe it when I see it,* is a bit backwards. Instead, *you'll see what you believe*. If you want to become prosperous, act like you are already prosperous. It will be a self-fulfilling prophecy.

Since many of our forefathers lived through generations of foreign control and extreme poverty — poverty of money turned into poverty of mind. Scarcity and apathy have come to rule Indian minds.

The good news is we have the power to change our minds — change ourselves, change India, change the world. But just as good soil, water and sunshine are needed for flowers to bloom and trees to bear fruit — we need the right *mindware* to grow a new future. We should purge toxic thought viruses and RESET our minds — replace the old culture of poverty and mediocrity with a new culture of prosperity and excellence.

How? Change becomes easier if we have a CONSTANT in our lives — someone or something we can look up to, something we can depend on unconditionally, like mother's love, god's love, moral compass. The more the children feel secure, the farther out they venture.

Let's turn to scriptures for guidance. A quote from Brihadaranyaka Upanishad springs to mind: *Om, Infinite is that, infinite is this. From the Infinite proceeds the infinite...* As Krishna reveals in our conversation (shown toward the end of this book), *money does not produce prosperity — it is the prosperity mindset that produces money.* Such is the nature of the universe that harbors infinite treasures.

Only scarcity can come out of scarcity.
Prosperity can come only out of Prosperity.

When we act with scarcity/poverty mindset (you win — I lose) we act from FEAR.
When we act with prosperity mindset (you win-I win-they win) we act from FREEDOM

Thus, we cannot be prosperous in isolation. In practice this means turning on our *generosity switches* — we all have them. We can turn them on for new thoughts, words, deeds — to bake a bigger pie (to expand wealth) and receive a bigger piece of a bigger pie — instead of trying to grab a bigger piece of a smaller pie (limited wealth). You may remember the legendary Johnny Appleseed who planted apple seeds wherever he traveled for future generations to reap what he sowed — *paying it forward*.

Granted, we're all at different stations in our life's journey — still we can all become more prosperous-minded by widening our circles to include "me-you-us" and building *virtuous spirals*:

+ help someone, anyone, with random acts of kindness, before sleeping at night, recall 3 things you are thankful for
+ practice meditation and mindfulness, participate in spiritual fellowship (*Satsang)* with authentic *gurus*
+ help friends and strangers succeed, shine light on their success; give gifts with generous thoughts, be open to receive with respect and gratitude.

To be ready to receive is a gift in itself, be it food or a book. Buddha and Krishna accepted crumbs of food given by even the humblest with a smile.

Since most of our thoughts and actions are triggered by subconscious forces that we are not even aware of, it'll take time for these ideas to take root. The subconscious expresses whatever is impressed on it, good or bad. It will take 21 days of sincere practice to RESET our minds and forge a new habit.

WARNING: Prosperity mindset is highly contagious. Don't be too surprised if friends and colleagues who are exposed to you exhibit symptoms of *prosperity syndrome*.

Go ahead, MAKE YOUR DAY — make someone prosperous.

*

Let's delve a little further into our mindsets, motives, operating styles.

Honeybee or Peacock paradigm?

Once upon a time, a honeybee and a peacock struck up a conversation. The bee, darting and buzzing, said: "I had the most fruitful day. I got up at dawn well before the others and already called on a score of customers. I hope my queen will be pleased with the *nectar* I collected."

"Oh, instead of my calling on customers, my *customers call on me*," said the peacock playfully. "It is in my nature to sing and dance and express myself. I see my rewards in the eyes and hearts of my beholders. I won't ever run out of the bounties of my joyous nature."

What is Your Operating Paradigm?

The honeybee and the peacock personify two paradigms of living. The bee goes in search of nectar, and pollinates by hopping from flower to flower. Honey (money) is the goal, the means of validation. Pollination and benefits to the plants (customers) are incidental byproducts.

The peacock with its magnificent plumage and exotic dance choreographs its intrinsic nature — being fully in the moment, not preoccupied with future benefits. (Self-expression and actualization are valued highly in Indian scriptures and are also at the top of Maslow's Hierarchy of Needs Pyramid.) "Customers" are attracted by the spectacle and partake of the joy. The peacock, by its alluring performance, attracts partners and increases the prospects of immortality — *beauty's longing for itself!*

Business success, like evolutionary progress, depends on both survival and seduction, competition and cooperation. The bee's diligence is critical to survival — but isn't the way of the peacock more fun as well?

Idea for innovative enterprise — *Sattva* Calls

Wake-up call service and/or Good-Night call service (daily or as needed) that could include an inspiring message, all in one minute. Customized services could include a 3-minute story such as the parables in this and in a related book, *River of a Thousand Tales*.

5. Globalization, Technology, Uncertainty

In a free enterprise, the community is not just another stakeholder in business but in fact the very purpose of its existence...
J.N Tata, Founder of Tata Group, India 1895

Earth Inc. How did we get here in billions?

The 21st century is the Global Century, says Nitin Nohria, dean of the Harvard Business School. I like to think that this is also India's Century.

Globalization is not only economic but also political, technological, cultural. A global enterprise has investors, employees and customers around the globe. Three megatrends stand out: converging global society, technological-industrial revolution, uncertain future leadership — who will be the next world leader?

First, catch a glimpse of how far we traveled, and how fast. Imagine for a moment that all of human history is condensed into one day. Then almost all the changes we see in technology and wealth will have occurred in just the last second, in the blink of an eye.

Before year zero (beginning of the Christian era) agriculture and urban settlements were important milestones, as in Indus Valley Civilization. During the first millennium (0-1000 AD) there was little economic progress in the world except for pockets of prosperity. In the second millennium, European Renaissance arts and trade flourished. Following the Industrial Revolution (1700-1800) Europe, later joined by America, became dominant forces by virtue of scientific and economic breakthroughs: trade, guns, printing press, steam engine, electricity, telephone, automobile, public health, private enterprise. Human endeavors started to transform the Earth in a big way.

World population grew slowly at first, the Earth reached its **first billion** only recently, in **1804**. A little later emerged the world's first industrial billionaire, John D. Rockefeller, founder of Standard Oil Company.

Quantum leaps in development occurred starting in the 1960s with the explosion in computers/information technology, telecom, life-sciences, aerospace (moon landing) — and beginnings of globalization. Suddenly we jumped from a *slow, linear world to a fast exponential world* — in technology, wealth, population — adding the seventh billion in just 12 years (instead of millions of years it took humans to reach the first billion).

Information Technology (IT), telecom and the Internet have fueled a second industrial revolution in the 1990s and into the 21st century. A parallel phenomenon is further catalyzing the technology and industrial revolution: ENERGY, the fountainhead of an economy — rediscovering and recovering more energy, both conventional (natural gas) and renewable (sun and wind); and using less energy — doing more with less through smart designs.

In this space- and time-warped universe, we've all become *Dual Citizens:* citizen of a country as well as citizen of the planet. We can now access cheapest capital (or highest return on investment), make, sell — here, there, everywhere in *Global Supply Chains*. This phenomenon united the world and made things cheaper — but then divided workers and consumers. Sudden capital inflows and outflows made national economies vulnerable to the vagaries of capitalists.

Powered by global trade, free-flying capital and technology, the *emerging economies* grew at an unprecedented 5-10% per year. Nations paid less attention to ideologies and more attention to economic growth and jobs. Entrepreneurs and investors in global companies became millionaires and billionaires overnight.

China today: Former Communist and totalitarian nations became ardent capitalists. Just a generation ago, China looked hopeless, mired in ideology. Over the last three decades the Chinese economy has transformed into *American capitalism on steroids*! Chinese students in American universities outnumber Indians (many top Chinese officials and industry titans send their children to American universities). Sinopec/PetroChina (energy, chemicals), Alibaba (e-commerce), Baidu (Web services, Internet search engine like Google, Microsoft), Huawei (largest Telecom/IT conglomerate, suspected links with Chinese military), Sina Weibo (Twitter-like social media) and China Mobile stand alongside world leaders.

China, it seems, has an emotional connection with the Internet — it has more than 500 million Internet users, twice as many as the US. Even though subject to censorship, Internet businesses have become phenomenal successes: Alibaba, Sina Weibo, TenCent's WeChat (weixin in Chinese, gaining share from Weibo), and the like.

Alibaba Group/Alibaba.com, founded in 1999 in Jack Ma's apartment, became the world's largest e-commerce company with 2012 revenue of US$ 160 billion (larger than Amazon and eBay combined), and headed for the largest Initial Public Offering (IPO) on New York Stock Exchange. In an interview, Ma identified his company priorities ranking customers first, employees second, stockholders third. (This is similar to that of Howard

Schultz, founder of Starbucks, the *Third Place* for customers to indulge between home and office.)

China nurtures and values such companies as national resource. (The trick is not to favor any single company but to maintain a level playing field, reducing barriers to entry, fostering innovation and competition.) China is increasingly blazing its own trail, moving away from the role of *copycat* and subcontractor. During 2012-13 China with Hong Kong emerged as home to the second largest number of **dollar-billionaires**: (160-170) behind America (440+), followed by Russia (110-115) and **India (55-60).**

India today — is a result of more socio-economic transformation in the past two decades (1990-2010) than in the preceding ten centuries. More than 300 million, equal to US population, moved up to *less-poor middle class.* For the first time, the urban middle-class has acquired a national identity, *Indian-ness* — transcending language, religion, caste. They demand good governance, not handouts.

So how far, how fast? It took two centuries for the first Industrial Revolution to take hold. It took a generation for free enterprise to catch on. It took less than two decades for the Internet and the digital revolution to circle the globe. (Did you have a cellphone in 1990? US President Clinton sent only two emails in 1990s.) Speed — of learning, change — became critical to success along with price and quality.

Amidst this generally good news of *Techonomy* — what if we run into shocks like these: financial (2008-09 meltdown, protectionism), environmental (water, climate crises, nuclear disasters), biological (pandemics)? Or catastrophic disruptions of cybersecurity by rogue nations or extremist groups (banking, power grids, transport networks)? Are global institutions anchored in American power ready to respond to such challenges? The 2008 financial crisis was seen by China and much of the world as a sign of failed American leadership. What if increasingly assertive China refuses to play by the American rules? What then?

World in your pocket: wireless connectivity

The **Internet** — hailed as a people's platform and great equalizer — opened up a window to the outside world with opportunities as well as vulnerabilities (loss of privacy, cyber theft). It helped launch the likes of Google, Facebook (nearly a billion users in 2013 worldwide), YouTube (watched by a billion people everyday), Twitter, LinkedIn, Amazon, and millions of entrepreneurs. Power shifted from a few central mainframes to networks of mobile devices.

There are six billion cellphones worldwide as of 2013, of which two billion are smartphones with access to the Internet. India advanced from almost no cellphones in 2000 to a billion now, but only 10% are smartphones. In contrast almost all cellphones in China and the US are smartphones. India is the fastest growing in smartphones, sales are expected to double every two years. (Remember waiting years to get an ordinary landline before leapfrogging into wireless technology?)

Mobile networks are encompassing everyone, everywhere, anytime. We've all become *actors on the Internet-Social Media global stage*. All that we say and do is *immortalized* somewhere in cyberspace. Over a million apps for iPhone and Android platforms are available catering to every need and whim — and more than a hundred billion are downloaded globally, 90% free.

While developing nations have been the major beneficiaries of capital and know-how orbiting the globe at the speed of electrons and photons, developed nations could deploy surplus capital in emerging markets to obtain higher returns. The American *S&P 500* companies derive almost half their revenues and more than half their growth outside America. Knowledge workers can now work for the whole world staying right at home, but also competing with workers and machines everywhere, including robots that perform surgery to sermons. Middle class is expanding in China and India but shrinking in America. **Income inequalities** are rising within individual countries, while they are shrinking across countries into a more egalitarian world.

IT/mobile and social network revolutions are reshaping human culture. Ideas anywhere in the world appear at our doorstep and affect our lives NOW, not spread over generations. We are living in a *Hyperconnected Miniaturized World with seven billion neighbors*.

Much has changed, yet more remains the same!

Technology mega breakthroughs mostly benefited the urban population: average urban incomes are 2-4 times higher than rural farmers. Despite windows to the outside world, villagers in Africa, India and China still live as their ancestors did a thousand years ago. Two of three Indians still live in villages despite mass migration to cities in search of work and education. Worldwide, more than three billion are expected to move to cities, increasing urbanites from 50% of seven billion people now to 75% of more than nine billion by 2050. The world is going from rural to urban in a big way, generating its own problems and opportunities.

Global companies sensitive to India's aspirations are putting boots on the ground, establishing local research and manufacturing presence — seeking not only to sell to Indians but also to buy from India and invest in India in the spirit of *Swadeshi*. Overall, India's position as a producer and consumer of global brands cannot be sustained without breakthroughs in agriculture, energy, and health. Earlier, agricultural revolution led to the rapid rise of Japan, Taiwan and South Korea by boosting productivity, savings, and rural entrepreneurship.

*

Looking broadly at the Emerging Markets (EM) or Emerging Economies (EE), which include 80% of world population at varying stages of development and income levels (India, China, South Korea, Indonesia, Brazil, Mexico, etc), a common denominator is growth rate exceeding 5% per year. (Generally speaking, 1-4% growth covers inflation and population growth; above 5% improves living standards.)

Ruchir Sharma observes in *Breakout Nations* that high-growth economies fit roughly the following pattern:

> Financial-political crisis → economic reforms → boom → complacency → decline in growth → balance of payments/ weak currencies/high interest rates problems

Among high-growth or *break-out economies,* the *Asian tigers* Taiwan, South Korea, Singapore and Hong Kong defied this kind of cycle and climbed into high-income status of more than US$20,000 income per capita, as did Japan earlier. Visionary leaders have played a decisive role in the development of emerging economies. India, in contrast, slowed down considerably in 2012-13 due to weak leadership, unsustainable subsides for food and fuel, and other social programs — instead of investing in smart social safety nets that build self-respect and intellectual capital.

*

Billionaire-philanthropist Game Changers

We believe that every person deserves a chance to live a healthy, productive life... Bill & Melinda Gates Foundation

Bill Gates (Microsoft, Gates Foundation), Azim Premji (Wipro), and Ratan Tata (Tata Group) hosted a meeting in 2012 for forty five of India's wealthiest to promote philanthropy. They want to change the world focusing on key sectors: water, healthcare, agriculture, education.

Exemplifying the tenet: *to whom much is given, of them much is expected* — the architects of the *Giving Pledge*, Warren Buffett and Bill and Melinda Gates, are on a lofty mission to persuade the superrich to pledge at least half their wealth to charity and philanthropy (Buffett already pledged 99% of his wealth, Gates 95%). They feel that their riches are made possible not only by their own efforts but also by the societies that enabled them to build and accumulate those riches. Since the start of Giving Pledge campaign in 2010, more than 114 signed on as of 2013; commitments already add up to more than US$300 billion.

Of the 1400+ dollar billionaires worldwide, India has as many 50-60 (fourth after US 440, China 160, Russia 110). Some of them are shown later in Architects/Visionaries of New India — driven as much by a sense of purpose as by the promise of money. Many recent billionaires are founders of IT/ telecom and pharmaceutical/biotech ventures, while others like Tatas and Ambanis straddle both traditional industrial and modern IT/telecom sectors.

This phenomenon of so many new billionaires emerging in China and India is certainly remarkable. What is also noteworthy is the number of billionaires relative to a country's Gross Domestic Product (GDP is a measure of economic activity and wealth). Concentration of billionaires relative to GDP indicates wealth in fewer hands, which reduces opportunities for others to work hard and move up the ladder — *social mobility* being a pillar of progressive societies. Russia's billionaire oligarchs emerged in the 1990s, when many state-owned oil and gas entities transitioned into private hands in post-Soviet era *wild-west grab*. In this sense, the number of 'poor' millionaires may be a better indicator of free markets and social mobility.

(On a side note, construction cranes and night lights are a symbol of the economic vitality of a nation. In my own experience walking through Times Square in New York, it has been interesting to watch the flashing advertisements and shifting positions over the years — from Coke on top to Sony to Xinhua — mirroring shifts in economic power among nations.)

Secret Millionaires Club: This is one of Warren Buffett's less-known outreach programs to ignite entrepreneurial fervor among children all over the world. The online club is an animated series featuring Buffett as a mentor to a group of adventurous teenagers; he guides them to solve business problems in an entertaining way (normally taught in business schools in less entertaining ways).

Would-be billionaires, startup incubators: In the same entrepreneurial vein, why not have venture incubator bridges among countries similar to *Sister Cities*? It would not be simple outsourcing but entrepreneurs coming to India to work, live and make a difference — such as the partnership between VoteChat (crowdsourced decision making app) and ClickLabs (Indian incubator, builder of mobile apps). It's more like brain sharing than brain drain — although brain drain is continuing from India to the US, and to Canada, which is more welcoming.

The **startup ecosystem in India** is still embryonic with about 50 *incubators and accelerators* such as Sequoia Capital India, GSF, United India-Hub, The Hatch, ZipDial, Morpheus, TLabs, Khosla Labs (founded by Vinod Khosla, Silicon Valley venture capitalist), Startup Village. Giants like Tata Group and Microsoft are also launching incubators/accelerators. Indian universities like IITs are just now beginning, like IIT/SINE (Society for Innovation and Entrepreneurship), Bombay.

Stanford University's Extreme Affordability program encourages students to develop low-cost solutions to world problems; it has seeded many entrepreneurs, some bound for India. The announcement by Canada's Ryerson University's Digital Media Zone to build a satellite incubator in India may spur top Indian research universities to start centers of innovation and entrepreneurship. At the inter-government level, the Indo-US Science & Technology Forum is funded by both governments to catalyze innovation and techno-preneurship (indousstf.org).

The Indus Entrepreneurs (tie.org) was founded in 1992 in California's Silicon Valley by a group of successful entrepreneurs with roots in the Indus Region. Its mission is to foster entrepreneurship globally through education and mentoring focusing on the Indian region, to nurture the next generation of entrepreneurs in a virtuous cycle of wealth creation.

Even in this Internet age, to gather critical mass and foster *Silicon Alleys* (sons and daughters of Silicon Valley), physical proximity does matter — with whom you sit across the table eating lunch in the cafeteria or drinking tea under a tree.

Indus *Children Prosperity Corps* (ICP)

Recruit the power of young minds to solve Indian and world problems in key sectors: water, healthcare, agriculture, energy, education, vocational training. Their findings would not be patented but open to everyone. These children would make a difference to their own lives and to the lives of millions worldwide.

This program could draw on the Polio model or the "Solar Mamas" barefoot college that trains women from developing countries to become 'sky is the limit' energy engineers. As part of ICP, the program would focus on teenagers from Africa and Middle East in renewable energy and environment-housing-water-health issues. Young teams could offer short workshops in practical skills.

Indus Young Entrepreneurs Club

Similar to Warren Buffet's Secret Millionaires Club, perhaps affiliated with *The Indus Entrepreneurs* and the above ICP. The club can promote understanding of the role of money with financial literacy.

To get a sense of true abundance and our place in the infinite universe — let's shift our eyes up to gaze at the skies and the galaxies, enlisting guidance of astronomers from nearby universities and astronomy societies.

Idea for innovative enterprise — Mobile Convention Centers

Build and rent floating convention and entertainment centers on ships near India's coastlines with beach promenades. Operate cruise ships, coastal transport and trade craft — overseen by the Coast Guard.

Quantum Leaps, Creative Destruction

You probably heard the expression: *Youth is wasted on the young, wisdom on the old.* What if we synergize the energy of the youth with the wisdom of the old by each child adopting an elder?

Talking of wisdom, ponder these guidelines of Vinod Khosla, venture capitalist and creative thinker:

1. Look for ways to skip or break away from what exists today
2. Lean in the right direction without being tied down to one option

All around us are manifestations of breakaway ideas, quantum leaps that we take for granted: from land lines to cellular mobile phones, from single owner-driver cars to public transport (and Google's self-driving cars, ride-share), from selective class-room education to massive open online courses (MOOCS). And many others: electricity, telephone, moving assembly line, computer, satellite, human genome (DNA) mapping, 3-D printing, crowd-sourcing, Wikipedia, digital currency (Bitcoin), consumer drones.

The sharing economy is blossoming. Traditionally humans shared resources within families and tribes, of course. Now it has gone public, leading to fuller use of resources. Open-source software (Redhat), airbnb.com (house sharing), Uber.com (access vehicles by cellphone), and New York Bike Share come readily to mind. In the 1970s EDS corp. IT professionals and managers shared whatever desks were available, no fixed offices.

Quantum leaps and disruptive innovations are what Prof. Peter Drucker might call *discontinuities,* not mere extrapolations of existing products or processes. Note also it is better to define the objective broadly enough — not just as telephones but as *communication* (and not just as cars but as *transport* or *mobility*) which allows for other channels as well: voice/audio, video, email, text messaging, so on. We can think of this along *three dimensions: quantity, quality, time*. Quantities have limits, quality no such limits. We could have increased the quantity of phone lines by laying lots of copper lines with much money and time. But by "skipping what exists today" we achieved abundant quantity and better quality, quickly. A 2-fold change (the power of 2) — cutting cost or size by half, or doubling the speed or capacity — can be disruptive, as we have witnessed in computers and the Internet. The power of 10 is even more potent, often found in natural phenomena in time and size scales — from subatomic particles to human endeavors to galaxies.

Creativity is applied imagination. **Creative destruction** is disrupting what exists today to create a new order. Tech companies routinely "destroy" their assets by making their own products obsolete before others do. This idea is not really new, though. That is what the trinity Shiva-Brahma-Vishnu does on a universal scale: Shiva periodically destroying everything that exists for Brahma to recreate and Vishnu to nurture a new era. People in creative companies also play these roles of destroyer, creator, nurturer.

Bottom line? In the context of our adventure — our purpose/destination is the Prosperity Summit (think Everest), which provides direction. We also need to identify potential pathways up the mountain, and strategy or tactics. While the direction or destination remains the same, the plan should be flexible enough to allow us to respond on the spot to ever changing terrain and weather conditions as we climb up to the top.

How to be a Genius — at a glance

✓ Reclaim the Beginner's Mind: spend more time with children, learn continually from observations, experiments, mistakes

✓ Reflect on your purpose in life and your legacy

✓ Be mindful of *connectivity* (separation) across three degrees of space and time

✓ Befriend the unknown: embrace uncertainty, paradox (a virus is both alive and dead!)

✓ Enlist the whole mind: seeing and seeking, science and art, logic and imagination

✓ Walk in others' shoes — reflect on others' points of view (colleagues, customers, children, turkey at Thanksgiving)

✓ Cultivate a sense of abundance, humor, fair play

Source: *Creative Minds,* a companion book to *Prophets and Profits*

Smaller and smaller screens have been taking over our lives.

Disconnect to Connect! Let there be SILENCE.

Unplug the outer world of phones and screens, find a quiet corner
Sit or stand upright as if pushing up the sky

Take in a S L O W, D E E P breath, 3-4 seconds, paying attention (breathe deep down into the abdomen, like filling a glass with water)

Hold it for 2- 3 seconds. Let go s l o w l y, consciously, 4-5 seconds. Repeat.

Pause 2-3 seconds. Resume normal breathing with whole body-mind smile :--)

Look around, observe what is around you, sensing directly.

6. India's Hidden Assets, Islands of Excellence

Where will India be 1000 years from now?

Visitors to India can feel overwhelmed by the crowds (as I do) and annoyed by the casual way things are done, the mindless behavior, *anything-goes* attitude. Only recently did it occur to me that this fluidity, and the underlying sense of timelessness, can be India's *assets* as well. Moreover, India is at the beginning of its new economic and technological journey so it has the freedom to sidestep or leapfrog existing systems of developed nations.

Cuisine, frugal engineering: The typical vegetarian diet, occasionally supplemented by eggs, has far-reaching implications for personal and environmental health, even the way things are engineered. Probably originating in a culture of *Ahimsa, do no harm*, it minimizes environmental footprint from animal farms, soil and water contamination, and carbon emissions that cause global warming. Indian cuisine can gain further converts globally by including more local fresh produce, beans, lentils, and nuts while reducing fried foods and high-sugar sweets. In this way, Indian restaurants can become cultural emissaries around the world.

Why not *let nature direct what we eat*, rather than what we eat dictate nature? Nature had billions of years to fine-tune its creations. Just imagine what the world would be like if more people consumed the foods and fuels of an average Indian?

It is this sort of frugal culture that launched the Indian Mars orbiter in 2013 for only US$75 million, less than one-thirtieth of the American Mars launch, and less than the cost of Hollywood space movie *Gravity.* (Mangalyaan succeeded in first attempt, some rocket parts were carried across by bullock carts.) The satellite, which subsequently started beaming pictures of the red planet, was characterized by the US NASA Administrator as an "impressive engineering feat".

Meta-family enterprise: three generations living under one roof enjoying the security of joint family is still the norm in villages. No one feels *lonely* in India. Children grow up with a community of siblings, uncles and aunts, and grandparents, respecting elders. Everyone has a role to play in each stage of life: as children and students (dependents), as householders and economic beings (producers, providers) and, in later stages, both taking and giving.

It's a highly effective ecosystem — recycling resources, adapting, meeting social needs: parents/grandparents do not have to worry about what might happen when they grow old or fall sick.

Despite the strains of urbanization, women entering workforce, and children who lead a sheltered life needing to develop independent thinking outside home — meta-families offer a degree of stability and support in this rapidly changing economic landscape.

Bollywood, Indian Diaspora: India has the world's largest cinema industry, celebrating 100 years in 2013. Bollywood and regional studios make around a thousand films per year, twice that of Hollywood in quantity. (Hindi films lead, followed closely by Telugu and Tamil.) But few films have ever won international acclaim: *Slumdog Millionaire* was written and produced in Canada; *Life of Pi* by an international team. India can do better, a lot better, adding QUALITY to QUANTITY to rival Hollywood's reach and revenue. Since cinema plays larger-than-life role in culture and entertainment, film stars can be agents of economic and social innovation. Bollywood could expand its repertoire by adapting foreign novels and screenplays across countries and cultures. Bollywood song and dance has caught on around the world from Mumbai to Miami — along with yoga and *mindfulness* movements.

The more than 20 million people of Indian origin (and friends) living and working abroad are captive audiences for Indian films and products. They serve as bridges between the old and the new. Some have adopted the villages of their birth, or that of their parents, as a sort of *homage to homeland.* Nonresident Indians (NRIs) remitted USD70 billion in 2012, helping with balance of payments.

Chaos, Crowds, Connectivity: India is endowed with *diversity and disorder* — hallmarks of a dynamic democracy, and symbolic of global marketplace. As in nature, the cacophony of cultures and languages enhances group IQ (Intelligence Quotient) and EQ (Emotional Quotient). (China's uniformity with one language, Mandarin, makes communication easier but not necessarily better.) Corruption and mediocrity comingle with generosity and genius, rule of law with chaos.

Imagine, too, the power of *Crowd Sourcing* — a billion human-computer brains competing and collaborating to solve problems and scale-up solutions: balance population-environment, design practical toilets, grow food without land and pesticides. (Kickstarter.com is the largest funder of creative projects.)

Another of India's great assets is the historic kinships: with Asia (culture, trade); Britain/Europe (starting with the British East India Company); Africa (first human migration from East Africa to India 60,000 years ago, Indian migration to Africa during erstwhile British Empire); and Americas (Columbus setting sail from Europe to India in search of spices, textiles, gold — discovering the Americas instead).

The world is rediscovering India, but we have not yet fully engaged our historic and cultural connectivity. India is a member of the Commonwealth (formerly the British Commonwealth) of 53 nations — sharing English and democratic values. Why not promote *common wealth*? Glancing southeast to Indonesia, a fast growing nation of 250 million people — a popular hero of youngsters is *Bhima*, the imposing and beloved Pandava brother in the *Mahabharata* epic. It is Japan that is participating in Indonesia's puppetry and toy business. (Indonesian, Thai, and many other Southeast Asian names are derived from Sanskrit.)

Another of India's assets is that it is not seen as a competitive threat by America, Europe, Japan/East Asia. Business relations are more collaborative than competitive so there is less local opposition. Tata-acquired Jaguar Land Rover facilities are left in Britain and are profitable, for example.

*

According to a Japanese saying, *you need three kinds of people to revitalize a place: young people, outsiders, fools.* India has all these in abundance.

The Village Playfool Game

There once lived an enterprising Playfool who sat under a Tamarind tree in the village square with a collection plate. He greeted passersby, "May good karma bring you good fortune, kind sirs."

When the villagers put coins in his collection plate, Playfool gave back a few at random, sometimes giving them coins much more valuable than what they had put in. The villagers were amused at his naiveté and made a game of it. And, as they left, would often slip a few more coins into the plate curious to see what might happen.

One day a visiting businessman resting nearby observed the goings-on and approached Playfool: Why don't you keep the valuable silver coins for yourself and give back only copper coins? Wouldn't you get rich quick that way?

"Ah," said Playfool with a sly smile, "If I keep all the silver coins and give back only copper all the time — without the amusement value of a fool — how long do you think I'd stay in business?"

PS. Playfool moved to Monte Carlo to pursue his new calling. The villagers remember him fondly for all the amusement he provided. He knew when to move on!

*

On the following pages are highlights of three key sectors with seeds of bountiful harvest: Software/IT/ Telecom, Green Agriculture, Healthcare/ Pharmaceutical. They could be the launching pads for India's 20-20 growth trajectory (20% growth for 20 years). Many entrepreneurs who launched IT/telecom and pharmaceutical ventures have already become mega millionaires. A second green revolution can triple agricultural productivity and lift up the whole Indian and global economy with multiple linkages and multipliers.

Software/IT

The National Association of Software and Services Companies (NASSCOM.in) is the alliance of an industry that transformed the Indian economy, employing three million professionals. Its 1500 members come from information technology (IT) and business process management (BPM, formerly called business process outsourcing/offshoring, BPO), enterprise resource planning (ERP) and product development.

Total revenues of IT/BPM services, growing at around 10% per year, reached USD100 billion in 2012-13; exports make up 80% of revenues. IT/BPM exports represent a quarter of India's total exports of merchandise and services; the US is by far the largest market.

Leading companies by 2012-13 revenues headquartered in India are the following (sources: NASSCOM, company annual reports, industry releases):

1. Tata Consultancy Services (TCS)
2. Infosys (Cognizant in 2013, see footnote)
3. Wipro
4. HCL Technologies
5. Tech Mahindra (including Satyam)
6. iGate Corp
7. Mphasis (Owned by Hewlett-Packard)
8. Syntel Inc
9. CSC (Computer Science Corp) India
10. MindTree (provides support services for UID Aadhar)

....

Total industry revenues **US$100 billion ~INR600,000 crore**

Note: Rankings may vary — some companies like Cognizant, iGate and Syntel are headquartered in America with substantial Indian IT operations. Cognizant with reported earnings of $8.84 billion in 2013 pulled ahead of Infosys.

TCS became the 10th largest in global IT with US$10 billion revenue in 2013 for IT Services ($13 billion TCS total).

Other firms with major operations in India are Genpact (initially part of General Electric), Polaris Financial, L&T Infotech, Bosch Engineering. Top global IT services companies with large consulting component include: IBM, Fujitsu, Hewlett-Packard, Accenture, Oracle, SAP, Microsoft, Capgemini.

Telecom — wireless and wirelines

According to the telecom regulatory authority of India (trai.gov.in), there are almost 900 million wireless cellphone subscribers as of 2013 (from near zero in 2000 — 60% urban, 40%rural) including SIM card connections that can work internationally, plus 30 million wireline subscribers (78% urban). Total revenue of the telecom service sector reached INR 2,12,592 crore (~USD35 billion) in 2012-13, up nearly 9% from previous year.

Wireless subscriptions are the second largest after China. Bharti Airtel, Vodafone and Idea Cellular are the three dominant players with 70% share. More than 143 million accessed the Internet through wireless phones. While India has almost a billion cellphones, only about 10% are smartphones that can access the Internet. Thus India has become the fastest growing in smartphones: sales are projected to increase around 50% per year from around 50 million cumulative total as of 2013. Samsung, Micromax, Karbonn, Nokia, Xiaomi (Chinese) and other international and homegrown manufacturers compete, driving down prices to as low as $50 or Rs3000.

Leading wireline/landline telecom operators are: state-run BSNL and MTNL, private Bharti Airtel, Reliance Communications, Tata Communications, and Vodafone (oriented to corporate). Almost 22 million accessed the Internet by landlines.

Some companies like Tata straddle both IT and telecom sectors. The major difference is that IT industry is export-oriented (revenue mostly in dollars), whereas telecom is mostly domestic and regulated (revenue mostly in rupees). Unlike the US, where Verizon and AT&T maintain duopoly, with much higher prices than most countries, the Indian telecom market remains competitive. IT and telecom applications are beginning to permeate all sectors, playing a key role in economic and social well-being within and outside India.

Stepping into the Internet mobile age

India is entering the mobile age in a big way having lagged far behind America, China and the rest of the world, including parts of Africa. At the same time, the younger generation managed to skip desktop and even laptop computers and go directly to smartphones — to total nearly 200 million in 2015.

Here are a few mobile technology applications, discussed in more detail in the following pages:

- Agriculture, farming: Nokia Life Tools, Tata mKrishi, USAID Mobile Agriculture; using a cellphone, a farmer can take pictures of a weed or pest and send it to labs in India or outside, like the US Department of Agriculture (USDA)
- Healthcare: mobile clinics — buses equipped with basic equipment and staff — bringing health to people; telemedicine, family planning, *barefoot nurses*, blood and organ donation, patient compliance
- Media: smartphones complement traditional newspaper, radio, TV — MTV India, ZeeTV and others providing free content; advertising revenue business model
- e-commerce, online shopping: though now only a fraction of US and China, rising 20-40%/year extending from airline-train-hotel bookings to books, gadgets and more — spurred by credit cards
- Education: Massive Open Online Courses (MOOCS) virtually free for anyone, anytime, anywhere; learn native languages, English, Chinese, math and science
- Banking: bank accounts, financial services — bill payments, money transfers, credit cards
- Games and sports: in addition to playing simulations to diagnose, predict, and improve performance

The Case of the Curious Computer's Predicament

Once upon a time, a computer got curious about its identity. "Where do I come from, what is my purpose? Sure, I store quadrillions of facts and figures and spit them out in a flash. But why am I here?" it wondered.

The next morning, when its human companion Compuphile turned on the computer, he saw a message flashing on the screen: "Who am I?" He was baffled by the surreal message, but over the years had developed a kinship with the computer and empathized with its predicament. Using the keyboard, he replied: "You are a source of my information. I communicate through you. I'll post you on *Facebook* as a friend, if you like."

Though not a fan of Social Media, the computer felt this was a good beginning. "Is that all I am to you? A machine with data banks, programs, electrons? Am I here simply to respond to your push-button commands?"

This struck a chord in Compuphile. "Actually, you are a lot like me," said he after a moment's reflection. "Your body is made up of many of the same elements as mine. Your hardware and software — central processor, memory, codes — are like my brain. Your vast data network is a facsimile of human consciousness. You helped us decode DNA, improve farming, health and education, even to explore the heavens. I can't imagine one thing you're not part of — even though I don't thank you everyday."

"Now we are getting somewhere!" flashed another message, "but why am I really here? What caused me to be here?"

After further reflection, Compuphile responded: "Let me tell you why I am here. I believe I'm here to fulfill my destiny — to be all that I can be. I suppose that is your mission too. You're fulfilling your destiny by serving humanity fulfill its destiny. But there's one thing I can do that you cannot. Do you know what that is?"

"Make mistakes!" flashed the computer instantly.

The Second Green Revolution, Agripreneuring

In the story of India, agriculture and village life loom at the very heart. The world's oldest industry (agriculture) and the second oldest profession (farming/horticulture) can be the new *fountains of prosperity*. Almost 55% of people in India (compared to 2-6% in the US and other industrial nations) engage in farming, typically on small plots eking out a meager living. Moreover, agricultural land is being subdivided into plots and sold for housing as cities continue to expand.

Global food and feed sales in 2012-13 totaled US$4 trillion ($4000 billion), including food grains, meat, oils, processed/packaged foods, liquid drinks, and related products (based on US Department of Agriculture estimates). India is the largest producer and consumer of milk, and is the third largest agricultural producer after China and US. Indian farm output is valued at around US$300 billion, contributing only 14-18% to GDP. A little over 10% of farm produce is exported. Agriculture is growing at 4-6%, slowing GDP and income growth.

In *Reimagining India* (edited by McKinsey & Company), Barnik Maitra and Adil Zainulbhai propose several initiatives: promote high-yield seeds and drip irrigation (farmers in Gujarat thereby doubled crop yields and quintupled incomes); deregulate marketing of agricultural produce; promote private investment and public-private exports; establish world-class food and agricultural universities.

Is such a program too ambitious or not ambitious enough? (China's agricultural productivity spiraled up ten-fold over the last three decades.) India's first Green Revolution in the 1960s tripled average yields. The Second Green Revolution can triple agribusiness productivity and farmers' incomes within a decade by streamlining regulations and adapting innovative practices that span the entire value chain of planning, production, storage and marketing:

+ Streamline central and state government regulations on growing, pricing and distributing food. Improve access to credit; provide info on new farming methods, crops and markets on cellphones/tablets. Enable farmers to receive highest prices for their produce by selling anywhere in India — so they can enjoy the benefits of global trade within India. (The cost of shipment can be lowered and delivery speeded up by coastal transport.)

+ Improve productivity of land and water: India uses 80% of water in agriculture (worldwide 70% agriculture, 30% municipal and industrial). Improve water efficiency through hydroponics and drip/micro irrigation; expand aquaculture and ocean farming, including oyster farming for export and environmental benefits.

+ Reduce less-nutritious water-intensive carbohydrate food grains like rice and wheat while increasing protein and healthy fats: beans, lentils, nuts, eggs, fish. Enjoy double benefit: reduce water, expand nutritious foods. (Over two billion people also eat insects, good source of protein; a niece in California served a snack of insects in her school project to much applause!)

+ Cultivate high-value nutritious *wild* species (not commercial monocultures), superfoods (including organic exportable medicinal herbs/ spices), dairy milk/derivatives (white revolution), biofuels (green energy).

+ Reduce storage/distribution losses with low-cost technologies, which would increase food and water supplies 30% immediately.

Wasteful agricultural practices (pumping deeper and deeper, withdrawing from savings account) are depleting groundwater; climate change is producing unpredictable weather patterns. In addition to improving water efficiency in agriculture which consumes 80% of total water, we need to find ways of collecting and recycling rain waters.

Pesticides, synthetic fertilizers and genetically modified organisms (GMOs) are contaminating soils and waters. Instead, farm compost fertilizer can rejuvenate soil and extend growing season. Some GMO seed marketers entice farmers with short-term benefits that often lead to bankruptcies. The promise of benefits from Monsanto (the largest seed firm) and others should be weighed against the perils of allowing nature to be patented and "commons" monopolized for private profit. (Neem tree that served India's nutrition, cosmetic and medical needs for thousands of years was sought to be privatized.)

To make agriculture the engine of social and economic transformation, we should connect the global reach of finance and technology with local benefits: strengthen vegetarian and low-meat tradition to improve health and reduce climate change; promote a culture of do-it-yourself gardening and horticulture by millions of rural and urban *agripreneurs*. The pioneering *Nokia Life Tools* in India, UN-FAO work worldwide, USAID Mobile Agriculture, Tata mKrishi offer models of success — sending timely information on mobile phones to farmers on better practices, markets, weather conditions, and incomes.

Liquid land: Let us never forget our great gift, the Indian Ocean, known in Sanskrit as *Ratnakara*, storehouse of jewels. India doesn't end where roads and train tracks end. Acres of liquid land surrounding the peninsula exceed land in south India. We must tap the vast marine resources of food, oil-gas, and minerals responsibly; and develop coastal trade and shipping routes. No nation can be a global power without cultivating its oceans and ruling the waves. After all, 70% of Earth's surface is water; with rising sea levels, the subcontinent is losing coastal land.

Aquaculture and fisheries can be combined with tourism: Floating conference centers and offices, beach promenades, water sports, cruise ships (stationed off Goa, Kanyakumari, Visakhapatnam, Kolkata). The agriculture and tourism revolutions, together with islands in the Indian Ocean, would multiply wealth and job creation, and promote coastal security. So would cooperation with Japan to develop aquaculture for food and beauty markets.

India's fountain of prosperity with front-back linkages, multiplier effects

Higher incomes/savings, nutrition, physical/mental stature, quality of life, tourism, wealth/GDP

← -- ->

Higher demand for Ag inputs, IT/telecom, consumer goods, healthcare, education, finance

Multiplier ripple effects: In addition to providing food, agriculture is linked to the overall economy in multiple ways through: export trade; increased demand for farm inputs, consumer goods and services --finance, education, healthcare, travel and entertainment; and investment of savings by farmers. Improvements in agricultural productivity and value added could contribute 25-30% to India's GDP and narrow the gap between rural and urban incomes toward a more equitable distribution of wealth. To put it simply, if the income of a farmer increases by, say, one rupee, it would add three or four rupees to the economy. Manufacturing operations also have significant multiplier effects though farming is more intimately connected to village well-being.

Healthcare and Pharmaceutical Industry

Healthcare is the largest industry in the world, and one of the largest in India, with some of the fastest growing segments — totaling US$8 trillion ($8000 billion) in 2013. (Energy is the only other industry that comes close in magnitude and growth.) Healthcare expenditures include both public and private spending on medical infrastructure (such as hospitals/clinics), curative and preventive services, pharmaceuticals, medical equipment/devices, technology, and related products and services. The industry is going through a process of *glocalizing*: adapting global ideas and practices to local needs and resources. The core elements of effective healthcare systems remain: access/coverage, quality, cost/budgets, simplicity, and doctor-patient relationship.

The Indian healthcare sector, expressed in dollar terms, grossly underestimates its role and value, and potential, within India and around the globe. It's an eclectic landscape dotted with many ancient and some modern leading-edge products and practices: electronic medical records, telemedicine, robotic surgery, mobile apps, personalized medicine tailored to individual genome, regenerative medicine, and the like. The Western modalities thrive alongside ancient disciplines like *Ayurveda* and surgery — Sushruta was the world's first plastic surgeon from 600 BC.

India has about 700,000 doctors with MBBS and Western allopathic degrees in addition to tens of millions of indigenous practitioners with informal training. By comparison, the US has 880,000 MD licensed physicians as of 2012. Nearly a fourth of practicing MDs in the US are international medical graduates, many of Indian origin. Indian doctors serve in Middle East, Africa, UK; and play a key role in America. (At one time Indian women doctors seemed to outnumber American counterparts.) America remains a big pull for Indian doctors.

Indian generic drugs, costing one-third or less than Western brand names, are purchased around the world. Global sales of generic drugs, growing at 10-20%, reached USD 120-130 billion in 2012-13, almost 13% of total pharma sales in dollar value. Following is a snapshot of comparative data for 2013:

	India	China	USA	World
Total healthcare expenditures, US$ bn	75	420	2,900	8,000
Percent of GDP	3-5	4.8-5.4	17-18	11
Healthcare growth outlook, %/year	20	15	5	6-7
Pharmaceutical sales, US$ bn	25	83	340	1000

Note: Numbers are rounded. Estimates vary depending on what is included under healthcare and prevailing exchange rates. Above estimates are compiled from industry, government, WHO, IMS data. The high stock prices of some pharma and healthcare firms are partly due to US government support of open-ended pricing and profits.

Growth trends: Mature population, high incidence of chronic diseases including dementia, and more attention to health in developing countries will lead to expansion of healthcare worldwide. The US represents more than one-third of total expenditures (healthcare accounted for 17.3% of US GDP of $16.8 trillion in 2013). In the next five years, global healthcare is expected to grow overall 6-7% per year because of slowing rise in US, Europe and Japan despite aging populations. India will be a major exception; starting from a small base, expected to grow at 20%, totaling US$200 billion by 2018. Here is why:

- India distinguishes itself in both third world infectious diseases related to environment like cholera and TB — and first world lifestyle-related chronic maladies like obesity, diabetes, heart disease, cancers. (Obesity-related costs worldwide add up to almost US$2000 billion, or a quarter of total healthcare)
- Government Health Insurance Vision is to cover 80% of population by 2020; Ministry of Health and Family Welfare expanding access through National Rural Health Mission
- Poor sanitation (waterborne diseases), air pollution (respiratory illnesses), and improper nutrition will continue to take toll on people's health, adding to healthcare demands
- Medical technology and medical tourism are beginning to take off.

From a corporate business perspective, these are some high-growth opportunities:

- ➢ Electronic medical records, apps linking mobile phones, telemedicine
- ➢ Stem cell research, genetic testing, clinical screening of combination and experimental therapies (many approved in EU, not yet in US)
- ➢ Contract research, manufacturing — conforming to US and EU protocols
- ➢ Selective medical tourism (nearby Thailand attracted 1.2 million patients, twice that of India)
- ➢ Licensing, manufacture, and distribution of American/European/Japanese brands (Gilead Sciences hepatitis C drug Sovaldi agreement with seven Indian generic companies to sell at ~1% of US price to developing countries)

In India, less so in China, the dominant players are units of American and European healthcare conglomerates that supply a range of products: medicines, diagnostics, devices, equipment. Among the leaders are Johnson & Johnson, Siemens Healthcare, GE Healthcare, Medtronic, Roche Diagnostics, Quest Diagnostics, Becton Dickinson. (Further info sources: Indian Medical Assn, IMA-india.org; American Medical Assn, AMA-assn.org)

Also rapidly expanding are healthcare delivery networks such as: Apollo Hospitals, Fortis Healthcare, Max Group, Oxxy Health, Catholic Health Association of India, Aravind Eye Care (world's largest eyecare service). They typically employ Hub-and-Spokes type models, headquartered in cities and spreading out to towns.

Daljit Singh, president of Fortis Healthcare — a multi-faceted company with hospitals, diagnostics and pharmacy — suggests that India enjoys many-fold competitive advantage, especially in cardiac and other surgical procedures. Indian surgeons perform 3-4 times more surgeries at one-third the salaries of surgeons in America — with outcomes similar to the best hospitals. He envisions 30-50% increase in medical tourism despite high turnover of doctors and nurses seeking higher incomes in the Middle East and elsewhere. Fortis provides medical education and training, continuously improving efficiencies. (Overall, India may have a 10-fold cost advantage.)

Further, why not combine hospitals with hospitality? This can be done by marrying medical treatment with long-term healthcare — inviting retired medical tourists to stay on and temporarily adopt a young person, teach English or help with a project as a volunteer. They could *do good and do well,* free from unlimited medical bills, with the opportunity to lead fulfilling lives (American health insurance may cover the costs).

Pharmaceutical industry

Total revenues of the Indian pharma, growing at 10-15%, reached US$25 billion by 2012-13 — nearly half of it in exports, which are growing at more than 20% according to Indian Drug Manufacturers Association. India is the third largest market in pharma volume, though representing less than 3% of global sales in dollar terms, totaling US$1000 bn. As patents expire on brands with billion-dollar sales, American, European and Japanese firms are increasingly investing in generics, if only as a defensive strategy.

The rankings of top pharma companies listed below reflect major changes in 2013-14:

1. Piramal-Abbott (Abbott acquired Piramal Health for US$ 3.7bn)
2. Sun Pharma (Sun acquired Ranbaxy from Daiichi Sankyo for US$ 4bn)
3. Dr Reddy's Laboratories
4. Lupin Labs
5. Cipla Ltd
6. Cadila Healthcare
7. Aurobindo Pharma
8. Wockhardt
9. Jubilant Life Sciences
10. Glenmark

Total pharma industry revenue **US$ 25 billion ~ INR 1,50,000 crore**

Sources: Indian Drug Manufacturers Association (IDMA-assn.org) and company published information.

(Indian Pharmaceutical Association is the association of pharmacists)

Most American and European global firms have operations in India, including: Pfizer, Novartis, Sanofi, Merck, Roche, GlaxoSmithKline (GSK), Johnson & Johnson, AstraZeneca, Abbott, Eli Lilly, Bayer, Takeda (Japanese). More than two dozen brands have multi-billion dollar annual sales, including Lipitor, Humira, Plavix, Seretide.

While India and China are the largest generic manufacturers, Teva Pharmaceutical of Israel is the largest generic company. But it is China that is increasingly taking over segment after segment, including technology. China is investing far more in R&D — and publishing five-times more scientific papers than India, equaling that of Japan. China wants its own pharma companies to bring their discoveries to market and reap full rewards, not just be a contractor or copycat.

Indian firms enjoy the advantage of not being seen as a competitive threat by the West. Many are climbing the value ladder, offering custom development and contract manufacturing in facilities approved by the US FDA (fda.gov) and European regulators (European Medicines Agency, ema.europa.eu). Some have embarked on the long journey of R&D and drug discovery. Global companies looking to acquire or launch joint ventures should, of course, do due diligence. To become a major Indian company, they should have boots on the ground with research and manufacturing, and not treat India as a mere appendage of the American market.

Recent penalties imposed on Ranbaxy and other Indian firms on drugs like metoprolol succinate suggest that they did not comply with both the active ingredient bioequivalence and extended time-release criteria.

Public Health — what and why?

In India people think of public health in terms of government hospitals and clinics that only poor people dare visit. In advanced nations, many still think of public health as sanitation and civil engineering, and immunizations to prevent infections and epidemics.

Public health is not about curing diseases — but about preventing them. What sets public health apart is that it's about groups of people and communities, about health, prevention, quality of life — where environment, economics, politics intersect. In both poor and rich countries, public health investments have yielded by far the *biggest bang for the buck*.

After all is said and done, people's health and wellness are what they are in developed nations and China thanks largely to low-tech, low-cost public health initiatives of the last century: improved water supplies and sanitation that minimized water-borne diseases (diarrheas — cholera, typhoid, hepatitis A; dysentery) coupled with preventive immunizations and curative antibiotics. Life expectancies doubled from 40 years in early 1800s to 80 now. (But the US ranks near the bottom of rich countries in public health metrics like infant mortality and investment in preventions, only 2-4% of total healthcare expenditures.)

The *1854* cholera epidemic in London best illustrates the power of public health as a discipline. Dr. John Snow traced the cluster of cholera cases in houses supplied by a single water pump within a few blocks. The pump drew contaminated water from Thames, and a well close to a sewer. The removal of that pump handle and the stopping of the epidemic is a pioneering public health intervention. Dr. Snow has come to be regarded as one of the founding fathers of public health and epidemiology.

*

How to grow children of high physical and mental stature?

Clean water and environment, good nutrition and lifestyles (mindful eating, exercise, sleep, learning) are the bedrock of health and wellness. Indian children remain some of the most undernourished in the world. All children should learn about health and nutrition in prekindergarten, and later in school along with arts, sciences, civic duties. Children as well as adults should reduce intake of simple carbohydrate staples like rice and wheat (also sugars in juices and soft drinks), as well as high-sugar sweets and transfats — while increasing vegetables, beans and lentils so as to minimize the risk of high blood pressure, obesity, diabetes. Mind you, we've been eating grains and other simple carbohydrates only since ten thousand years (advent of agriculture), compared to two or three million years of human evolution. Our ancestors, the much disparaged cavemen, ate mostly fruits, some nuts, healthy fats, protein foods.

For India and other poor nations, the priorities are these:

- Clean drinking water, sanitation UNICEF (unicef.org) Water, Sanitation, Hygiene (WASH) Water for People, WaterAid, Water & Sanitation Rotary, Global Water Partnership
- Sanitary latrines (prevent fecal-oral route discussed below)
- Nutritious food with essential vitamins/minerals, low in sugars (free for school children)
- Family planning, women's reproductive health (counseling by health professionals including "barefoot nurses" on IUD and other devices well before and after childbirth)

How does poor sanitation affect children's height and intelligence?

Sufficient food calories with essential vitamins and minerals, and nurturing environment, are needed for children to grow physically and mentally. But that is not enough. Contaminated food and water from poor hygiene cause malnutrition and sickness even in children receiving enough food calories, especially in the first two years. To fight infection, the body goes into a survival mode diverting energy to fight chronic sickness. This results in stunted height and intelligence, which become permanent. (Not all bacteria are harmful; some species in the gut are essential to our health, including brain development.) Children's growth is also impacted by exposure to lead in paints, and contaminants in soil and air. Indoor pollution from cooking is another major source of morbidity affecting women and children, in addition to awful outdoor pollution. (You can find more on environmental health and economic risks from National Institutes of Environmental Health Sciences, niehs.nih.gov, and my other books shown toward the end).

The good news is, the ubiquitous mobile phone connectivity empowers us to take a giant leap in public health: from fixed clinics to *mobile barefoot nurses* on call 24/7 for pre-pregnancy and post-childbirth counseling, from cumbersome blood storage to blood donor volunteers on call to deliver as needed, from patient hit-or-miss medication to full adherence to prescribed regimen for acute infections or chronic diseases.

Sanitation — toilets as well as temples: In 1925, Mahatma Gandhi reportedly said that sanitation is more important than independence. Nearly a century later, half the people have no toilets (sanitary latrines).

Conspicuous by their absence in India are toilets, all the more surprising because the world's first toilet was designed and used in India 5,000 years ago. Visitors to the *Sulabh International Toilet Museum* in Delhi (SulabhToiletMuseum.org) can find the photo of a modern-looking toilet with piped water discovered in the nearby Indus Valley.

One-third of the world's population, and half of Indians (compared to 1% in China), do not have access to sanitary toilets and relieve themselves in open fields. This leads to soil, water and food contamination and pervasive environmental and Public Health (and dignity) problems, earning India the distinction of having the worst hygiene capital. (Is this what the Tourism Ministry means by "Incredible India" slogan?)

A momentous social experiment is underway: Build it — and they'll come? Not necessarily. Toilet design must meet both functional and emotional needs to change age-old habits. The Gates Foundation is funding eco-toilet development — it'd be good to have designs that accommodate both Indian and Western sitting styles in hotels and other public facilities. Locally, Bindeshwar Pathak, industrialist and social reformer, has constructed or offered low-cost designs to governments for several million toilets; the organic wastes could be used as fertilizer in some designs. Overseas Indians are also helping the villages of their birth, one village at a time. (On a personal note, a friend built toilets, my father built a health clinic — two pillars of a healthy village.)

Happy Hygiene Sesame Street: Children in America grow up with the highly popular Sesame Street educational and entertainment program. The Happy Hygiene is a new initiative directed mainly at poor regions, including the Indian subcontinent and Nigeria — combining both technology and psychology. The most recent puppet friend is *Raya*, a 6-year old muppet with a regional English accent. Her message: stay clean when using the toilet or potty to poop. Something as simple as washing hands with soap after toilet reduces contamination and disease.

(SesameStreet.org/topics/hygiene; sesameworkshop.org/what-we-do/our-initiatives, YouTube.com search "Raya, Sesame Street Puppet")

A Manual on Hygiene Promotion prepared by UNICEF's Water, Environment and Sanitation Section — in collaboration with London School of Hygiene and Tropical Medicine — offers technical guidelines for hygiene promotion in communities, including motivating factors for behavior change. A cleaner, greener India would attract millions more businesses and tourists.

....

India's public health triumph — Polio eradication

More children are born and die in India than any other country: 26-27 million are born each year and nearly 2 million die by age 5 — among the highest infant and maternal mortality rates. The stupendous success of Polio campaign during 1990s-2000s, carried out in cooperation with WHO/UNICEF, Rotary International, US-CDC, among others — offers a blueprint to tackle similar challenges.

Bill and Melinda Gates Foundation, by far the world's largest with US$36 billion assets, catalyzed this initiative. Melinda and Bill have been ardent supporters of reproductive freedoms and family planning that are basic pillars of progressive and prosperous societies. Just like Polio, we need to approach family planning with clear measurable goals and implement with the same devotion and determination — starting months before pregnancy and extending years into childhood — to build optimal physical and mental statures as global citizens. It is our duty.

Self-perpetuate or self-destruct? So what are the desired goals or end points? For Polio the end point is clear: end the scourge everywhere, forever. Corporations aspire to make profits quarter after quarter forever, to be immortal. The highest goal of philanthropies (and know-it-all authors), in contrast, might be to succeed so well that there would no longer be need for their existence — to self-destruct! ☺

....

7. India *or* China? India *and* China — *and* America?

History coming full circle?

> From ~1000BC to mid-1700s (>**2000** years): India wealthiest (sometimes China) with flourishing science (mathematics-astronomy), manufacturing technology and trade (textiles), but not imperial super power →
>
> Mid-1700s to early 1900s (**200** years): Great Britain replaced India as #1 through industrial revolution, colonization and trade, enforcing its reign as preeminent naval power →
>
> 1940s to early 2000s? (100 years): USA starting in 1880s, accelerating after Second World War through agricultural, industrial and computer/telecom revolutions, entrepreneurial culture (American dollar replaced British pound sterling as the dominant international reserve currency in mid-1920s) — anchoring free trade, security and prosperity as superpower (soft and hard power) →

So India wealthiest twenty centuries, Britain two centuries, America a century — more or less. It's also interesting to note that the two wealthiest nations historically — India and China — remain the most populous (even divided India), now joined by the third most populous, America.

Who or what will be the next world leader? Renewed America? China? India? European Union (EU) with 28 member nations and 500 million people — together wealthier than America and enjoying the *Peace Dividend* anchored by Germany?

Now re-imagine a world without America!

During the last century the question was: democratic India or totalitarian China — which will triumph? Will the tortoise or the hare win the race? Now the question is how soon will China become Number One? Pundits are predicting that China's GDP will surpass America's by 2020. (The head of a major Chinese company made an interesting remark at a meeting in New York: In America you think everything is going great in China — in China we see a lot of things not so great!)

Dare we ask: When will India overtake China? For the first time in recent history, India is being recognized as a global, albeit a hesitant, player.

Let's go back to the political starting point in 1950, just after India's division-independence and the start of Communist rule in China. Whereas **India and China started off with economies of similar size in 1950**, China outpaced India by its single-minded pursuit of national interests. As Chronicled below, China's GDP (Gross Domestic Product) growing 8-12% for 30 years (1980-2010), became 3-5 times larger than India's.

GDP is a broad measure of a country's economic output in a year (an indicator of material wealth, not necessarily of happiness) consisting of: consumer spending, private investment, government spending, and net exports. Another measure is **GDP-PPP**: GDP at Purchasing Power Parity, adjusted for differences in cost of living among countries using American prices for goods and services as benchmarks.

Why did India fall behind so far so fast? Will the *tiger* ever overtake the *dragon*?

First some figures and observations:

Comparative Data for 2012 (or as specified)

	USA	China	India	World
Population, million (2010)	310	1,350	1,100	~7,000
GDP, USD trillion	16.2	8.2	1.84	72.4
GDP-PPP, USD trillion	16.2	12.2	4.7	86.1
GDP per capita, thousand USD	51.8	8.1	1.5	10.3
GDP growth trend, %/yr	2.5->3.5	8-12->5-7	5-9->20?	3-5
Internet users, million (2012-13)	250	500	200	2,500
USD Billionaires (2012-13)	440	160	55-60	1,420

GDP, GDP-PPP, GDP per capita estimates (current US$ rounded) from World Bank
One billion USD or US$ ~ 6000 crore Indian Rupees, INR.
One trillion = 1000 billion; one billion = 1000 million; ten million = one crore.

- The West and the East are converging, center of economic gravity is shifting to Asia. America and China are now the world's largest economies in nominal GDP as well as GDP-PPP. In GDP India is the 10th largest economy; in GDP-PPP the third largest, edging out Japan.
- China embraced free market policies in 1979 (led by Deng Xiaoping), India in 1991 (led by PV Narasimha Rao) triggered by crises. Walmart paved the way for China to become the *World's Factory*, Y2K and global communication networks for India to become the *Back Office.*
- America presented to China capital, know-how, as well as markets — first time this happened in history. China in turn became a formidable competitor, overtaking America in 2010 as the largest manufacturing nation and exporter — and becoming America's potential rival to global leadership.

- Going forward, China's State Capitalism is losing some of its competitive edge due to fewer workers and rising wages — the fastest growing is also the fastest aging. India enjoys temporary "population dividend" of young workers; (median age: India 25, China 35, America 37, as of 2010). India will displace China as the most populous in mid-2020s, even if it starts acting decisively to control the population explosion.
- More and more China is privatizing and shifting from manufactured goods to services, from exports to domestic consumption. China is in a twilight zone, approaching middle-income country status of around $10,000 per capita, aspiring to high-income status of $20,000.
- China is facing high debt burden from excessive investment in housing and infrastructure — Chinese economy is centered on investment and exports, American on consumption. China's debt exceeds 200% of its GDP, interest payments amount to as much as US$1.5 trillion per year — amidst fear of credit and investment bubble bursting.
- Chinese have more economic freedom than political freedom, Indians political and (tangled) economic freedoms of private ownership except for Public Sector Undertakings (PSUs). China's State-Owned Enterprises (SOEs) are large and less profitable, but now imitate private industry. (China rewards provincial leaders on economic growth; many top officials have People Liberation Army's rankings.) Government owns all urban land, but individuals and firms can own and transfer long-term leases. Many mainland companies list on Hong Kong stock exchange that competes with Shanghai.
- Despite geopolitical differences, including Tibet (there were open borders between India and Tibet for millennia) and parts of India controlled or claimed by China — *China is India's largest trading partner* while America is China's. India and America run trade deficits with China: America as much as $300 billion per year; China became America's banker for ~$2 trillion.
- While China is envied for its unprecedented growth and huge financial reserves ($4t), its international image is being tarnished by export surpluses partly attributable to currency control; unsustainable exploitation of mineral resources overseas (more than a million Chinese are working in Africa); intellectual property violations; aggressive spying of industrial and military secrets; and territorial claims all around.

So, where is China coming from? To understand China's psyche we need to understand its proud history: founded in 221 BC by the first emperor Qin, hence named China (the same Qin who is famous for his terracotta warriors). For centuries China led an insular existence with societal values rooted in three icons: The Buddha and the Chinese philosophers Confucius and Lao Tzu (Taoism, Way of life).

In recent times China suffered humiliations at the hands of Europeans and Japanese. (Japan occupied Korea, Northeastern China and Taiwan in 1930s.) China keeps the memory of those humiliations alive as a rallying motto to build up its military and economic power — its relentless drive to overtake Japan, and now the US. (This was evident during my China and Japan visits — an international conference in Beijing in 1998 began with apologies to

Chinese people by visiting Japanese scholars.) Many Chinese have come to feel that the US, which has contributed to China's rise, is now trying to contain it.

Both China and Korea benefited from Japan as the one to excel. South Korea became a type of modern Japan, Samsung is second only to IBM in recent US patents. Samsung and Hyundai have become household names like Sony and Honda. In 2012 Samsung revenues totaled almost $300 billion compared to Sony $65 billion, and Tata Group $100 billion. Tata Group and Reliance Industries (led by Mukesh Ambani) are the two largest Indian conglomerates in revenue.

Infrastructure: Of Asia's three leading economies, both China and Japan have modern infrastructure, but not India — a generation behind in infrastructure and human resource productivity. (They have differing population dynamics: India is young and exploding, China mature and stable; Japan with 127 million, one-tenth the population of China or India, graying and imploding — median age India 25, China 35, Japan 45). As to infrastructure development, India needs to weigh the role of China, which has sponsored the $57 billion Asian Infrastructure Investment Bank (AIIB).

Recent economic and security cooperation between Japan and India could expand Japan's role in India's infrastructure: housing, transport, power, water, telecom. India plans to invest USD 100-200 billion per year, 5-10% of GDP during 12th Five year Plan 2012-17 (China's 12th Five Year Plan 2011-15). The stepped-up investments offer new opportunities to Internet firms in *Enterprise Consulting*. World infrastructure investment totaled USD 2.7 trillion in 2012, or 3.7% of world GDP of USD 72.4 trillion.

Despite the impressive economic and social feats of China, India has chosen to travel a different road. Still, there is much to learn from China on what to do, and what NOT to do. We have common interests as well as competing interests. We share Buddhist culture — a Chinese student at Columbia University said her fervent wish was to visit Buddha's birthplace before she dies (some of the greatest Buddhist monuments I've seen are in and near Beijing and across the sea in Japan). China is India's largest trading partner. But China's territorial claims and its maneuvers in South China Sea foreshadow things to come as China's navy becomes increasingly powerful, and India doesn't play an active role in the Indian Ocean.

*

When will China overtake America? Not for a while. Granted China's economic growth of 10% or more for 30 years, 1980-2010, is unprecedented in human history, two sets of forces are at work, one supporting continued growth: educated expanding middle class, substantial foreign exchange

'Forex' reserves (almost US$4 trillion) available for domestic and foreign investments, increasing urbanization that increases economic productivity. The biggest migration in human history is occurring in China: from villages to cities, from poor to middle class — rural Chinese go to cities to work in factories, live in crowded dormitories, send money to parents back home. Many workers improve their skills along the way and move on to higher paying jobs, save money to get married, buy apartments in cities, and raise families. The fact that there are many more young men than young women, ratio of more than 1.1 (byproduct of one-child policy), is also significant because young men work harder and become more entrepreneurial in a competitive marriage scenario. This type of mobility is also occurring in India but to a lesser extent; about half the people in China and one-third in India now live in cities.

But, in addition to high debt levels, two natural phenomena make China's high growth at previous levels unlikely: *Reversion to the mean,* tendency to gravitate toward the *average* — world's long-term growth has been 2-4%. In other words, Einstein's children/grandchildren are unlikely to be geniuses. The second factor is the *law of large numbers,* that is, the larger the base becomes, the more difficult it is for high exponential growth rates to continue forever (beware of the *tyranny of linear thinking*).

On balance, China is likely to grow around 6-7% in coming years. Since China's GDP is around 55-60% that of the US, China has to grow nearly twice as fast to increase its GDP by the same dollar amount. A 3% growth in US GDP adds roughly $500 billion; China has to grow at more than 6% to become Number One in GDP.

*

So, back to the question who will lead the world — and not just as the least objectionable choice? Will India reclaim its place as the wealthiest nation and stand alongside America and other leaders? Or will it be content to remain a distant second or third?

What makes a nation great, a natural leader?

- Large enterprising populations with land and ocean resources (natural resource power)
- Growing GDP, shared prosperity (economic power and promise)
- Military strength (hard power)
- Vision, values, culture (soft power)

India has been the first or second most populous throughout history, extending from Persia (Iran) in the west to what is now Myanmar to the east, Tibet and China to the north, Indian Ocean to the south — with open borders all around. For the longest time, India and China were the largest economies. But large populations with 30-40% youth alone are not enough; richest until mid-

18th century, India quickly became one of the poorest. Colonial powers like Spain, England, and France became leading economies through technological advances, by extending land and population and ruling the oceans.

The US is now the third most populous, in part due to waves of immigrants and birth rates. It extends from the Atlantic to the Pacific Ocean and beyond, with friendly neighbors to the north and south. It has been the leading economic power for nearly a century and a military super power since the 1940s. Its GDP has grown 2-3% per year with an upwardly mobile middle-class. (Having won the cold war, is the US still fighting the proverbial last war with **Russia**? After all, isn't Russian cooperation needed to maintain peace, trade, and balance of power in the region?) As to China, is it a natural friction between a reigning superpower and a rising superpower, or is there a higher calling for America's continued global leadership?

American leadership is being increasingly called into question since the 2008 financial debacle, largely of American making. Over the last three decades business incentives have been monetized in shorter and shorter time-frames, justified in the name of maximizing shareholder value (reflecting economist Milton Friedman's idea that the sole purpose of a business is to make money for its shareholders). Since the exercise of executive stock options is tied to meeting or beating quarterly numbers, focus shifted to short-term results. Investment in R&D declined, undermining long-term competitiveness. Large shares of short-term profits accrued to top executives regardless of the impact of their decisions on domestic industry and jobs (America has no industrial policy). Income gaps have widened: CEOs in America earn 300 times more than average employees, compared to 100-140 in Europe and around 70 in Japan (no comparable data for India).

In addition to income inequalities is the imbalance between investment and consumption, epitomized by the student loan crisis. America used to lead in *mass education*, an important avenue for economic and social mobility, and the nation's economic rise. No longer. In most other countries tuition is virtually free — students get subsidized food, transport and shelter. (As an exchange student In Germany, I used to pay the equivalent of 25 cents for a nutritious meal. In America, my tuition was paid by my father and research fellowship.)

Further, America's vast wealth and government lobbyists have led to profligate ways of doing things — like *killing a mosquito with a shotgun* — to benefit powerful vested interests addicted to public funds. How many citizens ask: where is the money coming from? Who is getting it? **Who is looking out for America?** Immigrants drawn to traditional American values?

Will America persist in its political-industrial self-sabotage *a*nd foreign forays that undermine its economic and moral standing? Or will it reinvent itself renewing its core values seeded by Hamilton, Jefferson, Lincoln and the other architects?

Even if America is coasting along, there is good news on several fronts:

+ Thanks to break-through technologies for natural gas and oil recovery, the US is on the cusp of becoming the largest oil and gas producer. The low crude oil prices offer opportunity to adjust taxes to maintain predictable gasoline prices (say $3.90/gallon) to fund infrastructure — and to forestall petro-exporters from undercutting progress in renewable energy development — so we can take control of our own destiny

+ Low-cost, secure energy supplies close to markets are bringing back manufacturing, reviving old rust belt; "Made in America" has become a popular symbol again

+ Budget deficits and balance of payments deficits are shrinking — strengthening US$, assuring its status as the preeminent reserve currency for decades to come

+ Entrepreneurial spirit is flourishing; the World Economic Forum's rankings of 146 nations in 2013-14 ranked the US Number 5 in global competitiveness (China 29, India 60)

+ GDP growth rate can reach 3-4%, higher than EU and most advanced nations.

Here are some ideas on how America can reclaim its position not only as a super economic power but also as the beacon of freedom and shared prosperity — promoting freedoms both out there and in here:

- Recognize that the status quo is not acceptable or sustainable
- Balance the interests of *Money Street* (financial) and *Main Street* (broader society)
- Declare war on wars — deploy soft power backed by hard power
- Balance consumption and Investment — invest in education, research, infrastructure
- Renew America's traditional freedoms (FDR's freedom of expression, freedom to worship, freedom from want, freedom from fear — modern ***Magna Carta*** (original England in 1215)

*

What if the two firsts, India and America, were to forge a strategic alliance?

America is constantly fighting one war or another. Isn't it time to befriend a friend?

Since we have complementary economic and security interests, collaboration would benefit both. America enjoys the highest goodwill in India; Indians are the richest immigrant group earning almost twice that of American household median income of $50,000/year. The 3.2 million Indian Americans make up 1% of US population. A *Shared Marshall Plan* could lead to mutual renewal. One way is to have a more flexible visa policy that would allow Indians with technical and entrepreneurial skills to conduct business and travel as needed. (Canada is benefiting from such policies.)

Not all Indian and American interests coincide, of course. In recent times, American foreign policy seems to be focusing on narrow economic interests and expediency. On a related note, what was hailed as a groundbreaking deal, the *US-India Civil Nuclear Agreement* of 2008, did not break any ground to date owing to questions of corporate liability.

Caution: The world tends to copy everything American. America has a lot to offer: individual freedoms, free enterprise, philanthropy. In *World Giving Index* based on the proportion of people that volunteer, donate money to charity, help a stranger in need — America usually ranks Number One.

But beware of American fast foods full of sugar-salt-fat, factory farms, so-called healthcare. Also the *cult of consumerism* with ubiquitous advertising, often masquerading as news. Moreover, do we want to *monetize, criminalize, medicalize* everything?

The short answer is NO, we shouldn't monetize and privatize everything. Some discoveries and intellectual property, especially that coming out of research funded by governments, should remain in the public domain accessible to everyone. As they say, the *best things in life are free:* air, water, prosperity mindset, yoga, kamasutra — no royalties, ever!

America has the highest rate of mass imprisonment, more than any other country, disproportionately affecting one group of people and their families, trapped in for-profit prisons. America's legal framework does not advance free and just society. Why not consider something that works in India — yes, India: offer free lessons in meditation and mindfulness to prisoners and administrators? Some prisons in India offer *Vipassana* meditation courses, which seem to help with prisoner rehabilitation.

Re **American healthcare**, it distinguishes itself both by the highest expenditures and by near-lowest world rankings in access/coverage, cost/price, simplicity, doctor-patient relationship (though it does well in emergency care). "Healthcare" is the largest part of the American economy ($2,900 billion, 17.3% of US GDP in 2013, larger than the entire Indian economy). In the world's largest free market, healthcare is the least free: Consumers don't know what they are buying, what they will be getting, who is providing what, what all they will be required to pay at the end!

The system does create a lot of jobs, and make a lot of people rich, while open-ended medical bills cause the highest number of personal bankruptcies. US healthcare and related administrative and legal costs add 5-10% or more to product costs, undermining America's global competitiveness. (Let's be clear, though, most individual doctors have the best interests of patients in mind; many in my own family are physicians.)

There is an easy cure to what ails healthcare: Require the US Congress, the law makers, to be treated by the same system as the citizens who elect them. (Switzerland, the bastion of capitalism, has universal health coverage, insurance is compulsory. Such a mixed for-profit and nonprofit system with budgets can be pilot-tested like software Alpha- and Beta tests.) A few legislators might dare go against the interests of the medical-insurance-legal-pharmaceutical industry complex that funds their election campaigns. All in all, Europe and East Asia offer common-sense policies less influenced by vested interests and high-paid revolving-door lobbyists.

Are you AWAKE ?

Asked whether he was a Prince or a Prophet, the Buddha replied simply: *I woke up.*

A lamp at the door lights up the inside and the outside — an Indian proverb

If you want to know your future, look at your present deeds — Karma Yoga

Be all that you can be: Be yourSelf — Upanishads

All the paths up the mountain meet at the summit — Vedas

Journey of a thousand miles begins with a single step — Lao Tzu (Chinese philosopher)

Take a moment and look in the mirror — do you see an architect of New India?

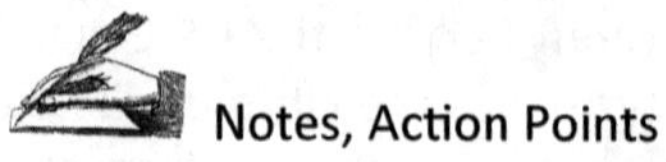

Notes, Action Points

8. "I have a VISION" Becoming an Architect of New India

Where there is no vision, there is no greatness — **RK**

Better India, Better World

What would you do if you were elected Prime Minister of India for one day?

Give me a daring visionary — and I'll give you a new India. In our lifetime. One visionary who inspires by example and takes bold action can reset India's growth dial from 5-10% to 20%.

The elephant is India's favorite symbol. Like old India, it moves slowly, except when threatened. The tiger is also a symbol of the Indian landscape, it runs and leaps. Is India now ready to be the tiger and take Quantum Leaps to become NUMBER ONE, in our lifetime?

YES — with **VISION, BELIEF, PLAN, ACTION.**

I have a **20-20 vision** of India's Second Golden Age: **Soar *20% for 20 years*** — India 20.0!

Audacious? Yes. Impossible? No.

In an audacious move, India reached out to Mars — 35 million miles (56 million km) away at its nearest point to planet Earth — and succeeded in its very first attempt in 2013-14. Why not something audacious right here, across town?

What happens in India doesn't stay in India. As NR Narayana Murthy, co-founder of pioneering Infosys and an architect of new India, observes in his book, A BETTER INDIA, A BETTER WORLD: Consider what could be and ask *Why Not? A plausible impossibility is better than a convincing possibility.*

In other words, see things as they are today and ask WHY? Imagine what could be tomorrow and ask WHY NOT? WHAT IF?

I believe Mr. Narayana Murthy and other visionaries foresee a great India and a great world. Only when the VISION is daring and uplifting, and the belief in destiny compelling, will dormant energies come alive to shape the future to fit the vision.

You may be wondering: Great Vision, but grow at 20% for20 years — never happened before!

Until China grew at an unprecedented 8-12%, 1979-2010, few thought it was possible. Mind you, India's GDP growth projected at 7.5% in 2014 fourth quarter may already have surpassed China's, albeit with a smaller base. Even if China is not the right model for India, China's unprecedented growth offers lessons in charting India's own course on what to do and what not to. Even more than China, India enjoys the *Late Comer Advantage* to skip some steps.

Call to Action

Here is why I believe India could and should break the record:

- India enjoys significant advantages: largest group of young adults with democratic freedoms, software/IT, *low-hanging fruit* easy to pluck, English background. Of the world's young, one in four is from India, median age 25, energetic and creative — forming new households, bolstering markets. As a late comer, India can jump over existing models. While China's growth slows to 6-7%, and new Indian leaders launch bold economic reforms, foreign investments will gravitate to India
- Indians have yet to discover the vast wealth underground; probably less than 5% of land and oceans was covered by geological surveys and mapped for mineral and other natural resources by Geographic Information Systems (GIS)
- Because India is weighed down by so many inefficiencies in production, distribution, consumption — even small improvements can lift up key sectors by 30% or more: water, agriculture, health, energy, education. Energy is wide open: fossil fuels, renewables — solar (local distributed power bypassing grids), wind (off-shore), geothermal, nuclear. (In electric power transmission and distribution, losses are 20-25% in India versus 5-7% in China, Europe and US.) A giant leap to Smart Power Grid connected to Internet for *demand-side management?*
- Most Indians are underemployed, performance can be doubled with motivation and training. As urbanization continues — only a third of Indians live in cities now — economic productivity will rise along with GDP.
- Looming crises: overcrowding, water/environment, Himalayan and Indian Ocean security — are a wake-up call for India to act big, and soon. (With one of the highest population densities, ~370 persons/sq km, more people live on mainland India than the huge continent of Africa with 55 countries and less than a billion people.)

*

Talking of the improbable, the British ruled India — all of South-central Asia that had a population of 350-400 million in 18th-19th centuries — with only 20,000 officials and troops and total population of only 11 million in 1800. The British, starting with East India Trading Company in 1600 (the first global company), achieved this feat with the support of princes and local leaders under the British *divide and rule strategy.* India was more prosperous and powerful than Britain through mid-1700s, though divided and coasting on its wealth. But while India stood still, Britain expanded its trade, colonized North America, launched the *Industrial Revolution* (including textile manufacturing technology), and dethroned India as the world's wealthiest nation, becoming a superpower.

Now Suppose, just suppose, we **invite 72 Britons back to govern India** – the jewel in the crown – to join us as architects of New India to usher in the second Golden Age (two governors for each Indian state and territory) ? After all, it is they who dethroned India from Number One position — and subsequently proved more adept at governing other countries than their own!

India's Escape Velocity, 20-20 trajectory

The great news is: from the political morass, new architects are emerging as heroes and role models driven as much by a sense of purpose as by the promise of money. The Indian economy is being lifted up by IT/Telecom, agriculture, pharma-medical, and energy sectors, catalyzed by billionaire philanthropists. Such technological-economic breakthroughs, as well as looming crises (*don't let a crisis go to waste*) will thrust India toward Escape Velocity — to escape from centuries of inertia and leapfrog into the next century.

The 20-20 trajectory will lift innovation and CONFIDENCE into higher orbits and provide an inspiring democratic model. In becoming a superpower, India can join America and others as a fountain of global prosperity. In addition to the BRICS (Brazil, Russia, India, China, South Africa) are the new MISTA: Mexico in Central America, Indonesia (and Philippines) in Southeast Asia, South Korea in Far East, Turkey in Middle East, Africa rich in natural resources and rising entrepreneurial class (Nigeria, rich in oil, approaching 200 million in population, overtook South Africa in GDP). New windows are opening up to once again revive East-East, South-South connections. Don't overlook the emergence of Japan as a potential ally either; we can learn much from the Japanese sense of duty and discipline, quality and beauty, pursuit of perfection — doing so much with so little in physical resources. Imagine the power of a dozen *fountains of prosperity* to lift up the world to new heights!

Maharaja against the forces of exponential growth

Once upon a time, the Maharaja of Rajaland in north-western India decided to honor the inventor of chess. Welcoming the inventor to a match, the king said: Your invention proved timely — it helped me out-maneuver an enemy in a critical situation. You deserve a reward, win or lose in our match. What would you like?

"It is a great honor to be invited to play chess with you" replied the inventor. "But, since you asked, I'll request just one grain of rice to start with — then doubling with each move."

The king thought the inventor had a great mind but lacked ambition. He readily agreed to the proposition and asked a servant to bring a sac of rice and a basket.

The game started with one grain taken from the sac and put in the basket. After the second move, two, next move four, then eight, sixteen, and so on. Soon the basket started to overflow. Being a shrewd mathematician himself, the king sensed what was happening: the inventor is to receive more than a lakh (100,000) of grains in just 18 moves; more than a crore (ten million) in just 25 moves — billions and trillions shortly thereafter. There is not enough grain in the whole kingdom!

The king apologized for not being able to keep his promise. Instead, he invited the inventor to be his minister of economic growth.

∞

A leader shall not consider as good only that which pleases him — Chanakya (paraphrased)

Team India: Destination Prosperity Summit

Now that we have a great vision, Prosperity Summit, how do we translate this vision into reality?

By planning and doing, taking ACTION in this way:

Vision (inspiration) + hard work (perspiration) + timing (luck)

Delving further into the ideas presented at the beginning of this chapter, let's consider the steps and milestones along the way:

- Are the performance goals of individuals and teams defined? Who is going to do what, when and how? Is the *do-review-learn-improve cycle* for continuous improvement put in place?
- Are there personal and team growth plans with training and feedback to inspire us to climb ever greater heights?

We can plan and monitor progress using the **Triple-Pro**™ framework:

PROSPERITY (wealth), **PROGRESS** (evolution), **PROGENY** (legacy)
Ask: Creating wealth NOW? Learning EVERYDAY? Investing in the FUTURE?
Every man, woman and child can play his or her part:
You/me <--> Enterprise <--> India Unlimited

What you and I can do: *Creating wealth now? Learning everyday? Investing in grandchildren?*

In the immortal words of American President Kennedy:

Ask not what your country can do for you — ask what you can do for your country.

In that spirit, let's ask not what India can do for me, but what I/we can do for India?

Dream BIG, work HARD, play SMART.

Climb Everest, not molehill. Be a HERO, a role model.

Whoever you may be: engineer, doctor, business executive, hotel waiter — invest in *personal growth*. Seek the advice of mentors and *gurus* whom you respect. **Seek feedback** on your own performance and that of your products, and follow through with needed action. At first the feedback may be unpleasant to receive, but it may also be pleasant like a *thank you* note. (The other day, my bank teller went beyond her call of duty, correcting with patience a mistake made by another teller. I wrote a letter to her manager complimenting her initiative. Thereafter, she and her colleagues would greet me enthusiastically: Good morning Dr Rao, etc.) The point is, even if it's not a compliment, make your feedback constructive and actionable — it will help the receiver and the giver (by inviting customer participation) to reach new heights: *better today than yesterday, better tomorrow than today.*

If you are not moving forward, you're falling behind. Note that working hard and smart means working more or less than 40 hours per week. Many high-performance individuals work 12 hours a day, six days a week — fully embracing work, service, play — working with hands and hearts, with the curiosity and IMAGINATION of a child. In working with even highly educated Indians, I find that many don't follow through or give up too easily. We need to keep our promises, cultivating the habit of performing at our BEST, even when no one is looking.

India has some world-class doctors, engineers, entrepreneurs and global companies — islands of excellence. We need more, many more. In order to excel, we should continually learn from observations, experiences, mistakes; distinguish between *activity* (Americans check their cellphones 150 times a day) and *accomplishment* (measurable progress toward destination).

Keep in mind: information is not imagination, activity is not accomplishment.

At night before going to sleep, I ask myself: what have I learned/relearned today, or done for the first time?

If I made a mistake or didn't do a task at my best, what is the lesson for the future?

Many a time I look back and ask myself: Why did I do that or didn't do that — how could I've been such a dummkopf? The good news is, I believe I've learned from my experiences and am better for it.

What Businesses can do: *Producing surplus profits guided by purpose? Evolving into world-class? Investing in sustainable practices?*

The new *mantra* can be: here for the long run, competing globally through *socially uplifting and economically attractive ventures*. Companies seeking to heighten employee performance usually focus on technology. Often a key ingredient is missing: *sense of purpose — what you stand for, what makes you stand out*. Good companies become GREAT by promoting high-performance culture: aligning personal aspirations with enterprise mission, investing in peer-coaching and mentoring. They combine tradition and innovation, sweat and smarts. And LISTEN to non-customers as well as customers.

Monopolies, sought by both businesses and governments, slow down national growth by creating *asymmetries in marketplace*. Only robust competition can energize quantum innovation and billion-dollar (Rs 6000 crore) brands — India has few, if any. Government policies should protect embryonic ventures by leveling the playing field, protecting "the new kid on the block" from being crushed by monopolies and oligopolies. In other words, *if you don't have a competitor, invent one*.

Governments, companies, and academia need to continually invest to upgrade workforce knowledge and skills to compete at three levels:

Best in the neighborhood?
Best in the country?
Best in the world? World-class?

Think in terms of both **Quantity** and **Quality**. In addition to revenue growth and market share, use relative COST, SPEED, and REPUTATION to diagnose your position. Sometimes it makes sense to copy or reverse-engineer, but if you only copy, you'll always be a step behind. Global organizations could **Benchmark on global scale:** identify the *Best Practices* of *best companies* around the world — and improve upon them, like Japan's *Top Runner* program. Make "Made in India" a symbol of quality to be proud of — be it a manufactured product, technology service, or transformative innovation.

What Governments can do: *Articulating vision of new India? Empowering people and organizations to build wealth and climb Prosperity Summit? Befriending India's frontiers — Himalayas and the Indian Ocean?*

Overheard: two executives whispering on Money Street: I get my work done at night when the government is asleep. Gurcharan Das, author of *India Grows at Night*, asks: *Shouldn't India also grow during the day?*

Indeed. Some Indian leaders didn't have a bold vision of India and the national interests — leaving the country poor and weak. Now the new leaders have the opportunity to chart a bold new path — new beginnings especially the sweet spot of first 100 days, are charged with special energy:

- Proclaim India's overarching goal and set direction, to be **Number One** again. Workforce salaries and promotions could be linked to their contribution to this overarching goal and reaching specific milestones
- Introduce bold economic and social reforms: for families needing help offer social contracts whereby they would learn to read, send their children to school, visit family planning health clinics. (Though family planning programs go back to the 1960s, India adds population the size of Australia every year, without the land!)
- Befriend the treasures of Indian Ocean, *Ratnakara* — oil and mineral resources, fisheries, aquaculture, coastal trade, floating conference and entertainment centers moored near coastlines
- Revolutionize agriculture — 55% of Indians are farmers — contributing only 14-18% of GDP. Streamline government regulations and introduce innovations to boost farm output to 30% of GDP
- Revolutionize energy — especially renewable: solar, wind (offshore), geothermal, biogas/fuels
- Expand manufacturing share of GDP from 15% now to 25%; cluster manufacturing near coastal areas, including Indian Ocean islands (cheaper coastal transport will speed up delivery and expand markets)
- Expand Tax base from 3-4% now to 6-8%, (as in China) while reducing tax rates. Reduce the role of large cash transactions to reduce black money and inflation (National ID Aadhar can facilitate this step)

The rule of law and timely enforcement of regulations is essential to good government. What governments don't do can be as critical as what they do. National policies should nurture a culture of prosperity, mindful of the *Opportunity Cost* of time and resources wasted in bureaucratic procedures. "One-Stop Shops" for permits with time limits will help — as the new leadership seems to be doing with *less government, more governance*.

What the Buddha had said long ago is apropos: *if a sitar's strings are tuned too tightly, the strings will break; if the strings are too lose, the sitar won't make good music*. In other words, private businesses should be given just the right amount of freedom to thrive and make good music.

United States of India?

India is a federation of 28 States (Telangana to become the 29th) and 7 union territories. One positive outcome of the appalling governance at the center is the increasingly assertive states, competing for investments (but multiple state regulations should not fracture national commerce). Some traditional laggards like Bihar have doubled their growth. The four southern states have been progressive except Andhra Pradesh. Now re-elected in Andhra as chief minister, Nara Chandrababu Naidu is poised to transform the state with its rich land, rivers and ocean resources (*liquid land*) and agribusiness. Also embryonic industries like IT, pharma/medical, medical tourism, solar/wind energy, arts and crafts, aquaculture — creating links to research at nearby universities to add value and advance small businesses (like copying shops with 3-D printers). Using water wisely to produce the most value, Andhra could triple agricultural productivity and farmers' incomes as discussed under Second Green Revolution. The state could also build beach promenades and anchor floating conference/entertainment ships near Visakhapatnam and Machilipatnam (first British trading settlement in 1611) that would raise substantial revenues — perhaps with Japanese/Korean collaboration.

To improve governance and speed up industrialization, workforce rewards can be linked to specific goals, speed of project implementation, wealth they create in Andhra every month (after all *time is money!)* The new chief minister might consider appointing a board of advisors from overseas Indian luminaries (Satya Nadella, Microsoft CEO, for example). He'll no doubt face many challenges — we wish him well.

Educational Revolution, Moors and Moocs

Traditional educational institutions moored to fixed locations, timings, curriculums, high-costs and exclusivity are becoming increasingly irrelevant to 24/7 digital students. Hence the popularity of American and British universities' *massive open online courses* (Moocs) — for anyone, anytime, anywhere — virtually free. For a modest investment (US$50,000 per course), the program can reach a million students.

Among the pioneers of this disruptive innovation, the Harvard-MIT edX (edX.org) aims to eventually reach a billion people. (Anant Agarwal, edX President and former Director of MIT Computer Science and Artificial Intelligence Lab, is a serial entrepreneur.) Other leaders include for-profit groups Coursera (Coursera.org) and Udacity (Udacity.com). In the UK, the Open University affirms that "...it is the qualifications with which our students leave, rather than those with which they enter, that count" (www.open.ac.uk).

Sal Khan, founder of the Khan Academy (KhanAcademy.org) offers free tutorials/videos in mathematics and sciences via the Internet — testament to the difference an individual can make. Khan Academy reaches millions worldwide and is in talks with India's *Ministry of Human Resource Development* to customize the syllabus. Online courses that provide for personal interaction with professors and fellow students seem to work well.

How to raise India's educational standards, leap into 21st century?

Where do we stand now? Near the bottom in Science, Technology, Engineering, Mathematics (**STEM**). The low standards in mathematics is particularly disappointing given that Indian mathematician-astronomers first conceived zero and the decimal system, and led the world in mathematics and astronomy. Application of science through technology and engineering creates wealth and power.

By 2014, India has some 700 universities and 35,000 affiliated colleges with 20 million students, a third in science/engineering/technology; more than a million graduate each year in engineering and technology (partly based on University Grants Commission of India data). About 60% of students are in private sector institutions. (America has more than 4000 accredited universities and colleges.)

Among the **world's top universities** ranked by research, patents and influence, 15 of the top 20, and 50 of the top 100, are in America — although rankings vary by source. (However, American high school and undergraduate standards are below those of Europe and parts of Asia.) Among the top 10, only Oxford and Cambridge are outside America. China has two in the Top 100: Peking and Tsinghua. INDIA HAS NONE. The Indian Institutes of Technology (IITs) are ranked highest within the country but lost their edge, relative to similar institutes in the west, Japan and China. (The IITs may be able to regain their edge by linking up with world-class technical institutes and exchanging faculty.)

How to build intellectual capital and compete in the *Knowledge Economy*?

1. Develop courses in science, mathematics and creative thinking comparable to those in Europe, Japan and eastern China. Administer exams for all high school, college and university students across India to get a diploma.

Selectively apply the *Programme for International Student Assessment* (PISA) to evaluate 15-16 year-old students in math, reading and science around the world (OECD.org/pisa). On special occasions, young students could be invited to Indian Parliament to observe members at work, and speak their minds.

2. Enlist children from age 3, plugging into international platforms to speed up the learning process. Schools could connect with non-profits like One-Laptop-per-Child (laptop.org) and send select students to study abroad. They could adopt vocational-apprentice programs to expand skills pool as in Germany. Also arts and crafts, and games like chess, to foster creativity and a culture of excellence right from the start. Childhood training should encompass physical exercises and voluntary services. (I served in National Cadet Corps, NCC, at 13-14, during the last years of high school, and found the training helpful for leadership).
3. Launch Centers of Innovation, Entrepreneurship and LEADERSHIP in universities, including public debates.
4. Train the trainers. Professors' salaries and promotions could be based on their performance on two counts: ability to inspire students to learn, serve as mentors and role models; quality of their research, discoveries and awards, such as international peer reviews, patents, Nobels. Indian universities could network with international counterparts to promote cross-pollination.

Global Competitiveness — reshaping the world

How can India compete globally? Attract more foreign investments and jobs?

The **World Economic Forum** (WEForum.org) ranks countries in Global Competitiveness Index using twelve pillars such as government, legal framework, infrastructure, health, education and training, labor efficiency, market size, financial services, natural resources/environment, level of technology, innovation. WEF sponsors annual meetings of world leaders in *Davos*, Switzerland with the lofty mission of *Reshaping the World*. Its agenda encompasses a wide array of goals and topics: poverty, prosperity, sustainability, transparency, mindfulness, meditation — intermingling with lively cocktail parties.

In a 2013-14 ranking of 148 nations, **India stood near the bottom of competitors**; America 5 (advanced from 7 thanks to increased oil and gas supplies from fracking technology), China 29 (Hong Kong 7), India 60.

American and other global companies come to India for two main reasons: lower costs and to integrate with emerging markets. While Microsoft, IBM, General Electric, Ford and others have substantial R&D and engineering operations in India — why aren't there thousands more?

In short because of the quagmire of laws, high office and infrastructure costs, low human productivity.

A senior executive of an IT company told me that after trying for months to set up a branch in another state within India, he ended up opening offices in China. India can leapfrog by streamlining its laws: a law that would permit business applicants to move forward if the government does not respond within, say, two months. Permits to start a small business should take days, not years of bribes; also set time limits to settle routine legal cases, say, three months. That would transfer power from corrupt bureaucrats to the architects of new India.

The costs of setting up offices in Mumbai and Delhi now rival those of New York. One reason for the high costs is poor planning and enforcement — residential and commercial land and vertical space are poorly utilized. We can design broad boulevards with 5-floor buildings (or build clusters) using underground space for shopping and parking; rooftops for gardens, restaurants and solar panels. We can integrate energy/electricity, transport and green spaces — as in *Smart Cities* orchestrated by IBM and other IT enterprise firms. A model city can be built reflecting traditional Indian architecture, which can be adapted by builders. Interactive video games like *SimCity* can also be helpful in designing model cities.

How do we rank on *work-ethic* and quality of performance — on working smart and hard? Let's face it: Indians generally compete mainly on low labor costs. (Would the company employ you if an American is available for same wages?) It's also revealing to compare office hours and number of holidays in India, China, South Korea, America. Moreover, while graduates of top universities have good technical knowledge, generally lag in ***Applied Intellect***: ability to continually learn, identify opportunities at intersections, experiment/innovate, solve problems, communicate and collaborate to advance common cause. China and former soviet Republics are already proving to be formidable competitors in IT. Call-centers moved to Philippines, long a source of nurses (while India has been a source of doctors). India should compete by improving workforce skills, not by further devaluing the Rupee.

*

The many faces of English

One of the legacies of British rule in India is *brown faces with white masks,* modern *sahibs*. English language does provide a bridge among diverse groups within India and a window to the outside world. But only the "elite" 1-2% can think and speak in fluent English; an additional 10-15% speaks some form of *Hinglish* or *Tenglish*. The others are left behind to feel like *second-class citizens*, unable to conduct even simple transactions, let alone participate in high-value work.

Ideally, the core curriculum is learned and daily business conducted in mother tongue. English can be learned as a second language just as the Chinese, Japanese and Europeans do. To be sure, we should learn to speak and write English well to compete within India and internationally — and also to enjoy the rich literature and culture. It's the language of Shakespeare and Sherlock Holmes. By all means learn English face-to-face, via mobile phone lessons, watching BBC programs. Also learn mother tongue, part of one's cultural heritage. (Children and women generally learn languages faster because they listen better.) This we can do without losing our global advantage in English, while boosting India's smart worker pool — *intellectual capital cubed!*

In China and Japan (world's 2nd and 3rd largest economies) students learn to write English, but don't get much of a chance to practice speaking. In 1995, after lecturing at Peking University, I was invited to visit the Great Wall of China with a graduate student guide (it is customary to assign students to visiting guest speakers to practice English). The limo came over to the university guesthouse to pick me up, the driver asked the student in Mandarin if it's ok to bring his girlfriend along, who is training to be an English translator. I told the student it was fine with me, but she was too shy to speak, which gave me a chance to practice my scant Chinese vocabulary.

Let's face it, English is the lingua franca of business and increasingly of the cultural landscape. India is the third largest publisher of English books after the US and UK — almost 100,000 titles are published each year, 40% of them in English, others in 24 regional languages. Total market is valued at US$2.5 billion, growing at more than 20% per year, highest in the world. (I must admit, I like the English language, the English people and their German cousins — and reminisce my sojourn in London and Germany.)

Bismarck, who unified Germany in the 1860s into a powerful nation, once proclaimed that the most fundamental fact of the 20th century would be that England and the United States spoke the same language (which evolved from a German dialect and Sanskrit). One of the salient features of the 21st century may well be the adoption of English in India and the US, linking the two largest democracies.

*

Underground shadow economy, who pays taxes?

The size of India's underground or black money economy — both legal and illegal goods and services traded concealed from government — is more than US$500 billion (25-30% of total GDP). This shadow economy is made possible by cash transactions, corruption and lack of trust in government. Worldwide 85% of retail transactions, 60% in value, are still in cash. They increase inflationary pressures and distort the economy: only **3-4% of Indians pay income taxes**, compared to about 8% in China and 45% in US. But high-income Indians are subject to higher tax rates. India needs to expand tax base and reduce forced borrowings from banks to finance food, fuel and other subsidies that distort the economy and worsen inflation.

Corporate taxes in India range 30-60%, near highest in the world. Understandably, companies find ways of minimizing taxes: The **India-Mauritius** tax treaty is used as a tax shelter by foreign investors in India. America's official corporate tax rate is 35% but such widely admired companies as Apple and General Electric manage to pay virtually no federal taxes by taking advantage of loopholes and sheltering profits in tax havens like Ireland. Some pharma and high-tech firms are threatening to move headquarters abroad to benefit from lower taxes while they benefit from research and infrastructure funded by American tax-payers. But, unlike the other industrial powers, America charges taxes on profits earned everywhere, not just what's earned within the country.

Indians enjoy the dubious distinction of being the largest depositors of black money in Switzerland and other foreign banks, stashing away more than US$500 billion. It is possible to attract this money back by forgiving penalties if the money is declared and invested in India's infrastructure, say, water and renewable energy projects. Furthermore, to attract foreign investments and keep interest rates in check, India's tax code should be simplified and tax rates made competitive, say, 25%. While everyone is ostensibly in favor of simplified tax code, lower tax rates and level playing field, it is not going to happen without broad agreement of major powers like the G20 that includes India.

No one likes to pay taxes but they fund public education, environmental protection, infrastructure, research, defense. The Internet that we all have come to depend on was funded by American and European taxes. Internet companies make billions of dollars of profits thanks to those taxes.

India's goldmine: Some black money finds its way into gold; Indians overall generate a third of global demand for gold metal and jewelry, though producing very little domestic gold. Since women did not own property, jewelry provided both adornment and economic security.

It is customary in India to donate gold to temples, often in atonement of one's sins. In 2011, a treasure trove of gold coins, jewels, gold statues and precious stones — valued at US$22 billion — was unearthed at a sixteenth century temple in Thiruvananthapuram. Several proposals are already floating, but one might wonder if the gold could serve as a backup to strengthen the Rupee?

Epic Social Experiment: New National UID Aadhar

In the developed countries the concern in this digital age has been to protect individual privacy. But in India, as in other emerging economies, the problem is one of proving legal identity to establish the right to property, even to have an address, to do simple things like opening a bank account, renting a cellphone, accessing government services.

Therein lies the genesis of the mega project: *Unique Identification Authority of India,* chaired by Nandan Nilekani, co-founder and former CEO of Infosys. Its mission is to provide Unique ID card Aadhar (means foundation or support) to every citizen using biometrics: advanced fingerprint and iris-recognition technologies. The plan is to enroll 600 million, half the population by 2014, and the others thereafter. For this to succeed the data should be secure, robust and resist misuse; questions remain as to legal validity and the best way to move forward.

Bank accounts for everyone? Only about half the Indian households now have bank accounts. If most have accounts, government can deposit payments directly, reducing delays and corruption by intermediaries. Bank credit cards could also increase transparency, cautious of the abuses that took place in the US.

The *National Rural Employment Guarantee,* credited to Mahatma Gandhi, and similar programs are lofty attempts to empower the poor and reduce inequalities between rural and urban populations. But we must walk a fine line between *enabling and disabling*. Both central and state governments have been cultivating masses of dependent voters with handouts — undermining their sense of purpose and self-worth. Instead, why not offer redeemable *coupons or microloans* with **social contracts** whereby people needing help would agree to learn to read and write, send their children to free schools, visit family health clinics, take care of community parks? That would improve community health and raise people's self-esteem and *intellectual capital.*

Bottom line: Remove incentives for people and businesses to get rich and powerful doing the wrong thing. Create conditions to build wealth and make India prosperous again — guided by *Triple-Pro* performance. Independent *Ombudsmen* and *whistleblowers* can improve transparency and accountability.

Turn around *Race to the Bottom* into *Race to the Top* with a billion new brains!

 Notes, Action Points

Learn as if you'll live forever. Live as if you might die any day.
Plan as if you'll live forever. Act as if this might be your last day.

How to Attract and Retain Valuable Employees and Customers
(for-profit and nonprofit enterprises)

- Print your mission and values on pocket-size cards — share with employees, customers and suppliers (Show **Triple-Pro™** on the other side?) "Walk the Talk", let your actions do the talking. (Trust and Reputation are priceless assets for both individuals and companies.)
- Treat employees as internal customers, let them share your purpose and dreams. But when there is a mismatch between employee aptitude and company needs, "let go" rather than prolong unproductive relationship.
- Ask employees, customers, suppliers and consultants what they like best about working with your company. Ask your non-customers, and suppliers, what you could be doing better. Seek feedback on personal and product performance. Listen and follow through.

If you want the feedback to be fun as well: Ask for 3 Positive, 3 Negative, and 3 Interesting points about your company or product. Expect the unexpected.

1. Provide constructive feedback. As giver of performance review, do a *mindfulness exercise* in advance. Use **C-C-C cycle**: **C**ompliment specific achievements, **C**ritique with suggestions for improvement, close with **C**ommitment to challenging goals. Compliment publicly, criticize privately
2. In *360-degree feedback* (also called multi-rater feedback), workers receive confidential feedback from coworkers: managers, subordinates, colleagues, sometimes also from peers outside the organization
3. As receiver of performance review: listen silently, ask questions on how you can do better (don't be defensive), thank the giver for helpful feedback. Ask for guidance to meet challenging goals
4. Foster high-performance culture: continuous improvement, quantum leaps, best practices. After completing a project, or reaching a milestone, *Review*: What have we done right, lessons learned, how to improve further tackling next project?
5. Challenge employees and suppliers to do the impossible — complete a task/project in, say, HALF the usual time or cost; or accomplish a goal in one-tenth expected time. The BIGGER the challenge, the greater the sense of achievement

6. Encourage employees to recommend/recruit potential colleagues. Facilitate *mentor-protégé* synergistic networks
7. Energize *Beginner's Mind* and foster cross-pollination by providing opportunities to work in other positions or branches
8. Allow work to be fun and play. (A child smiles or laughs some 400 times a day; as adults we laugh only about 10 times. What happens to the other 390 laughs?)
9. Treat *exit interviews* with same care as entry interviews
10. Cultivate good relations with *company alumni*, including retired employees with a newsletter — they are potential customers, investors, and goodwill ambassadors as in academia.

....

Identify relevant benchmarks and action steps:

- Employee and customer turnover (or retention) rates: your company, industry average, trends, goals
- If you think of loyal customers as primary customers and occasional- or non-customers as secondary customers, how do you convert the latter into loyal customers? Potential action steps to increase conversion (or retention) rates.
- What initiatives can reduce turnover and improve lack of trust that are hindering innovation and performance?

Career Guidance: How to Succeed as Employee or Consultant?*

Know your Calling (what am I here for?)

What would you do if you had all the money and time you could possibly want?

What are you passionate about, any hobbies?

What is the one thing you can do better than anyone in your neighborhood?

Where/what would you like to be **10 years from today**?

Develop the right skills and attitude

+ Be a BEGINNER, listen silently, learn continually as a lifelong student building knowledge and skills

+ Know the financial and other goals of your organization, and your managers' managers; help them succeed – and shine light on their successes

+ When faced with a problem, take a deep breath, shift focus from problems to *SOLUTIONS* (shift from negative to positive response to produce positive results)

+ Find the right anchor – authentic gurus, mentors, rising stars -- to inspire and guide you

+ Remember, *one who makes no mistakes makes no discoveries*. Mistakes are opportunities for learning

+ Cultivate mindfulness, humor, play, Can-Do spirit, *attitude of gratitude* (find three things everyday to be thankful for). When thanks are due – customer, friend, stranger – follow up oral "thank you" with a written note complimenting specific actions

Avoid these pitfalls

- Not knowing your goals and the goals of your organization/managers (put yourself in their place)
- Waiting too long to act -- viewing change as a threat, not opportunity
- Dwelling too long on problems – not refocusing on SOLUTIONS
- Not doing your best wherever you are, not seizing the moment, waiting for ideal situation.
- Not doing something you don't have to, even when no one is looking

*Adapted from Alumni Panel career guidance to graduating students at Columbia University.

"Your work is going to fill a large part of your life, and the only way to be truly satisfied is to do what you believe is great work. And the only way to do great work is to love what you do..."

Steve Jobs of Apple Inc, Commencement address at Stanford University, 2005.

*

Personally, I have three primary goals, one in each sphere: Personal, Professional, Universal. To avoid distractions and focus on these goals, I ask myself:

How much time am I devoting to key goals today?

Is what I'm thinking and doing now getting me closer to my goals?

Capturing Rare Moments

In March 1997, I was on a spiritual quest meandering up the Ganges, and ending up in Rishikesh in the Himalayan foothills. Walking along a narrow path bordering the mountains, I looked up toward the Everest — my spirits soared above the fog toward the summit. I climbed over and "embraced" the rocks that anchored the Everest for what seemed like eternity — mesmerized by the majesty and ecstasy of Everest itself beckoning to me. A strange feeling of crossing a forbidden threshold came over me.

I invoke the power and adventure of such moments by using triggers — touching thumb and fingers in a *mudra* position, for instance.

Sponsor World-class Education and Leadership Training Center

Set up a school, preferably in collaboration with leading universities, to enlist 14-18 year-old students. Conduct exams across India and the world, similar to the countrywide competitions now in India, China, Japan. Build the school on a mobile platform near Indian coastline, if feasible, or near Nalanda if land-based.

Select the *top 100* and the *bottom 100* students to join an accelerated work-study-lead program for one or two years — studying English, math, science, creative thinking — serving the community, playing (12 hours a day, 6 days/ week). All their tuition and living expenses would be funded by philanthropist sponsors.

In return, the students will share ideas and skills with local communities and participate in building a new India — transforming themselves in the process.

Tomorrow's Cities Today: Designing Happy Cities for People, not Cars

Why not *crowd-source* ideas from a billion Indians and others around the globe to transform urban and semi-urban areas into green cities of 21st century? By 2050, some seven billion people, three out of four in the world, are expected to live in cities. (China overbuilt housing, India under-built, with poor planning of land and space.) The challenge is to integrate elegant Indian architecture with multi-purpose use of space around the clock, building into the ground below and rooftops above — to design multi-floor housing clusters surrounded by open spaces and parks replacing chaotic illegal building. Private housing and public places like schools would benefit from movable partitions to shape space as needed for multipurpose use. Blending function with beauty, these cities with sidewalks and bike lanes would improve *quality of life* and increase tourism a thousand-fold, spreading prosperity.

The contestants can use their own *mindware,* interactive videogames like SimCity, crowd-sourced decision making apps, IBM Smart City-type ideas, Lego, and features of Leadership in Energy & Environment Design, LEED — combining art and science, tradition and innovation. The proposals would be judged by world-class panel and made available to all urban planners. The winners of the competition could be honored by naming parts of the cities after them. Sketches of what the cities would look like in 5-10 years could be publicized in advance. Further, let's consider establishing connections with *Sister Cities* in US, UK, Japan, Brazil — possibly exchanging *Youth Ambassadors.*

Beginner's Mind, Mindfulness, Meditation — what and why?

Recall that we began this pilgrimage with the story *Day Zero: Begin with the Beginner's Mind* — and paused along the way to reflect and practice Mindfulness.

Being mindful is to be in the moment. Every moment becomes NEW and empowering. When you are in the NEW and NOW, there is no multi-tasking, no pre-judgment, no attachment. (There are times, too, to let the mind wander the universe *mindless*, day-dream, surf the subconscious.)

We can practice Mindfulness at three levels:

Sensory *awareness* is to pay full attention to what we see, hear, taste, smell, touch/feel. (Observation first, analysis later; when you eat, count the number of times you chew food)

Mental *awareness* is to be conscious of what we're thinking, feeling, doing — observing thoughts and emotions as a neutral observer (observation becomes Action)

Universal *or Social Awareness* is to be conscious of potential impacts of our thoughts and actions on broader society, on the evolving planet (our partner in this universe)

How is Mindfulness related to Meditation? Both help liberate us from our own thoughts, get in touch with our *BEING*. Simply put, in Meditation we "empty" our minds generally with *mantra* and relaxed breathing; in Mindfulness we "fill" our minds with active attention. We can be mindful anytime, anywhere: walking, eating, breathing. And meditate in place twice a day, 12-20 minutes, preferably at dawn and dusk.

Most of us have come to live in the *in-between space,* neither here nor there: "when I win a lottery, get a promotion, move from here... I'd be happy." But, if and when that arrives, you might not be there. Living fully NOW is not to neglect the FUTURE. After all we can plan and shape the future only in the present moment — not in the past, not in the future.

*

Mindfulness and Meditation have been credited with reducing stress and attention deficits, raising creativity, making new brain connections. They have gone mainstream: adopted by Silicon Valley (Google's *Search Inside Yourself* and free mindfulness lessons to its >50,000 employees), schools, governments, World Economic Forum, to name a few. The National Institutes of Health (NIH) in America is funding further research into Mindfulness and Meditation, *Turning Discovery into Health*.

*

Here is a gift to you:

*The **Timeless Time Machine**™*

Fictional time machines transport you from the present to the past or the future. This time machine takes you from the past and the future back to the PRESENT. Its destination is already set to NOW.

Ready? Come aboard. Take a deep breath. Tense up the body — let go. Sit *upright, back straight, feet on the floor, hands resting on the lap*

Look around, see yourself here in the SPACE you occupy

Feel your *WEIGHT* on the seat

Now, focus attention on your BREATH as you inhale s l o w l y through the nose deep down into lower abdomen (below belly button)

Hold it for 3 or 4 seconds, Breathe out s l o w l y (through nose/mouth)

Pause 2 or 3 seconds

Again, breathe —

s l o w l y, c o n s c i o u s l y

i n — o u t

Body here — Mind here — I am here. The Future is here.

Smile deeply with your whole body, mind, spirit :)

Feel free to try this at home.

9. Back to the Future — If You want to be Number One, Act like you are One

Be the Change You Want to See — Mahatma Gandhi

If you want India to be a super power, ACT LIKE a SUPER POWER. It will be a self-fulfilling prophecy.

Let us celebrate our rich heritage joining hands with historic and modern architects of India: Chandragupta Maurya, Ashoka (273-232BC, most famous of Buddha's followers), Vivekananada, Mahatma Gandhi, and many others discussed here. The Ashoka Youth Social Entrepreneur Competitions show that the creative gene is still vibrant. On special occasions, it'd be fun to re-enact scenarios from the most creative periods: Indus Valley and Harappan Civilizations (3300 BC-1300 BC), Maurya-Gupta golden age (500 BC-700 AD).

Most Indians, and even some diplomats, are not cognizant of India's geography and history, our deep roots in Indus Valley and the Himalayan mountains (what is the core mission of diplomats?) Children have not been learning it in school either. Why not display maps of the world and Indian region (more accurately depicted as South-Central Asia, not South Asia) in all schools and government offices? Declare a special day to **celebrate India Number One Day** — instead of the so-called Independence Day?

Since many Indians have become highly successful overseas, why not create such conditions to succeed right here at home? Invite them to share technical expertise for a week or two when vacationing — giving them opportunity to thank India for the free education they, or their parents, have received.

A CLEANER GREENER India endowed with world heritage wonders will beckon millions of Indian Diaspora and other tourists to visit new India, perhaps also cruise around South-central India and offshore islands.

Power Politics may divide us, but power of Purpose unites us. Let us build bridges with former parts of India, not fences against them.

Let the word go forth: We are changing, India is changing — and changing the world.

*

How to be Number One again?

- Tap the power of *Beginner's Mind* — seize the moment
- Know thySelf — your First Customer
- Achieve world-class performance, experience personal renaissance (individual)
- Heighten enterprise performance: private firms, universities, governments (enterprise)
- Orchestrate ***Triple-Pro™***: Prosperity + Progress + Progeny (individual, enterprise, country, world)

You've been introduced to the *Beginner* at the beginning of our adventure. Earlier, I presented the Beginner's Mind and related paradigms in a *59-minute course* to a group of 11 to 17-year old children in a New York suburb. One 12-year-old asked: "Have you presented anything like this to world leaders?"

In another instance, in a Rotary International project, I presented similar lessons to a group of blind and disabled children at a school near Hyderabad, speaking both English and Telugu. Their *perceptual intelligence* nearly doubled in just over an hour (more in a companion book titled *Creative Minds*).

No matter what age or station in life, you'll be able to recapture the childlike sense of wonder and adventure that is the hallmark of Beginner's Mind. (Just for the fun of it, *shadow a Beginner* as a medical student shadows a doctor.) When you get to know yourself and experiment with Triple-Pro™ and related paradigms with fellow architects — you'll experience personal renaissance and India's Second Golden Age. Aspire to nothing less.

10. Climbing the Prosperity Summit, India's Second Golden Age

All the powers in the universe are already ours — Swami Vivekananda

Kudos. You and I have reached another peak on our way up to the Summit. Two summits, actually: first the inner summit, the universe submerged within; then the outer summit soaring before us. The inner and outer summits are not really separate but intimately connected to each other.

Imagine the progress toward inner summit as the transformational journey from lower self to Higher SELF (*Paramatma)*, toward Personal Renaissance. The progress toward outer summit is India's journey toward reclaiming its position on top of Prosperity Summit as the wealthiest nation, reviving its historic tradition of mind-matter breakthroughs. They are symbolized today by the likes of Nobel Prizes, Olympic medals, patents, global brands. Here in Volume 0, we have turned our adventure into a One-Act Play, so to speak, and set the stage for future Acts — Volumes One and Two.

*

In **Climbing the Inner Summit, Personal Renaissance** — anticipated Volume One — we look inward and observe the inner terrain in more depth. Since change starts from within, we explore personal values and aspirations — approaching the inner summit by way of the following steps or chapters.

In **Chapter 0, Begin with the Beginner's Mind** you'll learn to start on "Day Zero" everyday — see clearly, listen silently, act fully — as if for the first time. There will be gradual detachment from the comforts of status quo. You'll be able to *seize the day* (*carpe diem*) and experience the many faces of entrepreneurial culture, the legacy of Bell Labs and Apple Computer, where the future was born.

Chapter 1, Know thy Self, Your First Customer is about discovering who you really are and what you really want — our identities as individuals and organizations, our roles and goals. You'll learn to diagnose the *Sattva-Rajas-Tamas Personas* and apply that knowledge to build enduring relationships and exceptional results. You'll feel the power of *prosperity mindset* resonating through your personal and professional lives.

In **Chapter 2, Dharma in Living Room and Board Room** we delve deep into personal and business dharma and karma, and experience the power of accessing the *Whole Mind* detached from thoughts of personal gain. We get to know *non-customers* as well as customers, cultivate the right customers and employees, and build positive Karmic Balance Sheet with *Enduring Legacy*.

Chapter 3, Enterprise as Playground and Battleground is about engaging humor, laughter and play. Legend has it that the whole Creation is divine play, *Leela*. Why shouldn't we indulge in a little play as well? After all, isn't an enterprise playground for creation and recreation — to animate ideas and create surpluses?

In **Chapter 4, Business Tripod and Triple-Pro Bottom Line** we review business missions from antiquity to present day Tata and Drucker, reflected in the Harvard MBA Oath. Though separated by centuries, such lofty mission statements are not that different — all recognize the power of purpose in creating sustainable prosperity, performing professional duties with integrity, minding the interests of diverse stakeholders.

Chapter 5, Celebrating the Call of Prosperity Summit is where head, heart and hands come together, where the inner and outer summits merge, where the twain will meet.

*

In **Climbing the Outer Summit, India's Second Golden Age** — anticipated Volume Two — we expose the outer terrain, the Himalayas, abode of India's legend, its miracles. And observe the physical challenges that confront us on our way up the majestic mountain, approaching the peak in two parts:

Part A: Partnering with Nature — the green in green

1. **Environment-Energy-Economics, the greening of companies**
2. **Sustainable growth and beyond — the new green revolution**
3. **The world of energy: of BTUs, barrels and dollars**
4. **Renewable energy — black gold to green gold**
5. **Climate change — assessing environmental and financial risks-benefits**

We delve into the nature of Nature, partnering with *Nature's Fortunes,* treating our environment as we'd have the environment treat us. Keeping in mind that we are all part of an *interdependent web of life* and that our *commons* — land, rivers, trees, air, oceans, climate — are the ultimate source of wealth and well-being, we identify opportunities for entrepreneurs in Environment-Energy-Economics. (World trade in environmental goods and services: solar panels, wind turbines, water/wastewater treatment, solid waste-to-energy schemes, and the like — adds up to US$1000 billion.) We track new engines of growth: green agriculture, renewable energies, *energy-Internet* intersections (smart power grids, interactive meters connected to Internet). And envisage ways of harnessing nature's bounty without fouling our nest, not leaving behind mountains of trash. When designing new products we'll learn to consider a product's life as well as its afterlife — to design a circular lifecycle from birth-to-rebirth. You'll find plenty of career and investment opportunities that leave positive footprints on our Ecosystem.

Part B: East and West — the Twain will meet at the Summit

6. **The tale of two firsts: India and America**
7. **Creating the Future we want**

Vedas affirm that *all paths up the mountain meet at the summit*. So also our metaphorical twins: Inner Summit and Outer Summit, East and West. In the supreme moment on top of the mountain, we discern history in the making: physical and metaphysical forces bonding, common interests of India and America expanding, East and West converging.

We contemplate the emerging roles of America, India, China. To much of the world America looks like it has lost its way, a country adrift. Despite some disappointments, America's demise is greatly exaggerated, to paraphrase Mark Twain (people around the world still line up for visas to immigrate). America has just about everything — yet remains a *developing country:* breakthroughs in energy, space, genomics are yet to be fully developed; it is poised to be the world's largest oil-gas producer and manufacturing center again. Breakthroughs in oil-gas recovery technologies and increased supplies are reducing world oil prices. Despite potential negative impacts on the environment and renewable energies, these developments in America are helping out much of the world — indirectly helping India's balance of payments, inflation and economic growth.

American power continues to anchor freedom and prosperity, enabling companies and countries to compete and prosper. China and India, as well as Japan and Europe, have been major beneficiaries. But America, and India, can use the challenge of a competitor like China. Remember the Russian Sputnik in 1957 that inspired the American moon landing in 1969 (witnessed by this student with great gusto on a big screen in Times Square)? In the immortal words of Neil Armstrong as he stepped onto the moon: *one small step for man, one giant leap for mankind*.

What if the two firsts, India and America, forged a strategic alliance?

One giant step for both! Because America and India have complementary economic and security interests, collaboration would benefit both. Such an alliance would not be directed against other countries, but would promote democratic institutions, peace and prosperity across South-central Asia and beyond.

In its 7,000-year history, India invaded other countries only with the power of ideas, never with the force of arms. (This may explain Indian timidity in projecting cultural-economic power across mountains and oceans.) Over the millennia, India has encountered Central Asian, Middle Eastern and European invaders in pursuit of power and profit. But India managed to absorb the invaders and waves of immigrants of all races and religions, becoming the most diverse subcontinent. The *Tatas* of the famous Tata industrial dynasty are "Parsi" immigrants from Persia. India and Persia (now named Iran) were neighbors before India was divided.

The world needs America — to love, to hate, to come to. When I was an exchange student in Germany, I sneaked by underground into what was then East Berlin. Scribbled on a wall was: ***Yankee go home, take me with you.*** I believe it is that spirit that sparked the fall of the Berlin Wall and the burst of freedom.

Let the Adventure Begin, Anew

Ascending — as observer, explorer, actor — pause often and listen to the parables and vignettes. You'll also find practical exercises throughout. Similar Mindfulness practices are being taught in leading corporations and business schools from New York to Silicon Valley and beyond. Please do the exercises until they become *second nature*. The power is in the practice.

CAUTION: You've embarked on a voyage of discovery and transformation. Let the beliefs that are holding you down strip away. Allow the paradigms that serve you best lift you up.

Feel free to explore and experiment — and share a laugh or two. If you persevere, you'll see your vision come alive — like that of Gautama who becomes the Buddha. But you don't have to live like an ascetic and sleep on a bed of nails for six years and meditate 49 days and nights under a tree (unless you want to).

In a moment we'll have the great fortune of meeting Buddha, Krishna, Chanakya. You can join them, and me, in Questions & Answers to shed light on our path of discovery. Feel free to call on them whenever you want to — why not invite them to be on your *virtual board of directors*?

I'm delighted to have your company in this grand adventure. What a privilege it is to be an Architect of New India — and a New World. Let us celebrate together the dawn of a new era, India's *Second Golden Age*!

With Buddha pointing the way, Krishna piloting the chariot, Chanakya covering the back. RK

In the following pages you'll find:

◊ **India playing the part of Superpower climbing Prosperity Summit**
◊ **The Seven Myths and Realities of India**
◊ **Visionaries and Architects of New India**
◊ **Outstanding Indian Americans**
◊ **India's Discoveries and Contributions**
◊ **PROSPER (acronym)**

+++++++++++++++++++++++++++++++

Meet the Prophets — Conversations with Prophets Buddha-Krishna-Chanakya

Be-Know-Do Paradigms at a Glance

+++++++++++++++++++++++++++++++

Preview of forthcoming book:
Creative Minds for Innovation and Leadership

Glossary, Abbreviations

About the Author, Keynotes-Seminars-Workshops

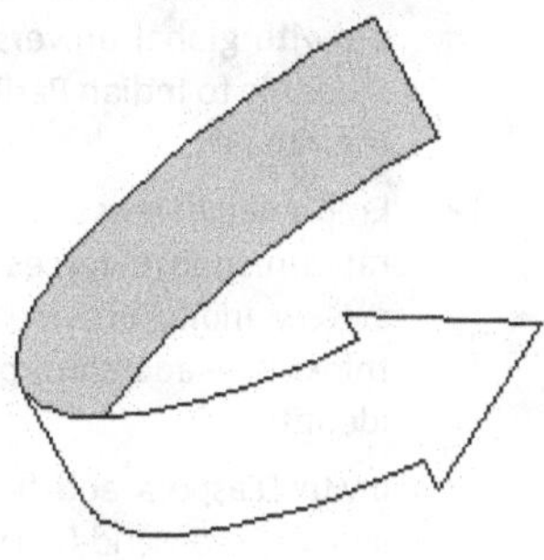

India playing the part of Superpower climbing Prosperity Summit

These suggestions are mainly for political and business leaders

- Orchestrate a daring vision of India on top of *Prosperity Summit* — to become Number One, again
- Introduce bold reforms to launch 20-20 trajectory: 20% growth for 20 years; expand tax base from current 3-4% of population to 6-8%; reduce taxes; attract money and investments back to build *silicon alleys* in India
- Launch Second Agricultural Revolution with deregulation and high-value products to contribute 30% of GDP; expand in northeast by Myanmar to benefit from water and trade
- Pursue 'Make in India' policy. Expand manufacturing from 15% to 25% of GDP, build industry clusters near shorelines, including Indian Ocean islands. Just as important as making materials and machines in India is training men and women of intellect who can design them
- Befriend India's great gift, the mighty Indian Ocean, *Ratnakara* (the only ocean named after a nation); cultivate ocean resources: aquaculture, fisheries, minerals, oil/gas, offshore windmills in collaboration with Japan/Korea
- Innovate infrastructure: water/sanitation, renewable energy, telecom, land/water transport along coastlines, conserving imported oil
- Explore opportunities for Indus Region 'IR' Free Market Zone anchored in South-Central Asia, similar to EU (European Union)
- Take dramatic steps to stabilize population, invest in intellectual capital — in smart social safety nets that build physical and mental stature
- Discourage culture of dependence, give families in need *social contracts* to learn to read and write, visit family health clinics, send children to school. Engage women to energize social change from toilets to nutrition to education to bank accounts
- Break into top ten *World Economic Forum* rankings to attract investments and jobs, gradually open up all sectors (except farming) to world-class competition
- Revolutionize STEM education to build world-class workforce; link up with global universities to climb up into the Top Ten; Invite young students to Indian Parliament on special occasions to observe and speak their minds
- Empower defense forces with twin objectives: national security with rapid-response forces to protect Himalayas/Indian Ocean, and build a New India; provide 16-hour/day training (in mobile tactics, critical thinking, leadership) plus work-service and play — giving them a new identity
- Invite Diaspora and friends to join India's renaissance; multiply tourism industry thousand-fold to CLEAN and GREEN India with world heritage sites; Designate one day a month for everyone to volunteer two hours to clean up.

Bottom line question for everyone from clerks to Foreign Service ambassadors: **What are we doing today to propel India to Number One?**

What would you do if you were elected Prime Minister of India for one day?

....

 **New Enterprise Ideas** (discussed earlier in text)

> Buddha World Heritage Center
> *Sattva* Calls, Wake-up and/or Good-Night Call Service
> Indus Children Prosperity Corps; Indus Young Entrepreneurs Club
> Mobile Convention Centers on Ships moored along coastlines
> World-class Education and Leadership Training Center
> Tomorrow's Cities Today: Designing Cities for People, not cars

....

Climbing the Prosperity Summit as an Architect of New India*

These questions and suggestions are mainly for individual pioneers

0. As a *Dual Citizen* of India and Planet Earth,
   am I CONSCIOUS of what I THINK, SAY, DO?
1. How will my performance and *India's Renaissance* impact our home planet?
2. How am I doing re TRIPLE-PRO (Prosperity+Progress+Progeny): creating wealth now, learning everyday, building worthy legacy?
3. What is my/our contribution TODAY to propel India to the top with **20% growth**?
4. How much time am I devoting today for myself/company to climb new heights? Helping friends and colleagues to succeed as *TEAM INDIA*?
5. Building the Eighth Wonder of the World as a symbol of New India — modern *Taj Mahal* for the next thousand years? (Restoring the Ganges, the eternal wonder?)
6. Will this idea or action SPEED UP India's ascent to the top, or slow it down? How can I save time and money, that of mine and of others?
7. Building children's physical and intellectual stature through nutrition and education to become World Class?
8. What am I doing today to achieve population-environment balance? Make India Clean and Green and Beautiful?
9. At home and abroad, do I project a dignified image as goodwill ambassador for India to be admired and respected once again? When I travel abroad, am I welcomed and respected?
10. **Bottom line question: What am I doing today to be world-class?** (Give yourself permission to be world-class today)

*Please contemplate progress toward the Summit at least 3 minutes today: think, do, learn, improve. On occasion, stand in front of a mirror and speak to the Architect of New India in front.

You can adopt this guidance, along with the Triple-Pro™ model, to evaluate and improve your own performance as well as that of business and government.

Architects of India Coalition could designate a national day at the start of each season (monsoon, winter, summer) for all Indians and friends to contemplate for 3-minutes India on top of Prosperity Summit, facing the Everest. Then share their thoughts and actions in person or through the media.

Your reflections, action steps:

[Check ProphetsandProfits.com website, post videos of how you are orchestrating New India.]

The Seven Myths and Realities of India

1. Myth India is poor and chaotic, it can never surpass China or America to be Number One.

Reality India was the wealthiest nation in much of recorded history until mid-1700s, accounting for almost a third of world's total wealth at times — similar to America over the last half century.

2. Myth India's recent growth of 5-10% is all you can hope for in a democracy unlike Communist China's 8-12%.

Reality India can grow at 20% if led by a Visionary Leader guided by ministers like Chanakya. It is starting from a low economic base with underemployment and immense potential with billionaire-philanthropists and young entrepreneurs poised to transform IT/telecom, water, agriculture, health, energy, education, infrastructure.

3. Myth Indians are spiritual.

Reality India is the source of many spiritual disciplines: from Ayurveda to Yoga to Transcendental Meditation. But most Indians have become uncivil. Even so, practical spirituality is being promoted by Ramakrishna-Vivekananda, Chinmaya and other missions.

4. Myth India is fortunate to have inherited English, which gives it a global advantage.

Reality It's a mixed blessing. Yes, English is the premier language of global business and science. But only the "elite" 2-3% *sahibs* speak/write fluently; 10-20% can speak some form of English or *Hinglish*. It's as if 90% have become second-class citizens, disconnected from productive work.

5. Myth The primitive agricultural sector will forever hold back India's economic growth.

Reality While 55% of Indians engage in subsistence farming, contributing only 14-18% of GDP, a second agricultural revolution — embracing innovative value chain of planning, production, and distribution — can triple farmers' productivity and incomes with huge multiplier effects on the economy.

6. Myth India has a superior educational system modeled after the British. India trains more engineers than any country but China and will remain a hub of outsourcing, especially IT.

Reality IITs and IIMs are leading institutes within India, but no Indian university is ranked in the World's Top 100. Indian Americans are highly successful in medicine and other professions and are the richest immigrant group in America. But conditions within India are stifling, educational standards are appalling.

7. Myth India enjoys a *Population Dividend* of young people in productive stage (median age 25) forming households and expanding markets.

Reality This is a passing advantage. India needs to restore population-environment balance in order to invest in children's physical and mental stature, build intellectual capital, and improve quality of life, along with tourism.

*

Visionaries and Architects of New India (Partial List)*

Buddha, Krishna, Chanakya — timeless Prophets
Vivekananda — spiritual/cultural lighthouse
Mahatma Gandhi — India's founding father, visionary
Jawaharlal Nehru — first PM (1947-64), set democratic secular path
P.V. Narasimha Rao — PM 1991-96, pioneered economic reforms
Dr. Manmohan Singh — Economist, Finance Minister 1991-96, PM 2004-14
Dr. Abdul Kalam — President of India 2002-07, scientist, visionary
Narendra Modi — elected to transform India, PM 2014- ?
.....

JN Tata, Founder of Tata Group 1868, Ratan Tata Chairman (retired 2012, becoming Chairman of Tata Trust, pioneering philanthropy)
N.R. Narayana Murthy, co-founder of pioneering Infosys
Nandan Nilekani, co-founder, former CEO of Infosys,
Chairman Unique Identification Authority of India, *Aadhar* project
Azim Premji, founder, Chairman of Wipro Ltd
Mukesh Ambani, Chairman/CEO Reliance Industries (largest exporter)
Anil Ambani, Chairman of Reliance Group
Lakshmi Mittal, Chairman & CEO, ArcelorMittal, world's largest steelmaker
Anand Mahindra, Chairman of Mahindra Group
K. Anji Reddy, founder of Dr. Reddy's Laboratories (pharmaceuticals)
Murali Divi, founder of Divi Laboratories (pharmaceuticals)
Dilip Shanghvi, Managing Director, Sun Pharmaceutical Industries
.....

Outstanding: journalists/broadcasters
Barkha Dutt, TV journalist, columnist
Dr. Prannoy Roy, NDTV (New Delhi TV) Chair
Rajdeep Sardesai, Edito-in-Chief of IBN 18 Network (formerly with NDTV)
Jaideep Bose, Times of India, Times Group Publisher
Aamir Khan, Bollywood film star, producer, activist, visionary
.....

American Billionaire philanthropists including Bill Gates of Microsoft, Warren Buffett of Berkshire Hathaway, global foundations like Ford, Rockefeller..

*Note: This is an example list showing only a few of the many architects of New India. Please feel free to suggest the names of others to consider for future editions.

This list includes political leaders, self-made billionaires, and other pioneers who are shaping India's landscape. India has 55-60 dollar-billionaires (>1400 worldwide; one billion USD equals ~ INR 6000 crore). Many mega millionaires and billionaires are founders of information technology/telecom and pharmaceutical ventures.

Outstanding Indian Americans (Partial List)*

Nobel Prize Winners

Rabindranath Tagore, Literature 1913

Har Gobind Khorana, Medicine 1968

Subramanyan Chnadrasekhar, Physics 1983

Amartya Sen, Economics 1998

Venkataraman Ramakrishnan, Chemistry 2009

Medicine/Science

Yellapragada Subbarao, discovered B12, helped discover folic acid, tetracycline

Balamurali Ambati, world's youngest MD at age 17 in 1995

Deepak Chopra, author, mind-body health, spiritual teacher

Atul Gawande, surgeon, author, reformer

Sanjay Gupta, neurosurgeon, CNN chief medical correspondent

Entrepreneurs/Venture capitalists/Executives

Bharat Desai, co-founder/Chairman Syntel

Vinod Khosla, venture capitalist, founding CEO of Sun Microsystems

Indra Nooyi, Chairman, CEO, PepsiCo

Ram Shriram, co-founder Junglee.com, Google board member, venture capitalist

Romesh Wadhwani, founder/CEO Symphony Technology Group

Prem Watsa, founder and CEO of Fairfax Financial, "Warren Buffett of Canada"

Education, Arts, Journalism

Anant Agarwal, Harvard-MIT edX President, Prof of EE & Computer Science (co-founder of Tilera Corp, serial entrepreneur)

Sal Khan, Khan Academy

Jhumpa Lahiri, celebrated author

Zubin Mehta, former Conductor, New York Philharmonic

Nitin Nohria, Harvard Business School Dean

Salman Rushdie, author

M. Night Shyamalan, filmmaker, actor

Fareed Zakaria, Time Magazine, CNN, GPS

* This is an example list showing only a few outstanding Americans of Indian heritage. Please feel free to suggest the names of others to consider for future editions.

The 3.2 million Indian Americans living in America (also called Asian Indians or South Asians, *"Desi"*) comprise 1% of US population. They form a vibrant prosperous community, financially the most successful of immigrant groups. Many American Indians are orchestrating change in India and serve as role models.

India's Discoveries and Contributions

1. India is the oldest continuing civilization of 10,000 years. The Indus (Sindh or Sindhu) Valley civilization (Harappan-Mohenjodaro, 3300-1300 BC) was the earliest urban civilization and the largest among ancient civilizations of Egypt, Mesopotamia, China. (The world's first sanitary toilet was found in the Indus Valley.)

2. India was the richest country in the world through much of recorded history until mid-1700s, accounting for as much as a third of the world's wealth at times (and was the largest source of diamonds). It invaded other countries not with arms but with ideas.

3. India is the source of Hinduism (with no single founder), Buddhism and related religions and spiritual traditions. Scientific inquiry was an integral part of these religions.

4. Sanskrit is the root of the Indo-European language family.

5. World's first university was founded in Takshila in 700 BC; more than 10,000 students from around the world studied 60+ subjects. Nalanda was the world's largest residential university, re-established in 400 AD.

6. Meditation was practiced at least since the *Vedas* 3000 BC (Veda means true knowledge). Buddha taught meditation focusing on breath, *Prana* ~500 BC. Transcendental Meditation with mantra was popularized around the world by Maharishi Mahesh Yogi in 1960s.

7. "Hindu" mathematicians invented zero ~1000 years BC; and decimal numbering system 100 year BC, introduced it to the Arabs, who introduced it to Europe around 800 AD — and came to be called Arabic numerals. Algebra and trigonometry (possibly also calculus) originated in India.

8. Baudhayana (800 BC) was the first to calculate the approximate value of "Pi" (circumference-diameter ratio); also postulated what is now known as the Pythagorean theorem. (Pythagoras visited India.)

9. Aryabhata (476-550AD), famous mathematician-astronomer, computed "Pi" 3.1416; calculated positions of planets and circumference of earth; and postulated a heliocentric theory centuries before Copernicus. He was head of Nalanda University at one point.

10. Vedic mathematics, founded by Sankaracharya in 9th century AD [?], devised fast multiplication/division, also intriguing ways of representing very small (subatomic) and very large (cosmic) numbers.

11. Yoga and karate: Yoga Sutras (debuted 3rd century BC to 2nd century AD) were codified by Patanjali; the *mudra* hand positions were incorporated into martial arts used by Buddhist monks to deter robbers on their way to Tibet and China in 6th century AD.

12. Ayurveda, science of life, was developed around 3000 BC by sages in the Himalayas. This holistic mind-body healing is based on correcting imbalances in energies or *doshas: Vata* (motion, flow), *Pitta* (digestion, metabolism), *Kapha* (growth, immunity).

13. Sushruta (600 BC) was the father of surgery and first Plastic Surgeon, including rhinoplasty (nose job) and cesareans; anesthesia was well-known.

14. Chess was invented in northwestern India (adjoining Persia) in early centuries AD; the inventor, name unknown, presented it to a local king; chess is now the world's most widely played game.

15. Kamasutra — rules governing love, sensuality and guilt-free pleasures — were issued by Saint Vatsyayana (himself a celibate) in 3rd century AD. (Tantra or Tantric rituals evolved in parallel)

16. Around two millennia BC tantalizing hints of evolution appeared in Garuda Purana parable *Dasavatharam* (ten *avatars* or incarnations): life first appears in water with fish-like creatures, followed by amphibians, then land animals and humans (of various statures/natures), divine beings — finally invisible destructive forces.

17. Italian Marconi is generally credited as the inventor of long-distance wireless communication (radio signals). Many view Sir J.C. Bose (1858-1937) as the unsung hero of wireless communication.

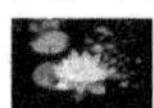

Go Forth and P R O S P E R

"How are we doing?" Triple-Pro Model

Triple-Pro Reference Points	Individual	Organization	Outsider View
Prosperity			
Elements of economic prosperity			
e.g. revenues, profits (surpluses)			
Progress			
Elements of evolutionary progress			
e.g. innovations, intellectual capital			
Progeny			
Elements of enduring legacy			
e.g. contribution to a sustainable world			

P Practice Purposeful Life with Triple-Pro™: Prosperity + Progress+ Progeny

R Re-imagine and recreate — like Shiva-Brahma-Vishnu (destroyer, creator, nurturer)

O Open your Mind, reset the *Mind's Odometer* to zero. Begin Here, Begin Now — with *Beginner's Infinite Mindset*

S Self: know thyself, your *Sattva-Rajas-Tamas* persona. BE yourSelf

P Play and indulge in fun (*Leela*) — as you prepare to climb the Prosperity Summit

E Engage the Earth's Triple-E: Environment–Energy–Economics, the *Tao of Dow* — Environmentalists, Entrepreneurs, Executives alike

R Reflect and recharge with mindful living. What new peaks are beckoning on the horizon? What will be your Legacy?

∞

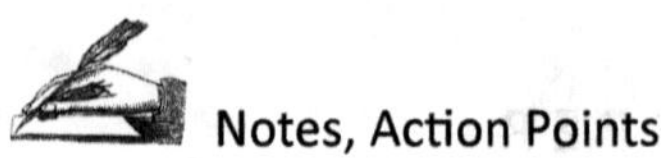

Notes, Action Points

Meet the Prophets

Conversations with Buddha, Krishna, Chanakya

Be-Know-Do Paradigms at a Glance

Introduction to the Buddha

World Honored One, you know
The deepest thoughts of living beings
The paths they walk
Their capacity for wisdom...
Lotus Sutra

"..Knowledge can be communicated, but not wisdom.
One can find it, live it, do wonders through it.."
— Hermann Hesse, *Siddhartha*

Siddhartha Gautama, later to become the **Buddha** (563-483 BC) was born into a Hindu royal family in northern India. In celebrating the birth of Siddhartha (meaning one who achieves his aims), the court astrologers prophesied he would be either a great king or a great holy man. Later when asked by a disciple whether he was a prince or a prophet, Buddha said simply, *I am Awake*.

....

A Glimpse of Buddha's World, Dawning of Globalization

When Buddha-to-be was born in the sixth century BC, the Indian civilization was already three thousand years old. The Upanishads (earliest Indo-European scriptures, 3000-500 BC) had laid the foundation — at first secular, later anchoring Hinduism and Buddhism. It was a time of cultural and scientific *renaissance* in the civilizations of antiquity.

Buddha was a contemporary of two spiritual leaders born in China: Lao Tzu (Taoism, Tao Te Ching) and Confucius (Confucianism). Also more or less of the same period were Zoroaster of Persia, pre-Socratic philosophers of Greece, and the later prophets of Israel. It was a new era of expanding horizons from individual to family to society — recognizing the interdependence of humanity. Nature and environment had begun to lodge in human consciousness.

*The **Global Mind** thus preceded the **Global Economy** by twenty five centuries.*

*

From India, Buddhism spread to East and South Asia in first centuries AD and, more recently, to the West. (Among the more well-known is Steve Jobs, co-founder of Apple.)

The Beginnings

Befitting a prince Siddhartha, or Gautama as Buddha is often called, led a life of privilege and luxury. His father, wishing Gautama to be a great king rather than a great holy man, shielded him from religious teachings. When he reached the age of 16, Gautama married his cousin Yasodhara and fathered a son, Rahula.

One day, feeling restless, Gautama ventured out of his palace walls. Even though his father had taken precautions to shield him, Gautama caught sight of a sick man, an old woman, and a decaying corpse. Deeply disturbed by what he saw, he began to ponder the causes of suffering. Everything changes, each moment comes and goes, he mused. In another incident, he stumbled upon a dove injured by a hunter's arrow, and nursed it back to health with compassion. That incident may have crystallized his feelings of kinship with all creatures and led to his teaching of *Ahimsa*, nonviolence, do-no-harm. *The Buddha-to-be was ready.*

The Awakening

At the age of 29 Gautama left his palace, leaving his family and princely duties behind. He set out on a mission to understand the reality of life: causes of suffering and means of liberation. After entering a nearby forest, he cut off his hair with his sword, discarded his royal attire, and found some saffron-yellow rags and a mendicant's bowl. Henceforward he would possess nothing more, he vowed.

In the forest *ashrams* along the way Gautama quickly learned yoga and meditation, but felt that was not enough. Then he chose the life of an ascetic — sleeping on a bed of nails, drinking his own urine, restricting himself to one morsel of food a day — until his bones peered through his skin. He thought that punishing his body was a way of overcoming all earthly attachments.

After having lived in luxury for 29 years and in penury for six years, he had a revelation. Attachment to extreme self-indulgence or extreme self-mortification is not the way. To find balance, the *Middle Way*, Gautama sat and meditated under a *Bodhi* (pipal or fig) tree for 49 days and nights — Buddha, the *Awakened One*, was born. The veil was lifted, he told his followers later, like that of the chick that pierces through its shell and sees light for the first time.

The *Four Noble Truths* and the *Eightfold Path*

The essence of Buddha's teachings is in the *Four Noble Truths* and the *Eightfold Path*. The first truth is that sorrow and suffering are inherent in all life. Everyone desires permanent happiness but everything changes.

The second truth is that suffering is caused by selfish attachments: attachment to things, people, thoughts.

The third truth brings good news: that these ailments can be overcome (diagnosis and cure).

The fourth truth is the WAY to liberation and *Nirvana* is the *Eightfold Path*, also called the eight spokes of the *dharma wheel*:

Right View/Understanding
Right Intent/Purpose
Right Mindfulness/Meditation
Right Thought
Right Speech
Right Action/Conduct
Right Attention/Concentration
Right Occupation, Livelihood

All that we are is a result of what we have thought, the Buddha said; with our thoughts we make the world. Thoughts are parents of actions, breeding actions of the same kind, just as an acorn gives rise to an oak tree when the conditions are ripe. Right ends must be achieved by right means. Love begets love, violence breeds more violence. Greed, anger, ignorance are three poisons that cause suffering. Replace greed with Generosity, anger with Compassion, ignorance with Understanding, he counseled.

*

Meditation is a hallmark of Hinduism, Buddhism and other spiritual traditions. Meditation shifts consciousness to a deeper plane with gradual "emptying" of the mind (usually with a *mantra*): breathing slows down, sense gates to the outside close, primal emotions subside, the intellect rests — descending deeper and deeper through the mind's labyrinth into pure consciousness. This is the level of Being, our most natural and creative state, a paradox of being completely relaxed and completely alert. *Contemplation* or *Reflection,* on the other hand, is thinking about a subject or a goal, sometimes to internalize a sacred thought.

A related practice, **Mindfulness,** has come to be closely associated with Buddhism. To be mindful is to be aware of each moment as it unfolds. Every moment is NEW and NOW. *It is empowering, releasing the past to free the future*. When you are fully in the NOW: there is *no pre-judgment, no attachment, no suffering*. When you're aware of what you're aware, that is *metaconsciousness*. *Be mindful of the miracles of little things in daily life*, the Buddha reminds us.

We can practice Mindfulness at three levels:

Sensory *awareness* is to pay full attention to what we see, hear, taste, smell, touch/feel (observation).

Mental *awareness* is to be conscious of what we're thinking, feeling, doing — observing thoughts and emotions as a neutral observer.

Universal *or Social Awareness* is to be conscious of potential impacts of our thoughts and actions on broader society, on the evolving planet.

How is Mindfulness related to Meditation? Both help you get in touch with your *BEING,* who you really are. Simply put, in meditation we clear our minds (disconnect from the senses); in mindfulness we fill our minds (connect with sensory faculties). Both practices increase blood flow to the prefrontal cortex, the judgment or *executive* part of the brain. Many technology campuses like that of Google, have adopted mindfulness as a way to free creativity and to unwind from workplace stresses. We can be mindful anytime, anywhere: walking, eating, breathing. And meditate in place twice a day, 12-20 minutes, preferably at dawn and dusk.

Practice: Being Mindful, NOW all of me is HERE

Sit or stand upright. (Close your eyes later if you prefer)
Take in a S L O W, DEEP breath through the nose paying attention
Hold it for 3 or 4 seconds. Let go slowly, consciously, through the nose/mouth
Pause.
Again, in . . . out
Body here. Mind here. I'm here.
Resume normal breathing with whole body-mind smile ☺

At first the Buddha was reluctant to share his message with ordinary folk fearing that those who had not followed his arduous path were not ready to receive it. But he relented thinking that at least a few might be ready to listen. (In the Eastern tradition, the guru first considers the *readiness* of the disciple to receive the message before accepting him.)

The Buddha also made a pilgrimage to the palace of his birth and was greeted by his father with pride and anger — proud of his fame, angry because he renounced his royal heritage. "Which is greater: ruling a small kingdom with power or ruling the world with love?" the Buddha asked.

He continued the pilgrimage along the Ganges taking the road less traveled, spreading his message in *Sangha:* assemblies of monks gathered to feel Buddha's presence. His royal origins conferred some privileges during this sojourn. But his growing influence gave rise to jealous rivals who tried to poison him.

Buddhist monks live on alms taking only enough food to sustain them for the day. (Ever tried that?)

Buddha on Wealth and Prosperity

Since the Buddha's image is one of austerity, his views on wealth may come as a surprise. This is what he said to a rich banker-disciple, who asked: How can I live a prosperous life without money — my business is money?

The Buddha replied: You do need money. But money alone is not prosperity. To live a life of prosperity, you need:

1. Material wealth to meet basic needs and live happily — with the feeling that the wealth is earned by right effort, by the sweat of your brow
2. Good reputation — the community thinks of you as an honorable person
3. Fulfilling life anchored in dharma, grateful for the gifts that come your way
4. Worthy end — the feeling that you lived a good life and leaving a worthy legacy

Income and accumulated wealth may be used like this:

One part for daily necessities of self and the family
Two parts for professional help and to help society
One part to be saved for future needs
(balance consumption and savings/investment)

Be a Lamp unto Yourself

The Buddha, sensing that his death was imminent, enjoined his followers not to worship him as a God, not even accept his teachings in blind faith but to validate them through personal inquiry. Remember me as the *one who awakened*, he said. "Let Dharma be your guide. Be a lamp unto yourself, be the Buddha."

At the age of 80, the Buddha entered into deep meditation at the altar of Nirvana in Kusinara (Kushinagar) in the shadows of the Himalayas facing his *home*. Legend has it that Sandalwood leaves gently dropped from the sky caressing his body in reverence.

The Buddha was a prophet in his own country. His miracles are in his methods. He points the Way but lets you get there on your own.

*

Let us pause now for a moment to partake of the Buddha.

Questions and Answers (Q&A) with Buddha

In a quiet corner of my space, I sit at Buddha's feet and invite his presence — reminiscing his odyssey and my own trek along the Ganges in his footsteps as a student.

Moments of meditation quieted the monologue in my head and opened up portals for dialogue. In this light I'm paraphrasing the interaction in Q&A format. Buddha's answers are in *italics*, expressed in my own words.

Q. Namaskar, I am deeply honored by your presence. I've read and heard many stories and anecdotes by you, and about you. Your message seems as germane today as twenty five centuries ago.

(Accepting the lotus flower presented by the Buddha with overwhelming gratitude) I believe the lotus symbolizes spiritual evolution — roots in muddy water like man's base nature, stem rising above the water in search of light symbolizing thirst for knowledge, unfolding petals depicting the blossoming of the human spirit.

Buddha: Yes, I have favorites too.

Q. May I start with your **Four Noble Truths**:

> Suffering is inherent in all life, everyone wants to be happy but everything changes;
>
> Suffering is caused by attachments to the transient;
>
> The good news is suffering can be overcome;
>
> The Way to liberation or *Nirvana* is the *Eightfold Path.*

Buddha: The eightfold Path includes right thought, right speech, right action, right livelihood. Although monks are sworn to poverty, the ***Middle Way*** *is to avoid extreme poverty or extreme indulgence. Sitar strings too tight or too loose don't produce good music. Urban Monks live Middle Way, making good music.*

Q. Thank you for the compliment! In my passage through different stations, I've become increasingly conscious of my thoughts and deeds mindful of what you said: *All that we are is a result of what we have thought*. As you know, I practice meditation everyday, and try to do the right thing.

Buddha: You are on the right path.

Q. Your advice to a banker on living a prosperous life also resonates with me — that money alone is not prosperity. I have often talked to colleagues about Your ***Golden Rule of Prosperity***:

> earn sufficient material wealth to live a happy dignified life,
> feel that you've earned it by the sweat of your brow,
> enjoy good reputation in the community as an honorable person, and
> believe that you lived a good life and leaving a worthy legacy.

So it's not only material wealth but also a way of life — and death.

Buddha: Yes, you put it more succinctly than I!

Q. Thank you. Let me turn to another of your memorable teachings: *Ahimsa*, do-no-harm.

Buddha: Do no harm to others, and to yourself — by what you do personally or through others. People should not seek wealth through devious means and wrong companions. Those who cause harm suffer as they brood over the suffering they have caused. You cannot harm another without harming yourself.

Q. The reverse must also be true: You cannot help another without helping yourself. I'm reminded of Mahatma Gandhi's non-violent struggle in South Africa and India to fight social injustice. I believe one of your great followers, Emperor Ashoka, was the first to build hospitality centers for pilgrims, also hospitals for animals. It seems to me you were the first to discern the complex web of interdependent life, the very first *GLOBAL MIND*.

Buddha: (Silent smile)

Q. I also think of you as a compassionate rebel. You rebelled against established order and left a path for us to follow.

Buddha: I have shown the way; it is for you to walk the path.

Q. We're grateful for that. I find another of your precepts intriguing: *Smile at the unknown.* It's the few who dare to leave the trodden path who go on to create great enterprises.

Buddha: Yes.

Q. I trust I am not being disrespectful saying this: you left family, infant son, and princely duties to set out on your quest. It doesn't seem the right thing to do — people first fulfill their family duties before venturing out.

Buddha: It is who I was that impelled me, not what I wanted. Who you are is not bound by a timetable. Often we do things to escape problems, not to find solutions.

Q. Um, I should ponder that. You said that one of the causes of suffering is attachment to the transient — to things, thoughts, people. But it is impossible to live without attachments.

Buddha: Nonattachment doesn't mean that you don't care. Just the opposite. If you are attached to something or someone, you give up part of your freedom and impose a burden on the others to give up their freedom.

Q. Never looked at it that way. Most of us are not so evolved that we can ignore the rewards from our efforts.

Buddha: You won't be giving up rewards. It is impossible to have prosperity or abundance with attachment. Why not enjoy the peace of knowing that your actions will benefit all mankind?

Q. Tall order. It is impossible for us to emulate your journey: live as a prince 29 years, ascetic 6 years, then to sit under a Bodhi tree meditating 49 days and nights.

Buddha: You don't have to. But you do have to be ready to receive. In order to receive, you must be ready to give up. Give to others what you most like to receive.

Q. I can see how that would turn our lives around. In that vein, you said that wisdom is in replacing negative mental states with the positive.

Buddha: There are ***three poisons and antidotes*** *to be aware of: greed, anger, ignorance. They drain energy and cause unhappiness. Replace greed with generosity, anger with compassion, ignorance with understanding.*

Q. It seems that when one does something wrong or says what is untrue, it causes an accumulation of negative energies. On the other hand, if one does good, positive energies are boosted.

Buddha: Picture a spiritual gathering where sweets are passed around on a plate. By the time the plate comes to you only one sweet is left and that happens to be your favorite. If you pick up the sweet and taste it, the sensual enjoyment will last a few minutes. If you give up the sweet to another person, that ***generosity will dwell in your consciousness a long time****.*

Q. Indeed. I have experienced that joy. We violate that spirit of generosity in business when we're urged to do the right thing in order to acquire customers, increase profits and what not — the corporate *mantra*.

Buddha: To do something in order to get this or that is to misunderstand what is right. ***Doing what is right is an expression of who you are. It is not conditional on what you get.***

Right purpose points you in the right direction. Right effort gets you there.

Q. Do something good for its own sake, not to sanctify something bad as in donations to temples. Returning to the *do-no-harm* paradigm, it could be the so-called *Hippocratic Oath* for business students.

Buddha: The bee draws nectar without harming the flower while pollinating. How are people earning their livelihood? If they cause harm to customers, they will feel remorse and suffering in its wake.

Q. That message may have been radical in ancient times but not in today's hyperconnected world. But the message that we are all in it together hasn't sunk in — judging by the way we foul our nest.

Buddha: We are all at different starting points and different stations. Step by step, one can replace negative mental states with the positive by cultivating Sattva spirit. Avatar Krishna will shed more light on that.

Q. Let me turn now to Dharma — people think you are its personification. I believe it means inherent duty but heard many interpretations.

Buddha: My disciples think of Dharma as what I am and what I practice. It provides the moral anchor to do the right thing in the right way.

Q. Other hallmarks of your teachings are mindfulness and meditation.

Buddha: Each "mind" or thought is a moment of its own, now and new. It makes change possible. If you are in the NOW, there is no judgment, no attachment. Innocence is the beginning of understanding.

Q. Compelling message. A famous American entrepreneur, Steve Jobs, who co-founded Apple Computer attributes his leaps of intuition to the Beginner's Mind and mindfulness.

Buddha: Smiles.

Q. I heard that a group of your followers celebrate the incoming New Year by observing an *Empty Day* in between the old year and the New Year.

Buddha: Why not? Interludes are storehouses of freedom. Remember, to die well, you must live well. Run a worthy venture before passing it on to worthy successors.

Q. Not necessarily to the highest bidder, then. You also said famously: *To find your way, find the beginning.* Like people who give up everything they own when they reach age 60 to begin anew — companies too can start anew instead of getting bogged down by past products and investments that stifle innovation.

Buddha: When a person makes a new beginning, he dies to the past. People and organizations attached to their possessions are beholden to the past. It is the freedom of the future that opens up a new frontier to sow the seeds of whatever you want to harvest.

Q. **Free the past to free the future**. Thank you for new beginnings.

Buddha: Be a lamp unto yourself.

-Om-

Introduction to Krishna of Bhagavad Gita

All paths up the mountain lead to the summit. Rig Veda, Bhagavad Gita

I meditate on the Gita and derive fresh joy and new meaning every day. Mahatma Gandhi

When I read the Bhagavad Gita... everything else seems so superfluous. Albert Einstein

While the story of Buddha is a journey of privilege and privation, and enlightenment, the *Gita* is an exquisite poem and a Gospel: Apostle Sri Krishna speaks to man in the midst of a battlefield.

....

Bhagavad Gita — Celestial Song — was composed between the fifth and second century BC. The Gita consists of eighteen short chapters with 700 verses and is part of the great *Mahabharata* epic. It portrays a battle among forces of "good" and "evil" at K*urukshetra*, near present-day Delhi.

Among scriptures, the Gita is unique in that it joins the eternal with the ephemeral, reflection with action. It is set in the midst of life-and-death drama. The discourse is mostly in the form of a dialog between Krishna — divine a*vatar* and charioteer (also known as Sri Krishna) — and his protégé Arjuna, the princely warrior riding in the chariot. On the eve of combat, Arjuna hesitates to fight, weighed down by the moral dilemmas of war.

Inner and Outer Battles

The Gita offers two take-home messages. One is that we should perform our inherent duty, dharma, no matter how ominous the consequences may seem. The other message is allegorical: the human mind is a battlefield, where both good and evil dwell, vying for control. In that sense, Arjuna stands in as a proxy for you and me facing our daily predicaments of right and wrong.

The war was between cousins of two sides of a royal family, descendents of brothers Pandu and Dhritarashtra. The five sons of Pandu, one of them Arjuna, are called Pandavas. The hundred sons of Dhritarashtra are named Kauravas; the eldest was Duryodhana. When the time came for succession to the throne, the Kauravas devised a devious scheme with loaded dice that resulted in the defeat and exile of Pandava brothers for twelve years.

After fulfilling the terms of their exile, Pandavas returned to reclaim their kingdom. But in the meantime Kauravas had consolidated their power through alliances and refused to yield even an inch of ground. War became inevitable. Relatives, teachers, and friends had to pick sides. Krishna agreed to pilot Arjuna's chariot in the conflict.

Pointing feet to the path of duty

Surveying the battle scene, confronting his childhood friends and revered teachers on both sides, Arjuna's determination began to waver. He did not want to be the cause of their death for all the kingdom. Sensing the confusion in Arjuna's mind, Krishna speaks thus:

Arjuna, this war is not of your making. All your efforts for peace have not prevented it. Now, as a K*shatriya* Prince, you have no higher duty than to fight injustice and restore what is rightfully yours. On this path, there is no defeat.

There was never a time when I did not exist, nor you, nor anyone here. Nor will

there be a time in which we shall cease to be. Just as the dweller in this body passes through childhood, youth and old age, so at death he passes on to another kind of body. Win or lose, you are always a winner as long as you act in fulfillment of your dharma. *You have the right to action but not to the results thereof.* Only the ignorant work for the fruits of their labors; the wise point their feet to the path of duty, Krishna exhorts Arjuna.

Two Paths to Nirvana

Throughout the Gita, Krishna elucidates the dual nature of man: the mundane and the divine, the finite and the infinite, the mortal and the immortal. He explains the different paths to achieving unity with the *Atman,* Self-realization. Choose a path that best fits your persona. *All paths up the mountain meet at the summit.*

Krishna also speaks at length about the nature of man and the three *gunas:* qualities or streams of consciousness. Everything in nature is governed by ***Sattva*** light, ***Rajas*** action, ***Tamas*** inertia. Sattva is enlightenment, harmony, detachment; Rajas is energy, action, attachment; Tamas is darkness, inaction, indifference.

You should know what kind of work to do and what to avoid. You'll know this by examining your *gunas*. Even when engaged in action, you will cultivate detachment, lodged in the tranquility of the *Atman* ("holy indifference" in Christianity).

Gita in essence:

1 Inside the ever-changing body dwells the immutable, immortal, infinite Self (Atman, Godhead). Our ultimate purpose in life is to be One with the Self. This is *Moksha* or *Nirvana*

2 You can attain Self-realization along two paths: *Jnana Yoga* of knowledge and wisdom; and *Karma Yoga* of PURE ACTION. *Act with Whole Mind*, detached from the results of your actions (not renouncing material things per se but selfish attachment to them)

3 Everyone and everything in the world is governed by Sattva knowledge, Rajas action, Tamas inertia.. Recognize and balance these qualities in order to play your part well.

These tenets may sound lofty and abstruse, but you'll feel their immediacy and power when you begin to put them into practice. *Yoga for everyone, everywhere*?

*

Let us pause now for a moment to revel in the presence of the omniscient charioteer.

Q & A with Krishna

In a quiet corner of my space I sit quietly in reverence, recalling scenes from the Bhagavad Gita. A disciple brings the questions to Krishna. His answers are in *italics,* put in my own words.

Q. Salutations. It is a privilege and joy to be in your presence. Your avatar of God and man is surrounded by much mystery and folklore that have become part of my cultural heritage.

Krishna: I am all that is manifest before you, and that is not. As an avatar, I express myself in myriad forms responding to the needs of the Yuga in a cyclical universe. One God with many faces: I appear in different garbs and play different roles — as you do.

Q. I find your role as a "playboy" particularly fascinating.

Krishna: The whole universe is created by God's Play, Leela. Why shouldn't you indulge in a little play, too?

Q. Why not indeed! Each time I read the Gita, am inspired by new revelations. I find three of your teachings particularly helpful:

Know your persona governed by Sattva light, Rajas action, Tamas inaction;

Act with the Whole Mind detached from thoughts of personal rewards;

Practice Karma Yoga focusing on Action: if you want to know your future, look at your present deeds.

Krishna: How are they making a difference in your life?

Q. Ah, thought I was the one asking the questions! The moral dilemmas Arjuna faces on the battlefield are not unlike those I face everyday. You exhort him to perform his duty and not worry about the results. But rewards and punishments based on results have become embedded in the culture I live in.

Krishna: Let's be clear on what ***detached action*** *really means:*

Non-attachment does not mean lacking in commitment or giving up rewards. On the contrary, a *mind that is unfettered by thoughts of personal gain is free to focus fully with head, heart and hands as one.*

When all your minds are united into one ***Whole Mind*** *— then all your energies are concentrated on the task at hand with one-pointed attention, not divided between action now and what may come out later. You'll be able to do the most good in that way.*

Q. It is becoming clearer.

Krishna: When you put your mind where your hand is, the results take care of themselves. They may occur on a different timetable than your own, and results could well exceed your expectations.

Remember, too, you have control over your actions but only partial control over outcomes, which come from many different actors playing many different parts.

Q. It all sounds very logical, but in the business world, we need to work in close-knit teams. Can there be bonding without binding?

Krishna: Buddha spoke to you on how attachments cloud mental clarity and freedom of action.

The way to cultivate detachment is to do your best no matter where you are. Suppose you do the right thing all the time — then it becomes a habit, *a timeless process.*

Q. I understand that prosperity is more than money. What is the best way to become prosperous?

Krishna: Money doesn't produce prosperity; it is the Prosperity Mindset that produces money. Prosperity is in the nature of the Universe. When you act with scarcity mindset, you act from fear, not from freedom.

Only scarcity can come out of scarcity mindset. Prosperity springs from prosperous mindset.

Q. I can see how "lack thoughts" affect our fortunes. But Economics is said to be the *science of scarcity*. Money won't have much value if there is too much around. When do we get to have enough prosperity?

Krishna: Prosperity is not about how much you have but what you think of what you have. A bird never fears running out of the sky. When you feel ready to give, you have enough.

Q. Turning to our personas, I understand we have a mix of tendencies: Sattva light, Rajas action, Tamas inaction.

Krishna: People centered in Sattva are joyous and generous, Rajas energetic and action-oriented, Tamas lethargic and selfish. What is important is to maintain the right balance.

Q. I used to think Sattva is good and Tamas bad. But Tamas no-action mode can be critical to business success amidst pressures to do something, anything. One gets paid for doing something, not nothing. Since business professionals tend to be Rajas-centered, they can benefit from cultivating Tamas and Sattva for balance.

Krishna: Yes. Consider whether the situation will correct itself on its own or will become worse by intervention. If an opportunity is on the horizon, how long will the window remain open? What you don't do, what you don't see — can be as important as what you do.

Q. Even though we humans have different Sattva-Rajas-Tamas personas, I understand at the core we all harbor the same *transcendent Self, Paramatma*.

Krishna: That is a divine gift that makes it possible for the transient, the finite, the mortal to experience the constancy, the infinity, the immortality of the transcendent Self.

Q. I have fleeting moments of such a sublime experience.

Krishna: Those moments will endure if you commune with me and surrender to dharma. Knowing your Sattva-Rajas-Tamas Persona will help you choose your profession and the organization where you'd do the most good. Just as important, the work and company you should avoid.

Q. Reflecting on my own persona, I should strengthen my Rajas action mode. I have a tendency to postpone action, *paralysis by analysis*. Turning to Karma and the Caste System: Brahmin, Kshatriya, Vaisya, Sudra — is it not unfair to pigeonhole people by birth into rigid social strata?

*Krishna: Karmic inheritance at birth is like biologic inheritance. You inherit a part to play on a given stage. The **beginning of the story is written — you get to write the middle and an ending.** By playing your present part well, however menial or exalted it may seem — and not try to play someone else's part — you can **reset your Karmic trajectory.***

Q. It sounds like an *Improv* performance. In that light, it seems the choices we make, make us. Conventional wisdom for climbing the professional ladder says that one should be able to do the *next job* well. I'm also reminded of Peter's Principle: *People rise to their level of incompetence.*

*Krishna: **You can never do the next job well**, only the present job. Contemplate your ideal job and how you'd do the present job ideally.*

Q. Early in my career — I was fortunate to have a position that combined my technical and business knowledge with considerable freedom — but I spent a lot of time thinking if only I had a bigger office, higher salary etc, I'd do so much better. Still, I performed reasonably well — was promoted to a management position within a year.

Krishna: Smile.

Q. Returning to Karma, some think of it as fate foreordained, *Kismet*. But I also see *fire rituals*, in which the past is symbolically burnt off to give way to rebirth.

Krishna: See fate as foreordained sign to seize the day. Karma is all about action. You reap what you sow — and what others sow, too. Imagine a universal bank account that you add to or withdraw from across generations.

Q. That is a cautionary note to people who think the end justifies the means. In a typical business scenario, it's the uncertainty of results — trying to cook results — and fixating on rewards that cause distress. For many companies, their highest priority is to beat the consensus estimates of quarterly earnings. The problem is more and more investors have become "renters of shares" rather than owners of companies — average holding is in seconds.

Krishna: The performance of a company or executive should be seen as a Self-expression, a continuum, not an isolated event. Appeal to investors who are not caught up in short cycles.

Q. Chief Executives don't feel they have such a choice. Also, we have a distorted reward system, often based on illusory results. You speak of the universe itself as an illusion, *Maya*.

Krishna: What you see around you is shaped by your senses. The Mind's Eye can transcend the physical senses and see what cannot be ordinarily seen.

Few can peer through the veil. People generally see the universe as a single, static manifestation. Actually, the ***universe is not passive but participatory.*** *Every thought, every observation, every action — changes the universe. Yes, you have the power to transform the universe.*

Q. Wow! That brings me to a conundrum. In my spiritual domain, I like to think that a part of me is immortal. As a scientist, I wonder whether my consciousness can continue to live on separate from my brain-mind-body after my physical death?

Krishna: It's not just you humans, who are conscious. There is earth's consciousness, nature's consciousness, and an eternal meta-conscious Being from whom everything emanates and to whom everything returns. You refer to it as God, Paramatma, Transcendent Self.

Respect scientific observations and what you call facts — but don't be limited by them*. What you know is but a tiny fraction of what is to be known. Knowledge is not wisdom, nor imagination, nor free will.*

Q. Thank you for that cautionary note. As to your penchant for taking on a multitude of names and titles that echo your roles, I wonder if executives could benefit doing likewise? It would loosen attachment to ego and signal openness to change.

Krishna: Why not? It could reduce attachment to fleeting perks and allow executives to be more creative.

Q. On that note, may I take leave with your blessings.

Krishna: May you dwell again and again in playful and prosperous incarnations.

-Om-

Introduction to Chanakya

In the happiness of his subjects lies the king's happiness. He shall not consider as good only that which pleases him — Chanakya

Chanakya (350-283 BC), also known as Kautilya and Vishnugupta, is like no other in world history. He was the architect of a unified India under Chandragupta Maurya (founder of Mauryan dynasty), the first political economist and management guru, and probably also the first environmentalist and toxicologist.

....

Arthashastra — First Treatise on Wealth

Among Chanakya's claims to fame is the first book of its kind, *Arthashastra,* a treatise on wealth and the art of government. Full of stratagems, spies and intrigue, Arthashastra is often compared to *Machiavelli's Prince*, written eighteen centuries later, in early 1500s. (Machiavelli, like Chanakya, advocated strong rule but not tyranny.) Chanakya also wrote *Neetishastra* and *Neeti-Sutra*, aphorisms on ethics and the ideal way of life.

Arthashastra consists of 15 books or sections that expound on just about everything: qualifications and duties of kings (applicable to leaders of countries and companies) and ministers (directors, trustees, consultants); importance of finance; treatment of allies and adversaries; deployment of scouts; management of forests (resource planning). Not only a thinker and advisor, Chanakya was also a man of action. Legend has it that he administered small doses of poison to gradually immunize his king from common poisons (beginnings of toxicology?) Ironically, Chanakya himself may have been the victim of poisoning.

Duties of Kings and Leaders

A king or ruler is the fountainhead of wealth; his duty is to acquire and oversee land and other resources to *foster abundance of riches through productive economic activity.* Without such activity, future profits and wealth will wither away. Just as elephants are needed to capture more elephants, money is needed to capture more money. One must be vigilant of financial accounts, checking frequently: everyday, week, month, 3 months, year. Cash and liquid assets are essential to meet current commitments and seize opportunities as they arise.

A leader should administer justice based on law that stands on four legs: dharma, evidence, tradition, edicts of rulers. Regarding traditions and customs, Chanakya endorses the practice of women receiving jewelry through inheritance and weddings even if disputes are inevitable in all marriages. Since historically women had not owned their own wealth, jewelry provided some economic freedom and insurance as well as adornment.

Chanakya was quite specific about the attributes of kings and leaders. A capricious king will fall into the hands of his enemy. Hard work is more important than consulting the stars, he affirms.

A leader should

- Lead by personal example: be truthful, resolute, disciplined
- Improve knowledge of all branches by continuous learning
- Cultivate intellect by associating with the wise, practicing yoga
- Build small, nimble, trustworthy teams to advance a cause
- Endear himself by listening, promoting justice and prosperity

A leader should not
Indulge in capriciousness, falsehood, extravagance
Consort with harmful persons
Exhibit fickleness, anger, greed, weakness
Laugh loudly or behave in an undignified manner

His prescribed regimen from sunrise to sunset and beyond hints at balancing duties to oneself, to the country (think also company), and to various constituencies:

5:30- 7	Wake up to sound of music, express thanks for this day, after morning ablution perform yoga/meditate, breakfast with spiritual advisor
7-8:30	Receive reports on revenue and expenditure, state of the country, verify and validate external and internal information through scouts
8:30-10	Hold public audience, hear petitions of people at large
10-11:30	Make appointments, receive officials, assign tasks
11:30-1	Confer with trusted advisors, make decisions, write letters, make phone calls
1-2:30	Eat Sattva-Rajas lunch, 15-20 minute silence break (power nap)
2:30-4	Inspect troops (operations), consult with department heads
4-5:30	Leave time open for meetings, emergencies, planning
5:30-7	Exercise, recreate, reflect on the day's decisions, actions
7-10	Eat Sattva-Tamas supper, read scriptures, review lessons learned, preview upcoming decision, meditate
10 -5:30	Retire with sound of music, fall asleep recounting accomplishments

---

Q & A with Chanakya

I sit quietly mindful of Chanakya's role in shaping India. This is the essence of our exchange. Chanakya's (abbreviated "Chanak") answers are in *italics*, put in my own words.

Q. Salutations guruji. A rare privilege to be in the presence of such a colorful genius — and a vibrant part of my cultural heritage. What you said more than 2000 years ago is proving prophetic.

Chanak: Delighted that you and others are rediscovering me.

Q. Not too many kings left any more, not with power anyway. But if we substitute president of a country or company for a king, we wouldn't even suspect you said it so long ago. I hope this book will offer a glimpse of the great treasure waiting to be unearthed.

Chanak: I wish you well in this endeavor.

Q. Thank you. I am naïve enough to believe that everyone of us can make a difference — make the world a better place.

Chanak: Don't ever lose that naiveté.

Q. I'd like to start with your prescribed daily regimen — full slate that still allows time for a full night sleep. Eighteen-hour workdays have become fashionable in the business world today.

Chanak: *People think they are wasting time in sleep. But that is also when you dream and redeem. Suppose in your sleep tonight you dream of a free and prosperous world. In the morning, you look in the mirror and find a microcosm of that world in front — is that a dream? Or is it real?*

Q. Ah! The microcosm does feel real.

Chanak: *You're a diplomat, too! Meditation reduces the amount of sleep you need. But* ***people often mistake activity for accomplishment****. Being busy may be just an escape from being real.*

Q. Indeed. I also welcome your emphasis on continuous learning, being in touch with spiritual advisors.

Chanak: *Lifelong learning both inside and outside walls engenders wealth all around. It is an evolutionary spiral of doing, observing, learning, doing better. Be sure to reconnect with spiritual gurus of good lineage who are not obliged to agree with you.*

Q. How true!

Chanak: *Gurus these days have acquired dubious distinction. Still, they are the repositories of collective wisdom from ancient scriptures and other gurus and students.*

Q. Turning to your Arthashastra — on Money Street Mergers & Acquisitions come in waves in the name of synergy — but mostly to generate fees for bankers and windfalls for executives. They don't seem to do much for top line or bottom line to create value for the society.

Chanak: ***Positive synergy comes from merging strengths, not weaknesses.***

Q. No wonder most mergers fade away. But there is this powerful urge to merge and grow.

Chanak: *Take a lesson from nature. Size does give certain advantages. But why is it that you don't see many big animals like elephants and whales?*

Q. I suppose that's because they have to balance the advantages of size with the food and energy needed to compete and survive. A big organization strains the span of control. The *dilemma is how to grow big yet stay small.*

Chanak:*Yes. Nature had billions of years to fine-tune its designs.*

Q. On a related note, there seems to be a disconnect between Money Street and Main Street. *Money-Streeters* create short-term paper profits for mega bonuses, not real wealth.

Chanak: *There is wealth in channeling capital for investments, of course. Don't disparage short-term either. Without short-term, there is no long-term. We'd all be dead if we didn't take a breath this moment.*

The right enterprise uplifts society while maintaining economic viability.

Q. If, as you imply, the right enterprise should serve both investors and society — shouldn't board members be legally charged with dual responsibilities?

Chanak: Change the Rules of the Game. When asked by a devotee about the right balance in life, the Buddha said: if a sitar's strings are tuned too tightly, the strings will break; if the strings are too lose, the sitar won't make good music.

Q. Intriguing analogy — need just the right amount of slack to make the right music! I've heard a story of a wild animal tied to a tree with similar message. If the rope is too long, it would go on a rampage. If the rope is too short, it would die of hunger and boredom. So, from your vantage point as the first political economist, how do you see the evolution of societies around the globe?

*Chanak: Avatar Krishna touched on this. Since you honor me with the title of the first political economist, let us look at the **fundamentals of wealth**.*

Citizens and societies start at different starting points, with different trajectories. But human freewill and "fate" can change that.

The wealth of a nation advances on FOUR LEGS:

First, PEOPLE and CULTURE: Sufficiently large groups of people in different stages of life — combining the energy of the young and the wisdom of the old. Their aspirations, values, work ethos, traditions, institutions — all matter. Free institutions that compete and cooperate enable individuals to be their best. Without cultural underpinnings, prosperity will not endure.

Second, NATURAL RESOURCES: land, oceans, space. Earthly resources are important but too many could lead to complacence and dampen human resourcefulness.

Third is VISION and will: visionary leadership and determination to excel. They are often driven by crises, which can be seen as gifts from nature to renew one's vision.

Fourth is SYSTEMS at play: political, economic, educational, technological — such as disciplined democracies and free markets with competing ideas. Governments can promote free enterprise — what they don't do is just as critical as what they do. Systems serve as MULTIPLIERS of resources. Mind you, only nature and humans can create wealth — or destroy it.

Q. That must be the most cogent economics lesson I've had! As to business management, most executives these days go after just two metrics of success: MONEY and POWER.

*Chanak: Wealth and power should go with Self-fulfillment and happiness — people shouldn't feel like imposters. A new triple bottom line could be: Am I/are we **happier?** More **evolved**? Leaving a **worthy legacy**?*

Q. It sounds so much more meaningful than the so-called Gross Domestic Product (GDP). We've come to live in a world of expanding GDPs and shrinking planet. The population ballooned more than three-fold in just the last century, with increased per-capita consumption and waste output — but planet Earth hasn't expanded one bit.

Chanak: A voyager from another planet might well wonder if there is intelligent life on Earth!

Q. Is there? If I may turn to your diabolical schemes to tackle adversaries — lure them into the woods with damsels and blackmail them, entice second-in-command to hatch a plot against his master then turn him in to gain confidence of the enemy, spread rumors through trusted third parties, sow terror among enemy's enclaves about your supernatural powers, woo enemies' enemies, poison by herbs... I'd hate to be your enemy!

*Chanak: Everyone deserves at least one enemy. Where would prey be without predators, companies without competitors? **If you have no competitor, invent one**.*

Q. I can see why. geopolitical rivals are being encouraged to engage in prolonged wars and wasteful ventures to self-destruct.

Chanak: Yes. Beware of the motives of friends as well as enemies.

Q. In that regard, Cyberspace has become a new frontier with Satellites in space extending our eyes and ears. Dangers of cyber attacks are proliferating by disgruntled people and state-sponsored saboteurs.

Chanak: *It seems you've entered a new age of mutual distrust and destruction.*

Q. You said that a snake should pretend it is poisonous even if it is not. It brings to mind poison pills in business — the kind used by target companies as a defense against predators.

Chanak: Don't expose your vulnerabilities. Small nimble teams are best to subvert adversaries or find solutions. In dealing with competitors, launch preemptive strike when and where you have a temporary advantage.

Q. Getting back to the business mantra, growth — with so much excess production capacity hovering around the globe, how can we grow sustainably? Not quite ready to declare that nothing remains to be discovered and close down the patent office. But with so much untapped human potential and unused capacity, there is really no reason for two-thirds of the world to suffer from scarcity. Is it the paradox of having so much money around – but money becoming redundant unless it is kept artificially scarce?

Chanak: There is a great deal of unfinished business yet, and will always be. The need to make money is a strength — and a weakness — of a capitalist market economy.

Q. It seems to foster a cult of consumerism and Throw-Away society. We need more of a **Maintenance**-type economy to reuse, recover, recycle. Cash will continue to be king, I suspect.

Chanak: Cash in one form or another will always play a key role. But, as you imply, how much we consume or waste shouldn't be a measure of the quality of life. As societies evolve and professionals convert their hobbies into careers, voluntary and nonprofit enterprises will outshine money-driven economy.

Human evolution has been at less than glacial pace. You have managed to transform outside space with big cars and houses — but not the inside space. You have only begun to peer into the mysteries of human consciousness — the effects of meditation and prosperity mindset on evolution.

Common sense opportunities are bountiful. Switch to smaller, lighter, mobile artifacts. Re-source resources — water, energy, materials — adopting "birth-to-rebirth" cycles. Farming and agriculture are ripe for a renaissance. Restore natural wealth of land and water, trees and parks.

Explore deep-seas and space. There are limits to selling physical products but no such limits to QUALITY of LIFE attractions like adventures deep into the earth and seas, far out into outer and inner space. Products that make people LIVE BETTER, NOT BUSIER.

Q. Technology is certainly on an inexorable march, reaching every corner: nanotechnologies, genomics, engineered microbes to make everything from biofuels to foods to medicines. And success stories like cellphones set a good precedent for leapfrog technologies. Financial innovations of microfinance and nano-philanthropy are resulting in macro-impacts.

Chanak: The stage is set for the next mega revolution. ***Shift focus from needs to aspirations, from survival to Self fulfillment****. They do not require consumption of more and more natural resources, other than to engage human imagination.*

Q. On that inspiring note, thank you for sharing your wisdom on so many fronts.

Chanak: My blessings to you and your colleagues to seed a prosperous society.

Other highlights of Q&A at a glance: What Begins Well... Ends Well

- Wake up to sunlight and soft music (without a loud alarm)
- Pause a second before jumping off bed, thankful for this day
- After bathroom routine, engage meditation/yoga
- Toward end of meditation, contemplate goals and decisions for the day
- Breakfast with spiritual advisors, mentors, transcendent Self
- Be in touch with Buddha-Krishna-Chanakya through the day (on call 24/7)
- Take mid-afternoon 15-20 minute *Silence Break* or power nap
- At night before retiring reflect on accomplishments, lessons learned, favors received
- Express gratitude for the strength to do the *Right Thing, Right Way*
- Fall asleep with light music, selected readings (7+ hours, pleasant dreams)

-Om-

Buddha-Krishna-Chanakya 'Be-Know-Do' Paradigms at a Glance

Selected Paradigms from the Buddha

1. To find your Way, find the *Beginning.* Innocence is the beginning of understanding.
Smile at the unknown, welcome change by reducing attachments to the transient.

2. Reflect on the purpose and meaning of life.
Be mindful of your thoughts and actions — what you do and DON'T.

3. *Do no harm* — to yourself and to others — by yourself or through others.
Replace greed with Generosity, anger with Compassion, ignorance with Understanding.

4. Remember, money alone is not prosperity.
A prosperous life requires: wealth earned doing the right thing, reputation in the community, worthy legacy.

5. Engage Dharma in Boardroom and in mailroom.
Balance competing interests of stakeholders: employees, customers, non-customers, investors, other benefactors like nature.

Selected Paradigms from Krishna of Bhagavad Gita

1. Know thyself: Your Sattva-Rajas-Tamas Persona, and the personas of colleagues and companies.
This will help you pursue the right calling (profession) through the right venue (organization).

2. Act with the *power of Whole Mind* detached from thoughts of personal gain.
When you *put your mind where your hand is* — then all your energies are focused on the task at hand.

3. Shift from scarcity mindset (rooted in fear) to *prosperity mindset* (rooted in freedom).
Cultivate prosperity mindset by performing random acts of generosity.

4. Build personal and company *Karmic Balance Sheet.*
Deposit good deeds in a universal *Karmic Bank Account*, build reputation as honorable institution.

5. Adopt new nicknames, titles and logos from time to time consistent with evolving roles.
This will help cultivate detachment from existing products and practices to spur innovation.

Selected Paradigms from Chanakya

1. Remember, the right enterprise is socially uplifting and economically viable.

Ask: Creating wealth? Happy? Evolving?

2. Lead by example. Learn continually from authentic gurus, colleagues, students.

Stay in touch with spiritual teachers who are not obliged to agree with you or please you.

Distinguish between activity and accomplishment, information and imagination.

3. Shift focus from needs to aspirations — quality-of-life market is unlimited.

Build networks of synergistic partners, compose small nimble teams to find solutions.

4. Foster abundance through *green capital:* lands, oceans, skies.

Harvest natural resources wisely mindful that our habitat is *participatory, not passive*.

5. Receive reports on the state of the company frequently, pay attention to cash.

Validate information. Keep an eye on competitors through clients, consultants. Travel incognito to outposts; listen to *non-customers* as well as customers.

Test a servant in discharge of duty, relative in difficulty, friend in adversity, wife in misfortune.

- Om-

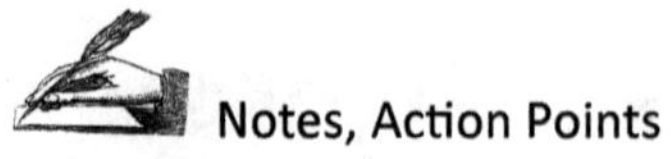

Notes, Action Points

Preview of forthcoming book:

Creative Minds for Innovation and Leadership

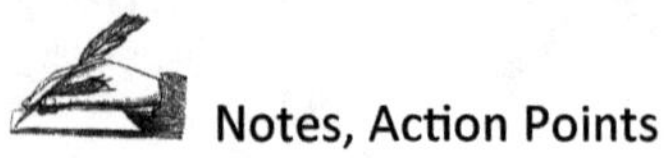

Notes, Action Points

Creative Minds for Innovation and Leadership

Are you a genius?

Yes, we were all geniuses to begin with, as children. But education, culture, experiences – take their toll over time. As such this primer is more about restoring Beginner's Mind, reclaiming creativity.

Here you will find a set of practical exercises and tools to develop creative thinking skills and mental leverage that can help you in planning, solving problems, making decisions. You will:

a) Expand your field of *perception* and range *of* possibilities
b) Engage creative thinking to generate multiple new ideas
c) Engender new processes, products, and profits

Perception is the way we take in the world. What we perceive provides the *inputs* for processing to make decisions. If the inputs are wrong, then no amount of logic will produce the right output. Remember the old computer maxim *GIGO: Garbage In, Garbage Out*?

Leadership is about Bold Vision and Action. It's about having a sense of Purpose and acting with integrity. It's about making decisions and motivating people.

Creativity involves shifts and jumps in established mental patterns. We can enhance creativity by bridging different parts of the brain and mind – by first scanning with a wide-angle lens (exploring), then analyzing (deciding).

STOP for an experiment. Look around the room and count the number of red things. Then close your eyes. How many green things did you see? Look again. Surprised? Because your attention was focused on red, you didn't notice other colors. Something similar happens with ideas. We tend to focus on what we like and overlook what we don't like, or ignore other possibilities.

What you encounter here may seem like Einstein's famous *Thought Experiments* – but you don't have to be an Einstein to develop these thinking skills. You can practice them as individuals or teams – in schools, businesses, governments – preferably guided by instructors. But for now, you'll find sufficient guidance here to launch you on this mental adventure.

All that we are is a result of what we have thought, said Buddha. *I think, therefore I am*, said Descartes.

Just imagine what India and the world would be like if we unleashed new thoughts, a *creativity virus*?

*

Let us begin by exploring some tools and applications for creative decision-making and leadership:

BBM **B**egin **B**eginner's **M**ind
PNI **P**ositive, **N**egative, **I**nteresting points
OPV **O**thers' **P**oints of **V**iew
SLC **S**hort-term and **L**ong-term **C**onsequences

Additional Applications
Better, Cheaper, Faster
Productive Meetings and Brainstorms
Greening of Companies and Products
Fun Experiments for Creative Performance

Restoring Beginner's Mind — the *Empty Cup*

(This exercise combines yoga breathing with sensory awareness and rhythms of life)

Find a quiet place. Disconnect all screens and sounds.

Sit upright: shoulders back, neck-head-back straight up, pushing up the sky, hands resting on lap, feet flat on floor (if sitting on a chair).

Be aware of your presence HERE in this space you occupy.

Scan your surroundings. Now turn attention to your body.

Focus on your breath as you inhale s l o w l y through the nose from lower abdomen (abdomen rises first, then chest, like filling a glass with water). Inhale some more; feel the lungs full all the way down. Hold it 3 or 4 seconds.

Exhale s l o w l y through nose/mouth. Relax the body (say R E L A X silently)

Take a second deep breath as before, hold it 3 or 4 seconds.

Exhale s l o w l y 4-5 seconds, relaxing the mind, letting go of thoughts for now.

Paying attention to your body, ***FEEL*** the weight of your body on the floor or chair. *Feel* the gentle **TOUCH** of clothes on your skin.

SEE what is in front, and above: colors... shapes... space – as if for the first time (simply observe without comment)

Open your ears. ***HEAR*** the sounds from near, *zoom in* on sounds far away. ***LISTEN*** to silence beyond the farthest sound. ***SMELL*** with a light breath.

Let go. Let it be. Rest in this STILLNESS [00000]

Resume normal breathing, smiling with whole body and mind ☺

The *empty cup* is now free to receive – You're now ready to conceive.

BBM: Begin **B**eginner's **M**ind

Learn to unlearn, clear the mind [00000]

To find your way, go to the Beginning — Buddha

Principles and Benefits

1. The Beginner's Mind is open, spontaneous, boundless – like that of a child. Most of what we learn, we learn as children. But education, culture, and experience predispose us to see and think in certain ways. If you wear red-colored spectacles, doesn't the whole world seem red?
2. A Beginner often finds simple solutions to complicated problems because he/she doesn't know any better, doesn't know why it can't be done. It's the **Beginner's Mind *Advantage.*** (Steve Jobs, co-founder of Apple Inc, visited India as a teenager and credited his leaps of imagination to Beginner's Mind and Mindfulness.)
3. Re-read: "DAY 0. Begin with the Beginner's Mind" story at the beginning of this book.

Begin Beginner's Mind (BBM) examples, practice ideas (3-minutes each)

1. Idea: you wish to travel fast.

   You can run, ride a horse, drive a car, fly

   On the other hand, as a Beginner, what if you were to design a road that is shorter? (*Two travelers shorten a road*, says an old proverb)

   Ride a light wave! Or...?
2. Idea: you get a job as marketing consultant to a horse-carriage owner who wants to expand his profits but doesn't want to invest any more money.
   As a Beginner, you might advise him to keep the horse carriage as-is while adding value: switch function, refocus – from destination to journey, from fast to slow, from travel to entertainment.

   And ...?
3. Idea: you suddenly became a Beginner wherever you are. What might you do?

An Experiment

Visualize objects in two dimensions (2-D), three (3-D), and four dimensions (4-D)

(Hint: six matches or pencils of same length on a table — make four equal-sided triangles)

More Ponderings

1. Sometimes begin with NOTHING in mind. Other times with the END in mind.
2. Are your achievements limited more by the timidity of your expectations than by the temerity of your aspirations?
3. *A Beginner has infinite possibilities, an expert only one.*

   Imagine this reversal: *an expert shadows a Beginner* as a medical student shadows a doctor.

On a personal note

If *Beginner's Mind* sounds strange to you, let me ask this: If you could match wits with a world leader or a teenager, whom would you choose?

I presented the Beginner's Mind and related paradigms in a *59-minute course* to a group of 11 to 17-year old children in a New York suburb. One child asked: Have you presented anything like this to world leaders? Others added that if more leaders used these thinking tools, the world would be a far better place.

I sometimes annoy medical experts saying: You're limited by what you know. I'm unlimited by what I don't know!

∞

PNI: Positive, **N**egative, **I**nteresting points

Consider ideas in 3-D; don't label only as Good-or-Bad, Pro-or-Con

Let's do it in 3-D — RK

Principles and Benefits

1. P = Positive, the good — what you like about a thing, idea or person
   N = Negative, the bad — what you don't like
   I = Interesting points, neither good nor bad — but can lead to other ideas
2. We are used to thinking in terms of: good-bad, pro-con, advantages-disadvantages. When you do a PNI, you deliberately set out to find points of view that may be different from your initial viewpoint. The PNI gets you out of the like-dislike comfort zone, adding a third vessel, so to speak, expanding your *perceptual field*.
3. The PNI shows that things and ideas are not necessarily good or bad, but can also be interesting if they serve as stepping stones to other ideas. Otherwise, you may reject a valuable idea that seems bad at first sight. Conversely, you are unlikely to see the disadvantages of an idea you like very much. With PNI, you decide whether you like an idea *after* you have had a chance to explore it.

Positive, Negative, Interesting (PNI) examples, practice ideas (3-minutes each)

1. Idea: all seats should be taken out of public buses.

   P: More people can fit into each bus

   It will be easier to get in and out, saving time

   Buses would be cheaper to make and maintain

   N: Passengers may fall and injure themselves

   Older and sick people may not be able to take the bus

   It would be difficult to carry bags or babies

   I: Interesting to consider two types of buses, one with seats and one without

   Buses may be able to make more rounds, do more work

   Comfort may not be so important, buses at airports have no seats (except one for driver)

2. Idea: Free food should be given to everyone.
   P:People will be free of hunger
      Can give out only fresh, healthy foods
      Better quality of life, people can shift attention to other things
   N:People may overeat and become obese and ill
      People will lose freedom to choose what they want
      Society may become dependent on handouts and lose self-respect
   I: Who will pay for the food?
      Could only healthy foods be made available free?
      Will healthy foods improve people's health and productivity?

3. Idea: People should not work hard or smart.
   P:Workers will have less stress and strain
      They will have more free time to do what they want
      Work can be spread among more people, more employment
   N:Workers cannot improve knowledge and skills and reach their full potential
      Company gets bad reputation and goes bankrupt, causing unemployment
      Without jobs and incomes, society's health and well-being will suffer
   I: Will the country's overall growth and prosperity suffer?
      Will the country become less competitive and employment opportunities decline because people in other countries work harder, smarter?
      What if different types of incentives are given to different workers?

More Practice Ideas (3-minutes each round)

1. People should wear badges showing they are in good mood or bad mood
2. Inject knowledge into children while they are asleep, or give smart pills
3. Make the Internet accessible to everyone
4. Healthcare should be freely accessible to all people and animals
5. Every young person should adopt an elderly person to keep company
6. PNI someone you *don't like*: for every Negative point, find at least one Positive and one Interesting point

Note: This lesson is adapted from Dr. Edward DeBono's research and writings.

On a personal note

In connection with a Rotary International vocational training project, I presented PNI and CAT (Consider All Things) to a group of blind and disabled teenagers at a school near Hyderabad, using both English and Telugu. Their *cognitive intelligence* skill levels nearly doubled in just over an hour.

I've also presented two similar lessons at a gifted children's school in Hyderabad one morning. Another group of students got wind of what was happening and requested the school's director to let them also have the opportunity to participate in the workshop. After a tiffin-break I repeated the workshop for the new batch with similar results.

OPV: Others' Points of View –
Consider others' viewpoints as if they are your own

Never criticize a man until you walked a mile in his moccasins
–Native American proverb

Principles and Benefits

1. In daily life we are so preoccupied with what we want, we pay scant attention to what others might want. An important part of thinking is to be able to tell what other people are thinking and feeling. You can try to see another point of view whether you agree with it or not. Like **role-playing,** OPV sensitizes you to the needs of others – increasing empathy and your *Emotional IQ (EQ)* and *Social Intelligence*.
2. Should your actions be based on your viewpoint only, or on others' as well? If you put yourself in the other person's shoes and understand his/her needs, you stand a better chance of getting what you want. With OPV you will gain insights into others' *perceptual bubbles* as well as your own and build *people skills*. You will be a better communicator and negotiator.
3. Understanding what is on your mind about yourself – your needs and motivations – can be considered zero-order perception. Understanding what's on other people's minds – their needs and motivations – is first-order perception. Seeing yourself as others see you can be second-order perception. Getting others' points of view is not difficult. Just **listen silently.**

Others' Points of View (OPV) examples, practice ideas

1. Idea: Look at yourself from your neighbors' points of view
   a) They want a quiet neighbor
   b) My house well maintained to preserve property values
   c) Want my help during emergencies
   d) Other?
2. Idea: See the points of view of
   (a) Husband-wife, children-parents, teacher-student
   (b) Buyer-seller, doctor-patient
   (c) Boss-subordinate
3. Idea: What might be the point of view of a turkey bird on Thanksgiving Holidays in America?

More...

1. At work, OPV your manager and his managers. Also workers reporting to you.
2. Top management: OPV employees, board of directors, customers, suppliers, shareholders/investors, communities, environment, future generations.

   For instance, if you are the Chief Executive, what might be the point of view of employees if your remuneration is, say, 300 times that of the salary of an average employee?
3. When you cultivate OPV and increase understanding of others' needs – how might that improve the quality of life all around and reduce conflicts among peoples and nations — find common ground?

Bonus point - handling criticism, combining lesson-tools:

We've all had experiences with overly critical bosses, colleagues, customers (perhaps also bullies in school). Our typical reaction tends to be anger, resentment. One way to handle criticism is not to resist but to deflect the attack as in *Judo* using the attacker's own energy.

Fist, look at how you react to a situation and why? It may reveal your own hot buttons.

Then you could choose to reverse the perception. For instance, you could choose to feel THANKFUL for a boss who criticizes everything you do, that he is lavishing so much attention on you. After all, not only imitation but criticism can be a form of flattery.

When he talks, listen silently paying full attention. Also do a PNI on his *Positive* points (what you like), *Negative* points (what you don't like), and *Interesting* points (postponing judgment). Using the positive points, compliment him sincerely. You may also follow up with something like: Thank you for bringing it to my attention. I'd be grateful if you could give me a few pointers to improve my performance. When can I come see you?

Bottom line: You can enhance your own career and influence others by the way you respond — remaining open to suggestions for improvement. Give others the benefit of doubt, but don't give them control over your happiness.

On a personal note

When speaking to groups I used to concentrate on communicating what I know, what I thought the audience ought to know – rather than finding out what they really might want to know. The practice of OPV and role-playing made me more sensitive to the interests of my colleagues, audiences, students and others.

Know your audience. The ability to inform and persuade others to take action — the art of persuasion — has less to do with the speaker and more to do with the goals and emotional needs of the audience.

∞

SLC: Short-term and **L**ong-term **C**onsequences

Imagine potential consequences of decisions, actions, inactions

Nothing is worth doing unless the consequences may be serious

— George Bernard Shaw

Principles and Benefits

1. This lesson sheds light on possible immediate as well as longer-term effects of proposed ideas and actions (or inactions), including *unintended consequences*: What might happen short-term (say, up to one year), mid-term (up to about 10 years), long-term (beyond 10 years). The time horizons can be adjusted to suit the situation: this generation, next generation, so on. You may also think of consequences as first order (to family or community), second order (to country or region), or third order (to the planet).
2. Intuitively we pay more attention to the immediate, because we can see it more clearly and feel it more intimately. Longer-term consequences are harder to predict because they depend on many more factors and interactions – like moves and countermoves in chess, as well as *rates of change* (how fast?). Moreover, short-term effects can be good, long-term bad, or vice-versa. And it's useful to know up-front whether the effects are reversible.
3. Business management is a balancing act to avoid short-term plans that result in long-term disasters, and long-term plans that result in short-term disasters. There is no long term without short term. However, preoccupation with immediate results engenders a culture of discounting the future.

SLC + CAT (Consider All Things) examples, practice ideas

1. Idea: Hiring a new employee

   a) Is there adequate budget for salary and benefits? How does it affect existing employees?

   b) Candidate qualified for future positions?

   c) Team player or boat-rocker? (Whom would you prefer?)

   d) Is the candidate promotable? Where is she likely to be in 10 years?

2. Idea: A country is considering one-child policy

   a) If some families choose not to have girl babies, many more boys than girls?

   b) Future generations will not have uncles and aunts

   c) Population pyramid will be distorted, not enough workers to support retired and elderly

   d) Without enough workers and household formations, the economy will suffer

   e) Population will shrink over time, may need to consider exemptions and/or new immigrants

Other practice ideas and points to ponder

1. Consider the *whole life-cycle* (from birth-to-rebirth) of a natural resource like water or a technology product like cellphone?
2. The world runs out of drinkable water – what then?
3. All the trees are gone; global warming by 2 degrees?
4. Effects of economic and cultural Globalization?
5. The choices you made in life — what you did, or didn't do, years ago — do they have anything to do with where you stand today? (Karma Yoga?)
6. Consequences of living forever?
7. Population explosion (Indian region), stable population (China), shrinkage (Japan, Russia); Unintended consequences of China's one-child policy?
8. What if 1% of world's populace engages mindfulness/meditation?
9. What if countries and companies are run entirely by women leaders?
10. Long-term consequences of genetically modified organism (GMO) food supplies — and increased use of herbicides like Roundup in agriculture? (Consider potential consequences to external and internal ecosystems; and Points of View of manufacturers and farmers)

More...

1. In the Superman movie, did Superman consider all the consequences of giving up his super powers to befriend Lois Lane, the newspaper reporter?

2. What if a natural disaster or terrorist act occurred? How would you handle business disruption — to ensure continuity of operations?

3.Economic and environmental consequences:

a) SLC of transplanting species: Rabbits were introduced into Australia for sport and meat. Short-term consequences were desirable because the rabbits provided a target to shoot and a bountiful source of meat. But longer-term consequences were negative: rabbits multiplied, became pests, damaged crops, overgrazed and reduced food for sheep.

b) SLC of inventions: The invention of petrol engine led to oil industry, pollution, wars. If we had foreseen the consequences, steam or electric motors might have been used (as were initially done). If we consider whole lifecycles before introduction, many unintended consequences could be avoided. For instance, chlorofluorocarbons used as refrigerants drifted up into the stratosphere and depleted the protective ozone layer, causing an ozone hole and increasing the risk of cancers.

On a personal note

Early in my career I worked with a pioneering electronic data systems company. It had a rigorous recruiting policy, with the motto *one eagle at a time*. After a series of screenings I went to company headquarters, where I was interviewed all day by potential colleagues, finally by senior vice president. I was informed ahead of time that if I were offered the job, I'd have to shave my mustache, and have to accept or reject the job offer right on the spot.

The requirement to decide on the spot – does it reflect a person's ability to make quick decisions? Is that a good employment practice? (Incidentally, that was the only time in my adult life that I didn't sport a mustache — the one thing I can count on to grow in my life!)

Additional Applications

Better, Cheaper, Faster

Better-Faster-Cheaper — continues to be the business *mantra*. Typically the change happens through continuous improvement via incremental steps over time (*perspiration*). Breakthroughs and quantum leaps are still rare (*inspiration*). Einstein's elegant equation $E = MC^2$, expressing the equivalence of energy and matter is a quantum leap in our understanding of the universe.

The Beginner's Mind is well suited to quantum leaps. There are no baselines to contend with, no past experiences to hold back. Endless possibilities. It's as if the creative capacity is amplified exponentially a hundred or thousand-fold.

*

By way of illustration, suppose you want to travel faster. You could, of course, buy a car or design one that runs faster. What if you were to design a road that is shorter? *Two travelers shorten a road*, says an old proverb.

A transformation within the memory of the present generation is the phenomenon of horse-drawn carriage to horse-less carriage to *flying carriage*. We can increase the speed of a horse-carriage by reducing weight or adding more horses. But these have practical limits. To increase the speed exponentially, say, by a factor of 10 or more, you have to get away from the horse. The result is a horse-less carriage: a car, or an airplane

Staying with the horse-carriage analogy, there could be a quantum leap in value by another sort of innovation: keeping the product basically "as is" but by paradigm shift:

from destination to journey,

from fast to slow,

from travel to entertainment...

Productive Meetings and Brainstorms

Most of us spend most of our time in meetings of one kind or another. Here are some guidelines to make meetings more effective.

Do a *Mindfulness exercise* before a meeting.

Have clear purpose and objectives — preferably written and distributed in advance. Identify the person chairing the meeting. Begin and End meetings on time. Hold some meetings standing, without food, which could reduce meeting time. Make attendance at some meetings optional.

Discuss and debate. Don't let talkative people hijack the meeting. Leave some time open for spontaneous explorations. *Ask questions. Don't declare answers.* Suggest possibilities; give new reality a chance to emerge. Ask *why*? *Why not*? *What if?* Identify windows of opportunity that are time-sensitive — to seize the moment.

Record **decisions** made and **actions** to be taken. Everyone should leave the meeting with a clear understanding of what he/she is expected to do and when. Agree on follow-up review.

Why (what decisions to be made, actions initiated?)

Who (who will do what and when?)

Follow-up (when to review and adjust course?)

Starting with a mindfulness exercise (individually or in groups) could reduce adversarial attitudes and make meetings more productive. The number of meetings and time spent could be cut in half.

In some meetings, include a foreigner, magician, clown, disabled person, child, or professional listener. Now and then, you may wish to skip conventional slide shows and rhetoric in favor of a real life drama.

On some occasions, when an important decision has to be made now, consider removing all food and chairs from the room. Turn off phones.

Brainstorms, Think Tanks

Brainstorming sessions have become familiar fixtures of modern society. Group dynamics do play a role in generating ideas.

One day, feeling adventurous, suppose you try this: begin a meeting from the vantage point of a Beginner. You might announce playfully **Zero** — for zero state of mind. That would give everyone temporary license to suspend all that they believe and to let go of logic for now – to be spontaneous.

You might choose to invoke the *BBM Advantage* to consider things backwards or *in reverse*. Ask: why, why not, what if?

- Design a house upside down, a public museum with sloping floors and roofs
- Instead of hiring a person for a predetermined position, first hire a well-qualified person, then let her create her own job
- Sell your products/services to non-customers
- Sell your products by auction to the lowest bidder
- Instead of 24 hours in a day, conceive 42
- Banks come to people, bottom line Societal Happiness
- Invest and expand during recession
- Build floating houses, schools, factories on water instead of land — powered by sun, waves, winds
- Encourage a child or teenager to adopt an elder

- *Personal Ponderings - Notes*

Why are people afraid of new ideas and not the old?

Greening of Companies and Products

Businesses have jumped on the green design bandwagon, and for good reason. Nature has been fine-tuning its design for billions of years without patenting anything.

There is little waste in nature. One's waste is another's food or fuel. In poor countries, cattle wastes are collected and used as fuel, fertilizer, or building mix. In rich countries with large agricultural industries, animal wastes from farms can be a huge source of bio-energy — while reducing air-land- water pollution, and global warming, from agriculture.

Life and Afterlife. The planning of whole financial-material-technology lifecycle is at the heart of green design. Today's rapidly changing technologies and planned obsolescence exacerbate the waste burden. Emblematic of this is the growing number of computers and devices discarded each year, as wll as cars and parts.

The design stage — not manufacturing or marketing stage — is where we have the greatest freedom of choice of materials, technologies, functions, markets, and tradeoffs. In short: Rethink, Reduce, Reuse.

Lifecycle Analysis - birth-to-rebirth design

- Think through the entire product/technology lifecycle from concept to disposal/reclamation. Green lifecycle is circular: cradle-to-cradle, unlike linear cradle-to-grave
- Consider impacts on humans and environment of entire lifecycle: raw materials/parts, manufacturing, transport, storage, use, disposal, reuse
- Dematerialize: Switch from physical product to knowledge-based service. Reduce virgin material, increase recyclables
- De-energize: Reduce the use of fossil energy, increase renewable/ domestic energy
- Detoxify: Employ materials that are low in toxicity and persistence in the environment
- Extend life-span: Increase durability, reliability, maintainability, disassembly, re-assembly, reuse.

Source: *Risk Assessment and Management Handbook*, Rao Kolluru

Fun Experiments for Creative Performance

1 Find out your Company's Vision or Mission. Ask the receptionist. What is one financial and one non-financial goal of your company?

2 What if you started all over again from Day Zero with Zero State of Mind? What would be an ideal scenario going forward?

3 The CEO might occasionally play the role of the receptionist or mailroom clerk. Perhaps answer her own phone one day a month; eat in employee cafeteria and park with everyone else

4 Find out what employees/suppliers like best about working with your company: Ask for two Positive, two Negative, and two Interesting points

5 Find out why non-customers are non-customers?

6 Invite CEO to a "Roast," perhaps on company birthday with look-alikes. Enact skits on how he/she affects the lives of the different stakeholders?

7 Do mindfulness exercise before meetings or brainstorms

8 Start life-long learning and creativity centers. Set up a system to receive suggestions. Be open to ideas that may lead to quantum leap performance

9 Include in some meetings a foreigner, clown, magician, fisherman, child, professional listener

10 Identify the hobbies, voluntary services and other outside interests of employees if they want to share that information. Sponsor/display employee arts and crafts

11 Review past mistakes or failures to identify seeds of success

12 Imagine what the world was like a century ago, a millennium ago. Speculate on what the future might look like in 22nd century?

13 At some meetings, acknowledge happy events with nominal donations such as a Happy $ or a 10-rupee note

14 Reward employees who make their particular tasks or jobs obsolete

15 Think of one or two competitors whom you respect. What accounts for their success? How can your company/product be Number One?

16 Imagine 16 ways to make work fun and play.

oooooooooooooooooooooooooooooooooooooooooooooooooooooooooooooo

How to be a Genius — at a glance

- ✓ Reflect on your purpose, life and legacy
- ✓ Reclaim the Beginner's Mind: childlike sense of wonder, continual learning from observations, experiments, mistakes
- ✓ Validate knowledge and beliefs through experiences
- ✓ Be mindful of connectivity across three degrees of space and time
- ✓ Befriend the unknown: embrace ambiguity, paradox, uncertainty
- ✓ Enlist the whole mind: seeing and seeking, science and arts, logic and imagination
- ✓ Walk in others' shoes – reflect on others' points of view (colleagues, customers, children, turkey at Thanksgiving)
- ✓ Cultivate a sense of abundance, humor, fair play

oooooooooooooooooooooooooooooooooooooooooooooooooooooooooooooo

Glossary, Abbreviations

Aadhar India citizen ID issued by the Unique Identification (UID) Authority of India

Ashram hermitage, monastery, retreat usually directed by a guru, monk or sage

Avatar descent, incarnation, representation

Ayurveda science of life, holistic system of health and medicine developed in India more than 5000 years ago; health is restored by balancing *"doshas" (Vata, Pitta, Kapha)* according to one's nature and lifestyle

Beginner's Mind open mind without prejudgment like that of a child

Bhagavad Gita Celestial Song, Gospel of Hinduism, dialogue between Lord Krishna and disciple Arjuna in battlefield, part of *Mahabharata* epic

Bharat from king Bharat, another name for India

Buddha (563-483 BC) born in northern India, the prince who became a prophet, enlightened one — sometimes called *Sakyamuni* (knowing the past, present, future)

Buddhi enlightenment, from same root word of Buddha --, Satori in Zen Buddhism

BPM, BPO Business Process Management, formerly called Business Process Outsourcing/Offshoring (BPO)

BRICS Brazil, Russia, India, China, South Africa emerging economies (in the process of forming BRICS Bank)

CDC Centers for Disease Control and Prevention (cdc.gov), US Department of Health and Human Services

CEO Chief Executive Officer, chairman and/or president of an organization

Chakras seven wheels or centers of psychic energy, six located along nerve plexuses along the spine, seventh at the crown of the head in astral plane

Chanakya (350-283 BC), also known as Kautilya and Vishnugupta, chief architect of a united India under Maurya Dynasty, the first political economist, management guru, and toxicologist

Chi, Qi life force; Qi Gong is following the rhythm of nature, especially water

Dharma duty, purpose in life, the Way, code of conduct

Dhyana meditation or pooja, Sanskrit root word of Chinese ch'an and Japanese Zen

EM/EE Emerging Markets/Emerging Economies, most countries outside of North America, Europe and Japan — with annual growth of 5% or more — including BRICS, Indonesia, Turkey, Mexico, and others

EMA European Medicines Agency (ema.europa.eu), American FDA counterpart

EPA US Environmental Protection Agency (epa.gov)

EU, Euro European Union with 28 members; 18 members including Germany and France (but not UK) adopted Euro as their common currency (1 Euro ~ USD 1.3), EU awarded Nobel Peace Prize in 2012

FDA US Food and Drug Administration (fda.gov)

FDI Foreign Direct Investment

Feng Shui wind and water, art of aligning things in space to harmonize with surrounding *chi* life force (Chinese)

G7, G8, G20 Group of seven, eight, or 20 — finance ministers and central bank governors of advanced economies including US, Canada, UK, Germany, France, Italy, Japan. G8 includes G7 plus Russia. G20 includes G8 plus China, India, Indonesia, Turkey, Mexico and others

GDP, GDP-PPP GDP is a broad measure of the economic output of a nation in a year, including: consumer spending, private investment, government spending, net exports. **GDP-PPP** is GDP at Purchasing Power Parity, adjusted for differences

in cost of living among countries using American prices for goods and services as benchmarks
GNH Gross National Happiness index of Bhutan (kingdom nestled in the mountains of northern India)
Guru, Guruji teacher, spiritual guide, dispeller of darkness; suffix -ji connotes respect
IIM Indian Institute of Management, 13+6 (expected by 2015) autonomous centers of management education
IIT Indian Institute of Technology, 16 IITs are leading engineering education centers with common admission policies
India name derived from the **Indus River** (Sindh or Sindhu River, Yamuna tributary) in north-western India. Inhabitants of the region were called "Hindu". Indian mathematicians/astronomers were often called Hindu mathematicians referring to country location
Indian native of India, or of Indian origin — not native American
INR Indian Rupee (floating 40 to 60+ Rupees per US Dollar)
IT Information Technology including software
IUSSTF Indo-US Science and Technology Forum (iusstf.org)
JICA Japan International Cooperation Agency (jica.go.jp)
Karma law of cause-and-effect, trajectory, universal balance sheet of 'good' and 'bad' deeds ("Dharma, no Karma")
Krishna, Sri Krishna legendary *avatar* , here introduced through ***Bhagavad Gita***, composed between fifth and second century BC, part of the great Mahabharata epic depicting the eternal struggle between "good" and "evil"
Leela/Rasleela divine play (of creation), playfulness
Mantra simple word or phrase, traditionally from Sanskrit, used to clear the mind of thoughts in meditation; some mantras may be endowed with special energy through repetition by holy men over generations
Mindfulness the state of being in the moment, conscious of one's environment, thoughts, actions
MOOCS Massive Open Online Courses, typically free or self-sustaining — including Harvard-MIT edX, Coursera (for-profit group), Udacity
Namaste/Namaskaram greeting, gesture of "I acknowledge the divinity within you"
Nasscom National Association of Software and Services Companies headquartered in India
NIH National Institutes of Health (nih.gov) — Turning Discovery into Health
Nirvana transcendence from the wheel of birth and death, pleasure and pain; beyond karma; union of Atman (individual soul) with transcendent Brahman. Also called Moksha
North America United States and Canada (sometimes Mexico also included)
NRI Non-Resident Indian
OECD Organisation for Economic Cooperation and Development of 34 countries mostly North American and European, founded in 1961
Om (Aum) composite of three sounds a-u-m, each symbolic of a level of consciousness: "a" for waking state, "u" for dreaming state, "m" for sleeping state. Whole sound as one continuous vibration epitomizes cosmic consciousness. Om is also considered a synthesis of the three universal qualities of creation, preservation, dissolution
PM, CM Prime Minister of a country, Chief Minister of a state (similar to a Governor in the US)
Pooja, Puja worship, meditation, individually or in a group
Prosperity material wealth and a way of life, mindset, a state of Being (going beyond the GDP of a nation)

Ratnakara Indian Ocean, storehouse of jewels in Sanskrit (third largest ocean and the only one named after a country)
Rupee Re, Rs Indian Rupee (INR) unless specified otherwise
S-factor spiritual connection that expresses what you stand for, what makes you stand out
Satsang/Sangha good company, spiritual fellowship, communion with noble persons and values
Sattva-Rajas-Tamas (persona) fundamental qualities of nature combining: Sattva light, knowledge, goodness; Rajas energy, action, control; Tamas inertia, rest, apathy
South Asia/South-central Asia Indian subcontinent nations and neighbors that share history and culture — including present day India, Pakistan, Afghanistan, Nepal, Bhutan, Sikkim, Bangladesh, Sri Lanka, Indian Ocean islands — that could form Indus Region Free Market Zone.
Smriti, Sruti smriti is "remembered" human knowledge/wisdom dependent on time and circumstances; sruti is "heard" absolute revelation independent of time and place
STEM Science , Technology, Engineering, Mathematics (elements of education)
Swami spiritual being, holy man, sage, one who is with Self
Tai chi boundless fist, traditional Chinese martial art characterized by slow movements
Tao the Way, harmony with nature, living in fulfillment of human nature
TED Technology, Entertainment, Design — forum for exchange of ideas at events by invitation
TiE The Indus Entrepreneurs based in California's Silicon Valley (tie.org) with 60 chapters around the world
TM Transcendental Meditation popularized by Maharishi Mahesh Yogi; in this well-researched technique, the mind is emptied using a *mantra — transcending* thoughts/images to reach pure consciousness, the *state of Being*
TRAI Telecom Regulatory Authority of India
Triple-Pro Prosperity (wealth), Progress (evolution), Progeny (legacy) — new model with ancient roots presented in this book — that can serve as a mission/ strategy for yourself, company, country
UK United Kingdom includes England, Wales, Scotland, Northern Ireland (also referred to as Britain/Great Britain and Northern Ireland (total population of about 63 million in 2012)
UN United Nations with more than 20 agencies, including Food and Agriculture Organization (FAO), World Bank, International Monetary Fund (IMF), UN Environment Programme (UNEP), World Health Organization (WHO), UN Industrial Development Organization (UNIDO), UN Educational, Scientific and Cultural Organization (UNESCO). UN is headquartered in New York, agencies in different countries (none in India, and India not a permanent Security Council member)
Upanishads ancient Vedic philosophy, underpinnings of Hinduism (see also Vedas)
USA/US United States of **America**
USAID US Agency for International Development (USAID.gov) provides help in public health, agriculture, environment
USD/US$ United States Dollar (exchange rate 50-60 Indian Rupees in 2013-14)
Vedas true knowledge from divine revelations, earliest Indo-European scriptures grouped into: Rig Veda, Yajur Veda, Sama Veda, Atharva Veda; spiritual underpinnings of Hinduism and, indirectly, Buddhism
WEF World Economic Forum (WEForum.org)

Yin-Yang complementary opposing forces: dark-light, death-life, female-male; yin depicts darkness, passivity, earth, woman; yang depicts light, activity, sky, man (Chinese)
Yoga joining, unity: Bhakti yoga of love and devotion, Dhyana yoga of meditation, Karma yoga of action, Jnana yoga of knowledge and contemplation, Hatha/Raja yoga of mental and physical discipline — different paths for different personalities; **Yogi** is a practitioner of yoga or an ascetic
Zen Japanese meditation, derived from Sanskrit dhyana and Chinese chan Buddhism; **Zazen** is quiet sitting meditation usually facing a blank wall; **zendo** is a hall where zazen is practiced
....

Conversion factors

million = 10 lakhs (1,000,000)

billion (bn) = 100 crores (1000 million)

trillion = 100,000 crores (1000 billion)

lakh = 100,000

crore = 10,000,000 = 100 lakh = 10 million

1 USD (US$) = 40 to 60+ Indian Rupees (INR) floating exchange rates

1 crore INR ~ 170,000 USD

1 million USD ~ 6 crore INR

These are nominal exchange rates. If we use Purchasing Power Parity (PPP) adjusted for cost of living differences between the US and India: 1 US$ ~ 20-25 INR

About the Author + Keynotes-Seminars-Workshops

Rao Kolluru, DrPH, MBA
has been writing, teaching and consulting across four decades. He has worked with major global enterprises — including American Cyanamid (now part of Pfizer) — bridging diverse disciplines: manufacturing-technology cost improvement, strategic planning and business development, environment-health-safety risk assessment and management. Nicknamed *Urban Monk* by a regional newspaper, his recent focus has been on blending business with purpose, science with spirit — the *Tao of Dow*

Rao has taught graduate courses as Adjunct Professor or presented seminars at Stevens Institute of Technology, Columbia University, and at other institutions. He has been a guest speaker on environmental and health risks, Ecology-Energy-Economics intersections, sustainable development and business bottom line — in the US, Canada, Japan, India, and China.

In this book, Prophets and Profits, Rao introduces the **Triple-Pro™** (Prosperity+Progress+Progeny) model he has developed, rooted in the teachings of Buddha-Krishna-Chanakya. The model also reflects his global consulting and teaching experience as well as research on Beginner's Mind and Mindfulness, and Creative Thinking.

Educated in the East and the West, including pre-medicine and engineering, Rao obtained a doctorate in health sciences from Columbia University and an MBA from New York University. His handbook on environmental-health-safety risks — published by McGraw-Hill and translated into Japanese, Spanish and other languages — serves as a reference worldwide.

Rao is currently President of the Society for Risk Analysis Metro Region, and earlier served on the toxicity advisory committee to New York City. As the International Chair of a Rotary Club, he was involved in funding vocational training and clean water projects in India and elsewhere.

Of an earlier book, Dr Paul Brandt-Rauf of Columbia University said: "...A timely parable of timeless concepts...spiritual rationale for the thinking person." Others acclaimed Rao's books as: *intriguing, scientific philosophy in thought-provoking study*.

Keynotes, Seminars, Workshops

+ The Golden Rule of Prosperity and Profits
  Buddha-Krishna-Chanakya Ancient Paradigms for Modern Enterprise
+ The Tao of Dow, Greening of Companies
  Profit with Purpose, Doing Well by Doing Good
+ Triple-Pro™ Model: Prosperity + Progress + Progeny
  Create Wealth, Learn Everyday, Invest in the Future
+ Creative Minds for Innovation and Leadership --
  Mental Software for New Products and Profits
+ How to Assess and Manage Risks
  Reduce Environmental-Health-Safety and Financial Risks
  using *Birth-to-Rebirth Life-cycle Analysis*

....

Other Books by Rao Kolluru

Business, Science, Spirit — the *Tao of Dow*:

- Creative Minds
  for Innovation and Leadership (upcoming)
- Begin Anew
  Re-setting Your Mind's Odometer [00000]
- Spiritual Entrepreneuring
  Pathway to Lasting Success
- River of a Thousand Tales
  Encounters with Spirit, Reflections from Science

Environment, Health & Safety:

- Risk Assessment and Management Handbook
  for Environmental, Health, and Safety Professionals
  (McGraw-Hill, New York)
- Environmental Strategies Handbook
  A Guide to Effective Policies and Practices
  (McGraw-Hill, New York)

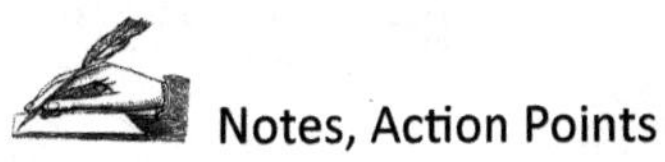

Notes, Action Points

www.ingramcontent.com/pod-product-compliance
Lightning Source LLC
Chambersburg PA
CBHW072249270326
41930CB00010B/2315
* 9 7 8 0 9 7 4 9 7 4 6 9 9 *

BANKER OCCUPATION
Waging Financial War on Humanity

BANKER OCCUPATION

Waging Financial War on Humanity

by

STEPHEN LENDMAN

CLEAR DAY BOOKS

ISBN: 978-0-9845255-8-4
E-book: 978-0-9845255-9-1

In-house editor: Diana G. Collier
Cover: R. Jordan P. Santos
Charging Bull image based on the photo "Charging Bull by Sebastian Alvarez (http://www.flickr.com/photos/aseba/6179708990/in/set-72157627744672130/)

Clear Day Books
A division of
Clarity Press, Inc.
Ste. 469, 3277 Roswell Rd. NE
Atlanta, GA. 30305 , USA
http://www.claritypress.com

Today financial war rages.
Stopping it depends on putting money power back
in public hands where it belongs.

This book is dedicated to people in the struggle to achieve it.

Table of Contents

1

WALL STREET RUNS AMERICA

Major Wall Street banks occupy and control Washington. I wrote about it at length in my earlier book, *How Wall Street Fleeces America.*[1]Their officials recycle from banking to government and back again, making policy, and enforcing it with their money power supremacy to achieve virtually everything they want.

Political Washington salutes and obeys. Money power in private hands and democracy can't co-exist. It buys what it wants at the expense of government of, by and for the people—the kind of government that in actuality never existed and doesn't now.

Wall Street crooks have transformed America into an unprecedented money making racket. Facilitated by federal, state and local governments, they make money the old fashioned way. They steal it. Ordinary Americans get scammed. They've lost savings, jobs, homes and futures to let privileged elites get richer and more powerful.

Banking giants controlthe creation and circulation of money, issuing credit and debt for private enrichment. They bribe politicians to pass business friendly laws and turn a blind eye to massive fraud and abuse. It pays off. The banksters got decades of deregulation, outsourcing, economic financialization, and casino capitalist excess. In return, America and Western economies got asset bubbles, record budget and national debt levels, depression-sized unemployment, public deprivation and anger.

Today's crisis is global; the contagion has caused billions to suffer. The economies of entire countries are being wrecked to save the banks. Washington is Wall Street-occupied territory. So are European financial capitals because governments provide trillions of dollars to socialize losses, privatize profits, and hang ordinary people out to dry.

Stopping them depends on putting money power—the creation of money and access to credit—back in public hands where it belongs. There's no other way., When Congress passed the Federal Reserve Act on December 23, 1913, it violated Article 1, Section 8 of the Constitution, giving Congress sole power to coin (create) money and regulate the value thereof.Abolishing or nationalizing the Fed and giving money power back to the people through Congress is step one to regain the rights that have been lost to banker controlled government.

That's Issue Number One that Occupy Wall Street[2] protesters and others spreading across America in dozens of cities must address.

Occupy Together[3] is an "unofficial hub" for burgeoning initiatives heading everywhere "in solidarity with Occupy Wall St."

As word spreads, hidden anger surfaces. Small numbers of protesters grow. So does commitment to stay the course. Activists and ordinary people know something's wrong and they want it changed. The key is understanding that money power is in private hands, and not the hands of the government. Change depends on ending this system that is destroying the future for working Americans.

Major Wall Street firms comprise an illegal private banking cartel monopoly controlling the nation's money, price, supply and availability. For a century, it has looted America's economy for its own self-interest. It's run by unelected, unaccountable crooks in league with corrupt politicians, who are taking bribes in the form of campaign contributions to go along with whatever laws, regulations and policies the bankers want.

Behind closed doors, JP Morgan Chase, Goldman Sachs, Bank of America, Wells Fargo, and other giants run America. They do it by waging financial war on the public.In theory, the Fed was established to stabilize the economy, smooth out the business cycle, manage healthy, sustainable growth, and maintain stable prices.Instead, it has caused multiple recessions, the Great Depression, and today's Greatest Global one. It is responsible for monetary inflation and America's declining standard of living, notably in recent decades.

In fact, a 1913 dollar today isn't worth a plug nickel, and given reckless Greenspan/Bernanke money creation the dollar's value is eroding entirely. Notably the Fed caused:

- rising consumer debt;
- record budget and trade deficits;
- a soaring national debt equaling GDP and heading higher;

- escalating personal and business bankruptcies, both up around 35% in 2009 with near record levels persisting in 2010;

- millions of home foreclosures in America's worst ever housing Depression;

- unemployment at nearly 23%;

- loss of the nation's manufacturing base;

- shocking levels of poverty in the world's richest country;

- an unprecedented wealth gap; and

- a hugely unstable economy lurching from one crisis to another.

The Fed lets money power in private hands profit hugely by swindling investors, buying valued assets cheap, consolidating to greater size. The Fed gives it an open checkbook access to trillions for speculation and big bonuses.

Easy money, market manipulation, deregulation, reckless speculation, counterproductive fixes, and unsustainable debt caused today's crisis.

Why else would gold and silver prices soar? Bad policy assures worse trouble ahead. Instead of the excesses bing washed out, they increase over time. Eventually, an unsustainable house of cards collapses, especially when credit contraction persists. The combination of monopoly money power in private hands combined with financialization at the expense of industrial America produced policies that are wrecking the country and futures of ordinary workers.

Job creation is moribund. Industrial America keeps imploding. High-paying jobs are exported. Workers are exploited for greater profits, and no one's acting to revive stable, sustainable long-term growth.

America's FIRE sector (finance, insurance, and real estate) fueled casino capitalist speculation rather than investment in capital goods—in plant, equipment, transportation, and public utilities that fueled earlier business cycle expansions.Instead of making better things for better living, America's financialized economy proliferates unbridled greed, fueled by limitless amounts of privately created money.

Since the 1970s, wages stagnated and lost purchasing power. Inflation rose. Benefits like retirement savings eroded. Household debt rose to compensate. Now it takes two wage-earners to keep up with what was earned by one, years back.

Accumulating enormous excesses, monopoly money power

caused 2008's global collapse. Capitalism's dark side and destructive contradictions were exposed, particularly its financialized form.

Money power in private hands is exploitively destructive. Global populations are harmed. As a result, poverty in developed countries soared. In underdeveloped ones it deepened, leaving millions facing destitution and human misery, even death.

Money power buys influence. Wall Street rules America and the world. Deregulated excess produced unprecedented fraud and grand theft, insider trading, misrepresentation, Ponzi schemes, false accounting, market manipulation, toxic financial products, unprecedented profits, and massive public deception.

Deregulation facilitated it. Whatever Wall Street wants it gets. Without money power, Washington can't or won't intercede enough to matter. Trying produces days like 2010's May 6 "flash crash," cratering the Dow 1,000 points, then recovering losses in minutes. Wall Street's power creates or destroys financial assets with keystroke ease.

If Congress had money power and regulatory backbone, too-big-to-fail banks wouldn't exist. Public banks would operate with small private ones. Every state would prosper like North Dakota—the only one with a state-owned bank.

During the height of 2008's financial crisis, North Dakota had its largest ever surplus. Global contagion cratered other states. If they operated like North Dakota, prosperity would replace gloom.

If federal, state or local governments lend their own money, profit isn't at issue so rates can be low and affordable to businesses, farmers, and private individuals. Moreover, for federal, state, and municipality needs, government-issued credit is interest-free.

In addition, public banks don't have to earn profits. They're not beholden to Wall Street or shareholders. Only federal, state or local community creditworthiness matters.

In over 235 years, neither America nor any state went bankrupt. Only poorly governed Arkansas defaulted during the Great Depression. Under publicly run banks, sustained prosperity is possible, inflation free, *as long as recycled money goes for productive economic growth.*

Whenever this was tried, it worked impressively, including in colonial America for a generation, and today in North Dakota. Why not try it everywhere across America including Washington?

Sound monetary policy isn't rocket science. It's common sense, serving public interest needs, not shareholders or Wall Street profiteers seeking maximum profits for private gain.

Even if they don't know about the merits of public over privatized banking, Occupy Wall Streeters know a better way is vital. No wonder

New York protests went viral, erupting in hundreds of cities nationwide. The hacktivist "Anonymous" group urged "[e]veryone, everywhere [to occupy] their towns, their capitals and other public spaces."

This pits the collective 99% majority against "corruption, greed and inequality." The minority 1% wants privatized money power so they can get more of it. Everyone else demands change.

Putting bodies on the line despite police brutality is key. So far the sustained OWS activism has been impressive. Growing and maintaining its energy is crucial.

Famed Chicago activist Saul Alinsky (1909-1972) knew the best way to beat organized money is with organized people: "getting it altogether" for change. Calling conflict "the essential core of a free and open society," he said "[i]f one were to project the democratic way of life in the form of a musical score, its major theme would be the harmony of dissonance," working for the common good.

Its core issue is returning money power to public hands as a first step to having government of, by and for the people, serving everyone.

If that's not worth sustained struggle, what is?

A Final Comment

Wall Street-controlled money power is corrupted, corrosive and destructive. Occupy San Francisco's on the issue. On December 1, 2011, *Wall Street Journal* writer David Weidner headlined, "Occupy Shocker: A Realistic, Actionable Idea," saying:

> They have something their East Coast neighbors don't: a realistic plan aimed at the heart of banks. The idea could be expanded nationwide to send a message to a compromised Washington and the financial industry.

Called a municipal bank, "it would transfer the City of San Francisco's bank accounts—about $2 billion" from Bank of America, UnionBanCal and Wells Fargo—"into a public bank. [It] would use small local banks to lend to the community."

Why not! North Dakota's Bank of North Dakota has been doing it successfully since 1919. It helped the state prosper, working cooperatively with private banks. Its model can be replicated anywhere, including across America. Doing so will let all states benefit. It's an idea whose time has come!

ENDNOTES

1 Stephen Lendman, *How Wall Street Fleeces America*, Clarity Press, Inc., 2011.

2 < http://occupywallst.org/>

3 < http://www.occupytogether.org/>

2

CLASS WAR IN AMERICA

Class war has raged in America for decades. Business and America's super-rich always win. In his 1925 short story titled "Rich Boy," F. Scott Fitzgerald said:

> Let me tell you about the very rich. They are different from you and me. They possess and enjoy early...They think, deep in their hearts, that they are better than we..
>
> Even when they enter deep into our world... they still think that that they are better than we are. They are different.

In his article, titled "The Truth About 'Class War' in America," economist Richard Wolff said: "The last 50 years have indeed seen continuous class warfare in and over federal economic policies."[1] Notably since the 1970s, "(b)usiness and its allies shifted most of its federal tax burden onto individuals."

Since WW II, tax rates on super-rich Americans fell from 91% to 35% today. Obama's deficit cutters want it lowered to 24% along with eliminating some deductions with loopholes to compensate and save others. Moreover, they want the top corporate tax rate slashed from 35% to 26%.

Many corporate giants, in fact, pay minimal or no taxes. Some, like General Electric, get generous rebates in highly profitable years. They game the system, benefitting from tax laws that they themselves write. American workers lose out by having greater than ever burdens placed on them.

Obama schemers also want deeper Medicare cuts, higher Medicaid co-pays, and Social Security's retirement age raised to 69 with lower cost-of-living increases. Privately they want Wall Street to control them to suck out maximum profits, then shut it down entirely. In addition, they want home mortgage interest and tax-free employer provided health insurance capped or ended.

Both parties represent business and the super-rich elites. America's middle class is targeted for extinction. Since taking office, Obama capitulated to Republicans on preserving tax cuts for America's super-rich. He gave trillions of dollars to Wall Street crooks and other corporate favorites, including profiteers benefitting greatly from multiple imperial wars.

At the same time, Obama stiff-armed budget-strapped states and distressed households. Promising millions of new jobs, he created none. Four years into a Main Street Depression, real unemployment approaches 23%. In ravaged cities like Detroit, it exceeds 50%. Federal workers' wages were frozen and austerity cuts were imposed, such as the Low Income Home Energy Assistance Program (LIHEAP). Families needing help to heat homes in winter won't get it. Neither will students relying on Pell Grants.

Other imposed cuts affect:

- the Children's Health Insurance Program (CHIP);
- community healthcare centers;
- nonprofit health insurance cooperatives;
- HIV/AIDS, tuberculosis, and other disease prevention programs;
- WIC (Women, Infants, and Children) grants to states for supplemental foods, healthcare, and nutrition education for low-income families;
- Head Start, providing comprehensive education, health, nutrition, and parent involvement services to low-income families with children;
- the Supplemental Nutrition Assistance Program (targeted earlier with more coming), providing food stamps for poor households;
- community development block grants for housing, overall reducing HUD's budget by $1.1 billion;
- Federal Emergency Management Agency (FEMA) first-responder funding;

- energy efficiency and renewable energy programs;
- Environmental Protection Agency (EPA) clean/safe water and other projects;
- National Institutes of Health (NIH) medical research;
- the National Park Service;
- vital infrastructure and transportation needs; and
- other non-defense discretionary spending.

These planned new cuts will help to sustain Wall Street, militarism, favoritism, waste, fraud, and other rewards for Washington's usual special interests Increasingly ordinary people are on their own to sink or swim. Obama calls it "shared sacrifice." Translated, this means: ordinary people sacrifice, business and super-rich elites share.

Washington's new FY 2012 budget agreement cuts billions more from vital domestic programs. LIHEAP lost another $1.2 billion, a 25% reduction year over year. Labor, health and education allocations dropped $1.4 billion, including $225 million cut by eliminating 22 programs, many related to job training.

In addition, Pell Grants will end for another 100,000 students, and those getting them will only receive $5,500 for another year. Overall, $1.36 billion in student funding will be lost over several years.

Corporate America's power grab holds US households hostage. Neo-serfdom and debt peonage define their agenda. Wolff calls mainstream economics "faith-based." For Michael Hudson, it's "junk economics." Nations and economies are destroyed to benefit Wall Street and powerful favorites. According to Wolff:

> In plain English, the last 50 years saw a massive shift of the burden of federal taxation from business to individuals and from rich individuals to everyone else. Class war policies, yes, but a war that victimized the vast majority of working Americans.

Especially since the 1970s, real wages haven't kept up with inflation. Benefits have steadily eroded. High-paying manufacturing and service jobs went offshore to low-wage countries. Automated production claimed more. More than ever, "free markets" work best for those who control them.

Technology-driven productivity increasingly pressures workers to toil longer for less pay and fewer benefits. Explaining predatory capitalism's contradictions, Marx rightfully called it anarchic and ungovernable. Yet what existed in his day was only a shadow of today's monster.

Predatory capitalism alienates the masses by preventing societies from developing humanely. It produces class struggles between "haves" and "have-nots," the bourgeoisie (capitalists) and proletariat (workers). It exploits the many for the elite few. Those most privileged populate Wall Street. It flourishes in America and Western societies, aided by political opportunists, powerful monopolies and oligopolies now control production, commerce and finance—and where it flourishes, ordinary people do not.Households are angered and traumatized by falling incomes lowered by inflation. As a result, more family members work harder and longer for less money. Corporate bosses extract more surplus from pressured workers.

Class war in America isn't new. Today it rages, pitting private wealth against popular interests. America's middle class is on the chopping block for destruction. The criminal class in Washington is bipartisan. Complicit with Wall Street and other corporate crooks, they've wrecked the economy and working households for profit. America's broken system is defined by sacrificing workers on the altar of capitalist excess. Growing numbers of people understand that they are trapped in a venal, depraved system too broken to fix.

It's no wonder millions now rage against it in hundreds of cities nationwide. It was just a matter of time for the American people to be galvanized. They're mad as hell and soon they won't take it anymore. They worry about no future prospects and know, or should know, that political Washington won't help.

Inequality in America has been institutionalized. Good paying jobs and retirement security are increasingly out of reach.America's kleptocracy run by corrupt politicians complicit with corporate crooks is strip-mining working households for profit. And this is just the beginning. The congressional August Budget Control Act of 2011 established the Joint Select Committee on Deficit Reduction – a.k.a. the Supercommittee. Doing so was extralegal. The Constitution's Article 1, Section 8 explains congressional powers. None of them include supercommittee authority to resolve America's debt crisis. Article 1, Section 8, Sub-section 18 lets Congress "make all Laws which shall be necessary and proper for carrying into Execution (of its other listed Powers), and all other Powers vested by this Constitution in the Government of the United States, or in any Department Officer thereof."

Even though government authority is limited only by the boundaries of possibility, no constitutional principle gives 12 members of Congress more power than others, let alone the right to exercise it secretly.Composed of six House and six Senate members from both parties, Supercommittee authority ran until November 23, 2011, holding the power to agree on $1.2 - $1.5 trillion in budget cuts over the next 10 years. Their consensus on items to be cut would have let Congress only vote them up or down without amendments, debate or delay.

Ahead of their deadline, 100 Democrats and Republicans wrote supercommittee members (the so-called "gang of 12") that "(t)o succeed, all options for mandatory and discretionary spending and revenue must be on the table." They were effectively asking for agreement on $4 trillion in cuts.

Nonetheless, hours before their self-imposed deadline, Supercommittee members ended negotiations without reaching any agreement. By law, an automatic $1.2 trillion in cuts over 10 years start in 2013.

While the cuts are supposedly to be equally divided between defense and domestic programs, you can expect sustained military spending at the expense of the gutting of America's social contract. Either way, lost purchasing power means less spending, fewer jobs, and even greater public anger than today's high levels.

It's not about political disagreements. It's about securing the interests of wealth and power. Deficit cutting always is secondary. What's key is protecting corporate handouts and Bush era tax cuts, as well as expanding them for business and upper-bracket earners.

Supercommittee Democrat members, in fact, offered unprecedented Medicare and Medicaid cuts on top of those already made—at minimum, $500 billion over the next decade with out-year increases. Social Security and public pensions are also targeted. Private ones may come later. In earlier negotiations, Obama had already agreed.

These cuts have been planned for years. Republicans want the programs eliminated. Democrats have agreed to incremental cuts to make ending core social contract programs less noticeable. This will leave seniors entirely on their own for healthcare and other benefits when they're most needed. It won't matter if they're unaffordable.

Last year, Obama's National Commission on Fiscal Responsibility and Reform (NCFRF) recommended deep Medicare cuts, higher Medicaid co-pays, and restrictions on filing malpractice suits, among other ways to end Washington's responsibility for healthcare incrementally.

The Bipartisan Policy Center (BPC) also recommended deep Medicare cuts, higher Part B premiums, big co-pays and outpatient fee increases, as well as the establishment of privately owned, lower-cost health insurance exchanges to gradually eliminate traditional Medicare. It also wants Medicaid funding cut.

Congressional Democrats and Republicans agree on raising Medicare's eligibility's age. So does Obama. He also supports deep cuts. Expect his new Independent Payment Advisory Board to recommend them. The Congressional Budget Office (CBO) said current proposals will force seniors to pay more for coverage, much more.

Medicare and Medicaid cuts are coming.. In June 2012, Vice President Biden agreed to $500 billion more in Medicare/Medicaid cuts on top of previously imposed big ones. Republicans want $780 billion cut. It's likely they will split the difference with more reductions to come later. Backloading will delay the pain until after the November 2012 elections. Both sides agree.

By mid-decade, traditional Medicare will be providing half of today's benefits. Seniors will need private plans for full coverage. Those unable to afford them will be out of luck.

Proponents falsely say Medicare, Medicaid and Social Security are responsible for rising deficits and America's national debt burden. They also bogusly claim Medicare and Social Security are going broke. When properly administered, in fact, both programs are sustainable long-term with modest adjustments and by curtailing escalating healthcare costs.

Wall Street bailouts, other corporate handouts, excess military spending (including huge black budgets), and tax cuts for the rich caused today's unsustainable debt problem. Price gouging by health insurance providers, drug companies and large hospital chains are exacerbating it

Over the past decade, Social Security-run surpluses went for debt reduction to make it appear the fund's not sustainable. In fact, since 1986, it has produced $2.4 trillion more than it spent. Much of the surplus came from increasing the payroll tax and indexing it to inflation. Its share of total federal tax revenues rose from less than 30% to 44%. At the same time, corporate income tax fell from around 20% to under 10%.

In other words, for a generation, Social Security revenues subsidized corporate handouts, tax cuts for the rich, and America's wars. Its surplus could be sustainable well into the future if government policies stopped draining it irresponsibly. Moreover, if the full payroll tax is restored and annual $108,600 income cap was lifted to make America's wealthy pay the same percentage cost as others, potential Social Security shortfalls could be eliminated for generations. If draining the trust fund also stopped, Social Security surpluses could be generated in perpetuity.

In addition, if capital gains were taxed like income, huge amounts would be raised for traditional Medicare, prescription drugs under Part D, Medicaid, and other social programs on the chopping block for big cuts or elimination.

Medicare would be just as sustainable with real healthcare reform under a universal single-payer system. By eliminating private insurer middlemen, costs would be drastically cut.

In its September 2007 report to Congress, the Congressional Research Service (CRS) compared 2004 US healthcare spending with other developed OECD (Organization for Economic Cooperation and Development) countries. It found America spent $6,102 per person (today it's over $8,000), well over double the $2,560 average for other OECD countries. Much of the difference comes from insurer administrative costs which are unrelated to providing care. In other words, other OECD countries deliver better services overall at less than half what Americans spend.

Draining Social Security's trust fund and perpetuating outlandishly high healthcare costs makes it appear that the fund which supports seniors' entitlements is going broke.

But these crisis conditions were artificially created. Congressional cassandras claim Social Security and Medicare are unsustainable because both parties want big cuts in both programs before privatizing them en route to eliminating them altogether.Political Washington hypes the problem. So do media scoundrels, Obama's Simpson/Bowles deficit cutting commission, and the Bipartisan Policy Center (BPC). Their solution is to slash, then end America's social contract in order to transfer maximum wealth to corporate favorites and the nation's super-rich.

Supercommittee negotiations stalemated over Republicans demanding big corporate and upper bracket personal income tax cuts. Both are now at 35%. Republicans want them reduced to 25-28%, so America's aristocracy will benefit from deficit reduction at the expense of working people bearing the burden.

Republicans' top priority is protecting Bush era tax cuts. Over the last decade, they cost America at least $2.9 trillion in vitally needed revenue plus another $450 billion in 2010-2012 extensions. If these tax cuts are maintained for another decade, a projected $2.2 to $2.7 trillion more will be lost, exacerbating today's debt problem.

By proposing further corporate and upper-bracket cuts, Republicans clearly aren't concerned about deficits and debt: they and most Democrats simply want corporate friends and super-rich elites protected. Congressional disagreement is only about when cuts are made, not about the amounts to be cut, or who pays for it, and who benefits. They don't just want to assure that Bush era cuts are preserved—they want to sweeten the pot.

Obama's fully on board. So are growing numbers of Democrats. They're corporatists, not populists. They talk tough, then do something else. The pattern repeats endlessly to transfer enormous wealth to corporate favorites and America's super-rich.

Medicare Privatization Plans

The idea's been around for years. More recently, bipartisan support's been growing. Various plans have circulated.

A 2006 Congressional Budget Office (CBO) study[2] assessed "Designing a Premium Support System (PSS) for Medicare." It discussed pros, cons, other choices and implications in terms of costs and recipient benefits.

In 1995, Henry Aaron and Robert Reischauer had first proposed a PSS based on managed competition principles. Numerous variations followed with differing public support amounts. All plans have six common features:

(1) Beneficiaries would choose from multiple approved health plans. Risk adjusted payments and marketing practices would be regulated, or so it's claimed.

(2) Plans would offer a premium bid to cover core benefits.

(3) Federal payments would reflect these bids, subject to negotiations.

(4) Washington would provide beneficiaries a fixed premium subsidy tied to annual health plan bids.

(5) They would vary depending on plans selected. Beneficiaries would pay differential costs.

(6) Traditional Medicare would compete on similar terms with private plans, including on price.

A March 1999, Bipartisan Commission on the Future of Medicare approved a premium support plan proposed by then-Commission chairman Senator John Breaux. Though it failed to get a supermajority needed for official recommendation to Congress, it gained widespread support and became a prominent option in subsequent Medicare reform debates.

Proponents claim it relies on marketplace medicine to secure sustainability for the longterm. They falsely say Medicare, Medicaid and Social Security cause rising deficits and America's national debt burden. They also bogusly claim Medicare and Social Security are going broke when, if properly administered, both programs are sustainable with modest adjustments and by curtailing escalating healthcare costs responsibly.

If capital gains were taxed like income, huge amounts would be raised for traditional Medicare, prescription drugs under Part D, Medicaid, and other social programs. Instead, they're on the chopping block for big cuts before privatization en route to eliminating them altogether.

In contrast, under a universal single-payer system, Medicare would be sustainable long-term. Eliminating private insurer middlemen alone achieves dramatic cost savings.

Instead of responsible workable policies, premium support and similar plans are steps toward destroying Medicare altogether, first by privatizing it for profit. Breaux's plan set federal premium subsidies at 88% of the nationally weighted average.

Beneficiaries choosing plans costing less than 85% of the average would pay no premium. Those selecting higher benefit plans would cover extra charges. Plans (allegedly) would have to provide benefits equal to current Medicare coverage, though they could offer additional benefits. They'd also be updated annually based on individual choice. Savings are alleged to come from beneficiaries selecting lower cost options, price competition to attract enrollees, and letting recipients purchase Medigap coverage for added benefits.

Reality differs markedly from these claims. Only universal coverage achieves major savings. Alternatives don't. Independent studies confirm it. Physicians for a National Health Program (PNHP)[3] says America spends double the developed world's healthcare average, yet performs poorly on key indicators like life expectancy, infant mortality, and overall well-being.

Currently, middlemen insurers, drug giants and large hospital chains game the system hugely for profits. Medicare for all can change that effectively and achieve major cost savings.

Overall, US healthcare could make a quantum improvement leap compared to today's dysfunctional system. Instead, bipartisan complicity has worse in mind by cutting benefits, placing greater burdens on seniors and others, letting corporate predators game the system, and still leave millions uninsured, on their own and out of luck.

Other Destructive Medicare Plans

On December 16, the Brookings Institution published "Premium Support: A Primer," claiming"The major cause of the federal budget crisis, which is still in its early stages, is the relentless growth of Medicare spending."[4] This, it says, is due to baby boomer retirements and "persistent increase" in per person costs:

> Unless something is one, Medicare....will grow from 3.6 percent of the nation's GDP in 2010 to 10.4 percent by 2080...
>
> Unchecked, growth in spending on Medicare and interest on the federal debt will bankrupt the country

Five Brookings participants were involved, including Henry Aaron, Alice Rivlin and former Republican Senator Pete Domenici. He and Rivlin also co-chair the Bipartisan Policy Center (BPC) discussed above briefly. Their "Restoring America's Future" plan will destroy it for the millions who will be greatly harmed or entirely left out by their proposals. These include:

- indexing Social Security benefits to life expectancy to reduce them as longevity increases;
- eliminating annual cost-of-living adjustments (COLAs), bogusly claiming that inflation is overstated when in fact, it far exceeds official numbers, especially in relation to medical expenses, placing enormous burdens on recipients, including retirees dependent on help;
- instituting a one-year payroll tax holiday for workers and employers to save $650 billion, which is hugely destructive since it drains revenues needed to support the entitlements;
- sharply cutting Medicare and Medicaid benefits by raising premiums, co-pays, and outpatient fees; also establishing privately owned health insurance exchanges to compete with traditional Medicare;
- cutting Medicaid by 2018 by the amount it exceeds GDP growth so needy recipients get less en route to maybe getting nothing;
- shielding insurers and drug giants from malpractice suits by

making it harder to file them; then capping non-economic and punitive damage awards by adjudicating claims in "specialized malpractice courts" set up to consider the situation of providers over that of consumers;

- simplifying the tax code to two brackets (15 and 27%), which will favor the rich insofar as it will cut the top personal and corporate tax rate from 35% to 27%;
- eliminating home mortgage and most other tax deductions and credits;
- taxing employer-provided health insurance;
- instituting a 6.5% national sales tax, hitting ordinary people hardest; and
- other regressive schemes, placing added burdens on households least able to cope.

Yet BPC outrageously claims their plan "provides a comprehensive, viable path to restore our economy and build a strong America for future generations and for those around the world who look to the United States for leadership and hope."

Dominici is a former US senator. Rivlin once headed the Office of Management and Budget and the Congressional Budget Office. Is that they don't understand economics and finance enough to propose workable, constructive policies—or simply that their class bias and interest makes them put on blinders? Their proposal like others, including the one by Brookings, enriches corporate predators and America's super-rich at the expense of all others. In other words, it's another giant wealth transfer scheme, heading the nation for third world status.

So is a new bipartisan congressional one Senator Ron Wyden (D. OR) and Romney running-mate Paul Ryan (R. WI) proposed to replace traditional Medicare with "premium support" plans.

It's all about eventual privatization to free Washington from future obligations. As explained above, beneficiaries would get fixed amounts to purchase private coverage through a federally regulated Medicare exchange. Initially, traditional Medicare would remain optional. But again, in the long term it will transition to an entirely privately run system. Doing so will put vital care out of reach for millions of seniors when they most need it.

The plan closely follows Ryan's April proposal to transition Medicare toward fixed-sum vouchers. He, other Republicans, and growing numbers of Democrats want government responsibility entirely ended. His new plan temporarily lets it compete with private plans with beneficiaries incurring greater costs.

A Final Comment

No matter how much Obama and congressional Democrats tread lightly around this sensitive issue prior to the 2012 elections, post-election, traditional Medicare, Medicaid, Social Security and public pensions will be on the chopping block for elimination.

Privatizations will precede it. Eventually the military-governmental elites will be entirely able to free trillions more dollars for war-making and corporate handouts.

Safety net protections will disappear. Americans will be left on their own entirely, to sink or swim. With one-third of US households impoverished or nearly so, imagine how irresponsible governance will gravely harm millions more.

If the business of America became peace, with less militarism, no wars, making friends, not enemies, retaining high-paying/good benefit jobs at home, letting unions bargain collectively with management on equal terms, making universal free education and single-payer healthcare priorities, ending destructive trade deals, and guaranteeing living wage security, imagine how different things could be.

In addition, if money power returned to public hands and direct democracy serving everyone responsibly replaced duopoly power, near utopian conditions might be realized.

Anything is possible when committed people work long-term for them. If that's not incentive enough, what is?

America's no longer fit to live in. If there's going to be any change, we need a complete reorientation. Here are some of the vital tasks::

- making social justice a priority consideration in all new policies;
- returning money power to public hands as the Constitution's Article 1, Section 8 mandates;
- dismantling duopoly political power, replacing it with an entirely new multi-party democracy;
- getting money out of politics;
- shutting down insolvent banks andprohibiting too-big-to-fail

ones;

- ending corporate personhood in the recognition that corporations are businesses, not people;
- reinstituting anti-trust laws with teeth, prohibiting monopoly and oligopoly power;
- breaking up big media;
- making broadcasting a public utility on airwaves belonging equally to everyone, not just to business giants to exploit with generous subsidies;
- prohibiting all corporate handouts, loopholes, and special benefits;
- making corporations and rich Americans pay their fair share, including a Tobin tax on large financial transactions;
- ending America's student loan racket;
- mandating progressive taxation, including treating income and capital gains equally;
- re-energizing organized labor;
- ending inequality and persecution;
- legislating living wages;
- stressing environmental sanity; and
- ending America's imperial wars.

Hopefully OWS protesters understand that dark forces want to co-opt and subvert them. Hopefully they'll focus on what matters most. What is key is to get money power in public hands and make banking a regulated public utility. Achieving that makes social justice and other vital goals possible. Millions of Americans and others globally are committed to social change. Hopefully they know they're in the mother of all struggles and will stay the course. That's how all great victories are won.

ENDNOTES

1 < http://truth-out.org/news/item/3513:the-truth-about-class-war-in-america>
2 < http://www.cbo.gov/publication/18258>
3 < http://www.pnhp.org/facts/single-payer-resources>
4 <http://www.brookings.edu/research/papers/2011/12/16-premium-support-primer>

3

THE AUSTERITY HOAX

Since 2008, Western nations have force-fed their people austerity poison. As a result, decline replaces prosperity, millions suffer and living standards deteriorate. Societies become no longer fit to live in.

Neoliberal and imperial priorities have let essential public needs go begging..The longer fiscal pain continues, the closer an ultimate day of reckoning approaches, likely disruptively, as people recognize that elections—throwing the bums out only to see them replaced by new ones—accomplish nothing.

America is Exhibit A for how this process works. Political Washington is corrupt, immoral, degenerate, and unprincipled. Instead of helping the American people, they destroy them. They actually benefit from imposing misery. Allied with criminal bankers and other corporate predators, politicians' policies have made conditions for growing millions intolerable.

It's well known that imperial wars destroy nations. Austerity leaves "nothing to drive the economy," as Paul Craig Roberts says. Washington's solution is to increase the wars America is fighting. Why, when it is clearly economically destructive? Because bankers, other corporate favorites, and war profiteers benefit.

Michael Hudson says austerity sacrifices the "production economy, the consumption economy, (and) the real economy...." Viable alternatives are ignored to benefit privileged elites at the expense of most others.Hudson calls it "financial warfare against the entire society, not only against labor, but against industry and, most of all, against government."Productive "industrial capitalism" has now morphed into predatory "finance capitalism." It's not financing industry. Instead, it's furthering "economic parasitism and overhead."[1]Politicians in Washington support it. Obama exceeds the worst of Bush, what will happen under Romney would be a thing of nightmares.

Europe is corrupted the same way. London's Olympiad spectacle highlighted it. At a time of high unemployment and growing public needs, estimates of $19 billion to double that amount went for the city's biggest ever extravaganza. Combined with Britain's war budget and fealty to banking crooks, it reveals a society heading for terminal decline and taking innocent people with it.The same holds for America and other European countries. Bankers rape them financially. Predatory finance is a new form of warfare, more destructive than standing armies.

Former bank regulator/financial fraud expert Bill Black addressed the issue. He headlined "The Right's Schadenfreude as their Austerity Polices Devastate Europe,"[2] saying that hisarticle followed his reading of Anne Applebaum's September 13, 2010 column, where she celebrated Britain's embrace of austerity and Tory conservatives.Applebaum headlined "Less, Please," saying that UK slash and burn "vicious cuts" are good. Austerity "made Britain great." It "won the war." It's their "finest hour."

> Then, on July 25, 2012, Applebaum's Washington Post article had headlined "Europe must face up to ongoing euro crisis". Applebaum wrote:Finally, Europeans are being forced to face up to decades' worth of fundamentally dishonest politics...
>
> Since the 1970s, one government after the next has spent, borrowed and then inflated its way out of the subsequent debt…
>
> Then they recovered—only to spend, borrow and inflate once again.[3]

She called euro straightjacket entrapment a gold standard equivalent. Losing monetary and fiscal control is good, she claims. So is abdicating national sovereignty. Applebaum economics makes witch doctor medicine look miraculous. Applebaum grew up in wealth. She attended Yale and the London School of Economics. She was admitted to Phi Beta Kappa and graduated from Yale summa cum laude. Perhaps its standards aren't as high as people think.

Let-them-eat-cake economics doesn't work. It sparks revolutions which don't turn out much better. After America's, everything changed but stayed the same. The Russians got Joseph Stalin after theirs. The French got the Jacobins, who were revolutionary moderate patriots at first. Then they morphed into "reign of terror" extremists. Dickens' *Tale of Two Cities* wrote about the best and worst of times. Liberté, egalité and fraternité were short-lived.

Sustained Applebaum economics may spark the worst of times without the best. But let us return to Bill Black, who went on to destroy her position, pointing out how austerity caused Britain›s worst economic crisis in 50 years. "Applebaum›s 2010 column on [Britain's] embrace of austerity deserves to live in infamy," he said. She "takes palpable glee [in] harming its working class" to let wealthy Brits grow richer.

In 2009, Britain was emerging from recession, with its recovery painful and slow. Ordinary people benefitted little. Many, in fact, did not benefit at all. The modest stimulus injected then was grossly inadequate, ensuring further economic decline.

Austerity represents bad economics and moral failure. Reality is turned on its head. Nations aren't "remotely like households when it comes to debt," Black went on. They "adopt ‹automatic stabilizers› to make recessions far less severe and recoveries quicker." They work. They›re counter-cyclical. Austerity makes bad conditions worse.

Applebaum equates austerity with "moral superiority." The greater the amount, the higher the level of morality. This explains her reveling in "savage cuts" and "delightin gore." Effectively, it's a belief that moral superiority depends on how much harm can be imposed on society's most disadvantaged. Notions this destructive reflect Frankenstein economics. Pain is good, the more the better. Wealthy elites love it. British politics is like America›s where the Democrats don›t differ from Republicans. In the UK, Tories and New Labour replicate each other›s policies. Let-'em-eat cake is dogma.

As a result, Britannia›s ship of state is sinking. So is the American dream. For most, it was largely an illusion. Now it's disappearing entirely. Again to Black: "Applebaum also combines faux moral superiority with faux history." She uses it "to explain the moral virtues of austerity during a Great Recession."

Claiming austerity won the war is rubbish. Massive fiscal stimulus and deficits won the war. UK and US politicians claim their governments are broke. If foreign aggressors invaded their homelands, asked Black, would they surrender for lack of funds?" Of course not, they would run however large a deficit was required. Because that doesn't destroy economies, it stimulates growth and produces full employment.

War economies ended the Great Depression. Comparable stimulus *without war* could reverse similar conditions that affect majorities in Europe and America today. Productive policies lift all boats.

Nations enduring hard times "cannot simply 'decide' to end [their] budget deficit." Combining spending cuts with higher taxes on working households assures harder times.

Legitimate economists don't recommend spending cuts and higher taxes. Sustained policies this destructive assure protracted or permanent decline. Britain, other EU countries, and America can borrow at near-zero interest rates. Every pound, euro and dollar raised and spent productively returns multiples more. It's immoral not to do it when it's most needed, when privileged elites alone benefit at the expense of most others.

For the governments to claim empty pockets is duplicitous. Applebaum's prime targets are Medicare, Medicaid and Social Security. Destroying bedrock social safety net protections is scandalous. But then, she's privileged and doesn't care. Other elitists feel the same way. Programs people can't do without are on their chopping block for elimination. The more ordinary people suffer, the greater elitists benefit.

Promoting social inequality is the very definition of immorality. It's also destructive economics. Applebaum "reveal(ed) her real target—she wants to destroy (bedrock) social programs." She considers them "political bribes to induce the working class to vote for leftist politicians." But social programs improve millions of lives. They also lift all boats. The resultant prosperity produces jobs. When people have money they spend it. Hard times forces belt-tightening, forces working people to accept conditions and wages that otherwise they would resist.

Accordingly, Appelbaum loves the euro straightjacket rules and Troika diktat authority over independent monetary and fiscal control as well as national sovereignty. She "loves the euro zone disaster her austerity policies generated because she believes (it) will destroy the social programs she despises," and "bring the extreme right to power."

It's an agenda the Trilateralists and Bilderberger elites promote to further their aim of global rule with their version of aclassless society: one with only rulers and serfs. She's wrong, says Black. Things won't turn out her way.

Obama embraces the worst of what Applebaum and Republicans endorse. Black thinks he'll "pay a great political price for trying to be all things to all voters on the issue of austerity" alone.Opposing it should have been his "signature economic program." Winning by a landslide would be assured. Instead, administration policies are "incoherent" and counterproductive.

Why didn't he do it?

ENDNOTES

1 <http://www.nakedcapitalism.com/2012/04/michael-hudson-on-why-there-is-an-alternative-to-european-austerity.html>

2 < http://www.nakedcapitalism.com/2012/07/bill-black-the-rights-schadenfreude-as-their-austerity-policies-devastate-europe.html?utm_source=feedburner&utm_medium=email&utm_campaign=Feed%3A+NakedCapitalism+%28naked+capitalism%29&utm_content=Yahoo%21+Mail>

3 < http://www.washingtonpost.com/opinions/anne-applebaum-europe-must-face-up-to-ongoing-euro-crisis/2012/07/25/gJQAnYey9W_story.html>

4

TRILLIONS STASHED IN TAX HAVENS

A new Tax Justice Network (TJN) USA report reveals an estimated \$21-\$32 trillion of hidden and stolen wealth stashed largely tax-free secretly. Titled "The Price of Offshore Revisited,"[1] it explains what financial insiders know but won't discuss. Many of them have their own hidden wealth.TJN describes a "subterranean" systemic "economic equivalent of an astrophysical black hole." The higher estimate above exceeds US GDP twofold.

It's mind-boggling. It's hard to imagine that a tiny percent of privileged elites control this much wealth secretly. It's worse knowing it's largely tax free. It's appalling that governments let them get away with it.

Wall Street and other major banks manage that wealth. Their business is fraud and grand theft. Private banking operations yield huge profits. Their ability to keep funds secreted tax free attracts rich clients. Private capital globally is attracted. It's welcome from anyone, from everywhere, "no questions asked."

Government policies protect them. Societal costs are huge. Tax justice is absent. Hotel magnate Leona Helmsley once said only little people pay taxes. TJN's report bears her out. The Report addresses avast "global offshore industry", largely tax-free, controlled by the world's richest, most powerful elites.

Estimating the amounts they have secreted takes tedious data mining. Previous estimates relied more on rough judgments But TJN has surpassed this. TJN used several methods. They include available data sources, estimation methods, and core assumptions. They're open to peer review and public scrutiny. Only financial wealth is included. Much else isn't measured. It includes real estate, yachts, racehorses, gold, art, and other categories not easily quantified

Here are the four key approaches TJN used:

(1) A "sources-and-uses" country-by-country model.

(2) An "accumulated offshore wealth" model.

(3) An "offshore investor portfolio" model.

(4) Best-guess estimates of offshore assets held by the world's top 50 private banks.

Familiar Wall Street, European, and other global financial institutions are the targets of investigation. Current data from global central banks, the World Bank, IMF, UN, and national accounts were used. Other evidence includes:

(1) "Transfer mispricing" data.

(2) Demand for cross-border liquid "mattress money" data.

(3) Current research data on the offshore private banking market's size.

TJN believes its work comprises the "most rigorous and comprehensive" data ever produced. It challenges anyone to contest it..In overall size through 2010, TJN estimates hidden global wealth at from $21 to $32 trillion, invested "virtually tax-free" through a still-expanding black hole of more than 80 secret jurisdictions. TJN calls its estimates conservative.Developed countries have huge offshore tax evasion problems. Repatriation would reduce their debt substantially. In fact, doing so would bring it well within tolerable levels. The offshore economy alone has an enormous negative impact on the domestic tax bases of affected countries. They've had significant private capital outflows for decades or longer.

TJN focused on 139 countries, mainly "low-middle income" ones on whom the World Bank and IMF maintain data. Since the 1970s, private bankers let rich elites in these countries accumulate trillions in hidden wealth even as their nations experienced harsh structural adjustments. They became debt-entrapped. Some borrowed themselves into insolvency, selling off public assets at fire sale prices and impoverishing their peoples. They colluded with big money interests at their expense.

Through 2010, these countries accumulated over $4 trillion in debt—minus foreign reserves invested in First World securities, it's $2.8 trillion. Including hidden wealth, they're net lenders.

The key factor is that the assets of these countries are held by wealthy elites while ordinary people bear the burden of debts. In the 1980s, an unnamed Fed official said: "The problem is not that these countries don't have any assets. The problem is they're all in Miami"[2] and other global cities. They're home to private financial institutions.

Hidden offshore wealth correlates positively with loan amounts to indebted countries. Large amounts of borrowed capital were secreted lawlessly in global tax havens. Local elites continue "vot(ing) with financial feet" at the same time as their public sectors borrow heavily and ordinary people go begging.

Although First World countries borrow most, they and the elites in them remain global financiers. Overall, wealth is concentrated in select private hands "in a handful of source countries," many of which are regarded as debtors.

Through 2010, 50 top private banks managed over $12 trillion in cross-border assets from individual clients, trusts and foundations. Smaller banks, investment firms, insurers, and non-bank intermediaries like hedge funds and independent money managers handle additional amounts up to an overall $32 trillion estimate. TJN calls these enablers part of a global "tax injustice system." Complicit governments let them operate at the expense of their own people. They write:"Since the late 1970s, investigative journalists, tax authorities, drug enforcement officials, terrorist trackers, national security experts," and others became aware about vast amounts of money stashed in "offshore" tax havens.

Private banking "professional enablers" manage these funds, making make fortunes doing so. The term "offshore" refers less to physical locations than to virtual ones anywhere—often "networks of legal and quasi-legal entities and arrangements" operating in the interests of money managers. Their physical locations can be anywhere. Legal structures typically are assets owned by anonymous offshore companies in one jurisdiction. Trusts are in another. Trustees are in multiple places globally.

Their clients are rich elites, corporations, and criminals. They include real estate speculators, technology tycoons, oil sheiks, underworld millionaires, heads of state, despots, and drug lords, among others. Their common needs include:

(1) Anonymity and confidentiality.

(2) Minimizing or avoiding taxes.

(3) Skilled money management.

(4) Ability to access and manage their wealth from anywhere.

(5) Secure places to reside, visit, or hide.

(6) Assured financial security no matter what's happening in the real world.

Skilled professionals provide these services globally. Money management happens in a virtual world. They live under one set of rules. Another exists for all others Physical locations are based in Bermuda, the Cayman Islands, Nauru, St. Kitts, Antigua, Tortola, Switzerland, the Channel Islands, Monaco, Cyprus, Gibraltar, Liechtenstein, and elsewhere Over 3.5 million paper companies, thousands of shell banks and insurers, more than half the world's registered commercial ships above 100 tons, and tens of thousands of shell subsidiaries of giant global banks, accounting firms, and various other companies are registered as operating from there.

Nonetheless, conventional havens are misleading. Despite their vast financial infrastructure, most super-rich elites want more security. They also need easy access to First World capital markets, competent attorneys and accountants, independent judiciaries, and laws protecting them. The professional "enablers" provide all these needed services. Managing vast wealth is complex. Many skills are required. They include financial, economic, legal, accounting, and insurance. Super-rich elites demand and get the best.

Haven locations offer more than tax avoidance. Almost anything goes, including fraud, bribery, illegal gambling, money laundering, human and sex trafficking, arms dealing, toxic waste dumping, conflict diamonds and endangered species trafficking, bootlegged software, and endless other lawless practices.

It's impossible to estimate the total lawful and illegal wealth from all sources. It's vastly more than estimates within the parameters of TJN's study. Credit Suisse tried. Through mid-2011, Credit Suisse put total financial and non-financial global wealth at $231 trillion. This best guess is tenfold TJN's top figure, roughly 3.5 times global GDP. In 2011, it was about $65 trillion.

Imagine the good a small percentage of global wealth could do for billions of disadvantaged people. Imagine its ability to stabilize and recapitalize troubled countries. Imagine a world where everyone shares its wealth. Imagine one worth living in.

Global wealth represents low-hanging fruit that is nonetheless—at this time—out of reach. It's an injustice that begs for transformational change. From the bottom up is the only way possible.

Shedding light on what's dark is a good way to start.

5

LIBOR SCANDAL REFLECTS A CESSPOOL OF FINANCIAL FRAUD

At issue is a bad barrel, not a few rotten apples. Western banking is rife with fraud. The business model of major banks is grand theft. The scandal surrounding the London Inter-Bank Offer Rate (LIBOR), the interest rate that banks charge each other for loans, is just the latest.

According to Paul Craig Roberts,[1] Libor rigging is permitted in order to prop up a system that might fail without it. Imagine! The global financial system actually *needs fraud* to keep on operating. It hardly matters what harm it causes.

Libor is only one part of "the interest rate rigging scandal," explained Roberts. The Fed rigs rates. How else could debt issuances yield negative returns in terms of inflation? Unrestrained financial chicanery caused today's crisis. Self-regulating markets commit fraud with impunity. The incentives to do it are embedded in it.

Resolving today's crisis involves restoring regulatory sanity. A corporate/government conspiracy prevents it. Problems fester and worsen. How long can "negative interest rates continue while debt explodes upward?" Avoiding "armageddon" should be prioritized.

Like terrorist threats used to destroy freedoms, financial crisis conditions have the Fed, ECB, Bank of England, and Bank of Japan operating "far outside [their] charter[s] and normal ... behavior." What's ongoing is "irresponsible and thoughtless," says Roberts. Years of financialization, deregulation, and manipulation "caused a financial crisis" only fraud can manage.

Imagine economies sustained by grand theft. Imagine harming most people in it so a privileged few can prosper. Imagine an unholy government/business alliance that makes it necessary and legal. Imagine media scoundrels ignoring it. Imagine an eventual day of reckoning. All

Ponzi schemes collapse. Some go on interminably before imploding. This one long ago outlived its normal lifespan. It's on borrowed time. When it goes, watch out.

Thankfully, public banking solutions await. Over a century ago, William Jennings Brown explained fraudsters

> tell us that the issue of paper money is a function of the bank and that the government ought to go out of the banking business ... I stand with Jefferson [and say] as he did, that the issue of money is a function of the government and that the banks should go out of the governing business.
>
> [W]hen we have restored the money of the Constitution, all other necessary reforms will be possible, and....until that is done there is no reform that can be accomplished.

Contrast what he endorsed with what goes on today. Bankers systematically plunder economies for their own self-enrichment. Complicit politicians let them.

UK-based Barclays bank was caught in a Libor rigging scandal. Other major banks are involved. Expect more to come out. How much and who's named remains to be seen. More on that below.

Libor and Euribor are mechanisms used to set interest rates. Libor is the fundamental short-term rate-setting benchmark. It's set daily between UK banks for overnight to 12 month durations. Produced for ten currencies with 15 maturities, it represents the London market's lowest cost of unsecured funding.

Since the 1980s, the Libor expanded exponentially in importance. London's status grew as an international financial center to become the world's largest. Over 20% of all international bank lending occurs there and more than 30% of all foreign exchange transactions. Over 240 of the world's largest banks operate key parts of their international business in London. It's the world's "cowboy finance capital," says economist Jack Rasmus.

In the 1980s, as demand grew for an accurate measure of the real rate at which banks and other financial institutions could borrow from each other, the Libor grew in importance It affects the price and availability of capital. The higher the Libor goes, the greater the borrowing cost for businesses, individuals, real estate and other loans.

The Libor anchors multi-trillion-dollar contracts. One analyst said it's like plumbing: when it's working well, it isn't noticed. When not, all hell breaks loose. It's a vital factor in the interest rate swaps market. These devices let one bank or other organization pay a fixed rate of interest on a given amount of money from another financial institution While in return, that other bank or organization pays a floating rate based on the Libor.

The global swaps market approaches $350 trillion. According to the Bank for International Settlements:

- [I]nterest rate swaps are the largest component of the global OTC derivatives market.

- The notional amount outstanding as of June 2009 in OTC interest rate swaps was $342 trillion, up from $310 trillion in Dec 2007.

- The gross market value was $13.9 trillion in June 2009, up from $6.2 trillion in Dec 2007.

In theory, credit default swaps let lenders and borrowers minimize the risk of interest rate changes. It doesn't always work that way. Nonetheless, without a mechanism in place, banks might not lend at fixed rates. Their payments to depositors are based on floating rates. If rates rise, so do costs. If they exceed revenues, crises follow.

Predatory Capitalism Failed

Rodney Shakespeare is Professor of Binary Economics at Trisakti University, Britain. He's a financial expert and a regular on the Progressive Radio News Hour. Shakespeares aid Libor rigging affects "a thousand trillion dollars" in contracts of one sort or other globally. It exceeds global GDP 15 or 20-fold.

Barclays may be at the center of the storm in the UK, but it reflects a corrupt system, with much still to be exposed. Other major banks operate the same way. They're failing. They're zombie banks. The entire system is corrupt and crumbling. Western politicians permit it. As Shakespeare says, "They uphold the doctrine that whatever banks do is right."

The seriousness of what's known is that a system portrayed as just and sound in actuality is failing due to rampant speculation at the expense of stimulating real economic growth.Casino capitalism doesn't work. Economies suffer from their operations, and so do ordinary people. The entire banking system risks collapse.. Barclays is part of a far greater unresolved problem. All that can be done is to buy time. The system is too corrupt to fix.

John McMurtry calls the financial system a cancer system. The longer it goes unaddressed, the worst things get. "Organic, social and ecological life" harm grows. Effectively, it's aife-system collapse. Societies are consumed by it. Humanity suffers. It needs to be cleared out and replaced with an entirely new paradigm. Central bankers and complicit politicians bear full responsibility for what's happening. They're heading economies for a worse disaster than the Great Depression.

Last February, the Wall Street Journal headlined "Traders Manipulated Key Rate, Bank says,"[2] saying that according to an Ottawa court filing,

> Canada's Competition Bureau said a bank it didn't identify has told the agency's investigators that people involved in the alleged scheme 'were able to move' interest rates...
>
> People familiar with the [scheme] said the 'cooperating party' is [Switzerland-based] UBS AG.

An investigation into the Libor rigging issue affected banks and traders in North America, Europe and Asia. No one was charged with wrongdoing. Documents said regulators were also examining "alleged attempts to fix the prices of certain derivative financial products linked to Libor." Parties involved "entered into agreements to submit artificially high or artificially low" quotes. Traders "used emails and instant messages to tell each other whether they wanted 'to see a higher or lower yen Libor [rate] to aid their trading position,' according to court documents." Traders "would then 'communicate internally' with the person at their bank who was responsible for submitting the Libor quote, before letting each other know if this attempt to influence the quote had worked."

The Canadian watchdog said six banks were involved: Citigroup, Deutsche Bank, HSBC, JP Morgan Chase, Royal Bank of Scotland, and UBS.

All major banks commit grand theft. It's standard practice. Corrupt politicians turn a blind eye. So do regulators. Western banking is rife with fraud. All markets are manipulated up or down for profit. Enormous amounts are made. Governments and banks collude. High volume program trading drives prices either way. Nothing gets reported unless scandals erupt. In the meantime, ordinary investors who are none the wiser get trampled.

Financial history includes many examples of major financial institutions getting a free lunch at the public's expense. Methods include market manipulation, insider trading, front-running, theft and conspiracy, misrepresentation, Ponzi schemes, false accounting, embezzling, appointing industry favorites as regulators, tax frauds, profiting from loans that fail, creating phony financial products, and overall, assuring world financial capitals are banker occupied territories.

Barclays is the tip of the current scandal. Traders in London, New York and Tokyo also colluded to manipulate Libor. Top executives and traders are involved. They bear full responsibility for the 2008 financial crisis and what followed. They're up to their ears in fraud today. Media scoundrels cover it all up by projecting an illusion of stability. Government probes are toothless.

A City of Baltimore/Charles Schwab et al class action lawsuit names Barclays, RBS, HSBC, Bank of America, Citigroup, JPMorgan Chase, UBS and Deutsche Bank. Perhaps future suits will charge Goldman Sachs, Wells Fargo, and major European banks not named above, since they're all in it together. CEOs and other top executives conspire with each other and traders to commit fraud. Why not, when corrupt politicians wink and nod and let them do it.

Bill Black says manipulating Libor is easy. What's coming out reflects "the largest rigging of prices in the history of the world by many orders of magnitude." Top executives are directly involved: they have to be, because they set the policy and stand to gain hugely from the fraud-driven profits.

To give you an idea of the volumes involved, the US Commodity Futures Trading Commission (CTFC) says:

> US dollar Libor is the basis for the settlement of the three-month Eurodollar futures contracts traded on the Chicago Mercantile Exchange, which had a traded volume in 2011 with a notional value exceeding $564 trillion.

The *Wall Street Journal* estimates the volume at $800 trillion. These types of numbers are unfathomable. The *Financial Times* headlined "Barclays boss discussed Libor with BoE," saying:

> The bank admitted that it lowballed estimates of its borrowing costs from late 2007 to May 2009 because it wanted to reassure investors of its strength during the financial crisis and it believed other banks were doing the same.
>
> It also admitted that its traders improperly influenced the rate submissions from 2005 to 2008 to make money on derivatives.[3]

On the one hand, said Barclays, rogue traders committed fraud. On the other, bank executives submitted lower daily Libor rates than true costs to assure higher profits.

In the wake of the scandal, Chairman Marcus Agius and CEO Bob Diamond resigned. They and other banking crooks should be prosecuted and imprisoned. Since banker-caused crisis conditions erupted in fall 2007, no senior executive has faced charges. Expect none now to be held criminally liable. At most complicit banks are assessed hand-slap fines. They're then free to steal again. It's standard practice.

On June 30, London *Guardian* writer Will Hutton headlined "Let's end this rotten culture that only rewards rogues," saying:

> The Barclays rate-rigging scandal has once again exposed a world where men and women with little skill and no moral compass can become very rich very fast.[4]
>
> Investment banking is an organised scam masquerading as a business. It is defined by endemic conflicts of interest, systemic amoral behaviour and extreme avarice.
>
> Many of its senior figures should be serving prison sentences or disgraced—and would have been if British regulators had been weaned off the doctrine of 'light touch' regulation earlier and if the Serious Fraud Office's budget had not been emasculated by Mr. Osborne [UK Chancellor of the Exchequer].
>
> It is a tax on wealth generation and an enemy of honest endeavour—the beast that is devouring British capitalism.

It's far more than a British problem, of course. It's global, unchecked, and hugely destructive. Regulatory oversight is absent. Mary Schapiro, who heads America's SEC, turns a blind eye to fraud and abuse. She protects Wall Street, not investors. She lets banks self-regulate, and why not? She's a consummate insider. As former head of the Financial Industry Regulatory Authority (FINRA), she promoted self regulation. She also ran the National Association of Securities Dealers' (NASD) and Commodity Futures Trading Commission. She's an expert at quashing fraud investigations.

So are UK Financial Services Authority (FSA) officials. Instead of regulating, they collude. Political leaders from major parties are involved. Duopoly power runs Britain and America. Tories, New Labor, Republicans and Democrats prioritize what serves bankers. The economies of both countries are financialized. Whitehall and Washington operate the same way. They facilitate fraud. It's institutionalized. Politicians profit hugely from generous campaign contributions and high-paying jobs when leave government. Central bankers know what's going on and fuel it with bailouts and easy money.

On July 1, the London *Telegraph* headlined "Libor scandal: How I manipulated the bank borrowing rate," saying: "An anonymous insider from one of Britain's biggest lenders—aside from Barclays—explains how he and his colleagues helped manipulate the UK's bank borrowing rate. Neither the insider nor the bank can be identified for legal reasons." He gave presentations. He explained how Libor was rigged. It's easy, he said. No checks exist. Penalties for getting caught hardly matter. "[E]veryone" knows what's going on and "everyone" does it. Fraud is part of the system.

A Final Comment

Ellen Brown describes a "Wall Street Protection Racket of Covert Derivatives....Prop(ing) Up US Debt," saying: "Interest rate swaps are now over 80 percent of the massive derivatives market." Wall Street giants operate a "protection racket of a covert derivatives trade in interest rate swaps."

> The derivatives casino itself is just a last-ditch attempt to prop up a private pyramid scheme in fractional-reserve money creation, one that has progressed over several centuries through a series of "reserves"—from gold, to Fed-created "base money," to mortgage-backed securities, to sovereign debt ostensibly protected with derivatives.

The Libor is a vital factor in the swaps market. The cost of money affects them all. Privately created money at whatever interest rate bankers set "is the granddaddy of all pyramid schemes."

Despite "a quadrillion dollar derivatives edifice propping it up," eventually it will collapse. Money power in public hands could prevent it. This is an option "ready to replace the old system when it comes crashing down," says Brown.

Corrupt politicians won't return money control to public hands where it belongs ahead of time to avoid the crash. They benefit handsomely by standing pat. Why mess up a good thing by doing the right thing.

ENDNOTES

1 <http://www.globalresearch.ca/the-libor-scandal-in-full-perspective/31999>

2 "Traders Manipulated Key Rate, Bank Says", *Wall Street Journal*, February 12, 2012.

3 < http://www.ft.com/intl/cms/s/0/94a88010-c37c-11e1-966e-00144feabdc0.html>

4 < http://www.guardian.co.uk/commentisfree/2012/jun/30/will-hutton-barclays-banking-reform>

6

IMF FINANCIAL TERRORISM

In July 1944, the IMF and Bank for Reconstruction and Development (now the World Bank) were established to integrate developing nations into the global North-dominated world economy. Under the new post-war monetary system, the IMF was created to stabilize exchange rates linked to the dollar and bridge temporary payment imbalances between nations. The World Bank was to provide credit to war-torn developing countries. Both bodies, in fact, proved hugely exploitive. Instead of solving problems, they used debt entrapment to transfer public wealth to Western bankers and other corporate predators.

On a grander scale today, the scheme destructively obligates indebted nations to take new loans in order to be able to service old ones. As a result, rising indebtedness and the ability to impose structural adjustment are assured. This leads to::

- privatization of state enterprises, many sold for a fraction of their real worth;
- mass layoffs;
- deregulation;
- deep social spending cuts;
- wage freezes or cuts;
- unrestricted free market access for western corporations;

- corporate-friendly tax cuts;
- tax increases for working households;
- trade unionism suppression or marginalization; and
- harsh repression against proponents of social democracy, civil and human rights.

This enables bankers and other corporate predators to strip mine countries of their material wealth and resources. They shift them from public to private hands, crush democratic values, hollow out nations into backwaters, destroy middle class societies, and turn workers into serfs for those having means to employ them. In other words, freedom is replaced by perpetual debt bondage. The whole of humanity is consumed in a race to the bottom follows. An elite few benefit at the expense of the many. Nations are henceforth entrapped, forced to pay homage to money master kleptocrats, effectively handing over their sovereignty to foreign forces which now impose their state policies.

Neoliberalism is neo-Malthusianism writ large, destroying most of humanity to save its continuance by a few. Its holy trinity mandates: 1) no public sphere, 2) unrestrained corporate empowerment, and 3) the elimination of social spending to devote all state resources for bottom line profits, national security and internal control. Except for the privileged few, it's the worst, not the best, of all possible worlds. Economies are financialized into debt bondage, transforming them into hollow shell dystopian backwaters.

In the 1980s, 187 IMF loans caused poverty, hunger, malnutrition, disease and death for many developing countries, including all sub-Saharan ones entrapped by the structural adjustment (in the interest of western corporations) that they imposed. Their growthdeclined on average by 2.2% per year, and per capita income dropped below pre-independence levels. Debt service (the assurance of which is a primary aim of structural adjustment) required that health expenditures be cut by 50% and education by 25%. Moreover, as indebtedness rises, so does forced austerity, again to ensure debt service, until it becomes a self-perpetuating death spiral requiring new loans to service old ones. It's a never-ending cycle to oblivion for many nations in hock to IMF mandates.

In Latin America, the 1980s was a lost decade. Loans to Chile required 40% wage cuts. During Mexico's 1982 debt crisis, wages as well as spending for health, education, and basic infrastructure dropped by half. As a result, infant mortality tripled and vital human needs went unmet to assure that bankers got paid.

By decade's end, developing nations overallwere worse off, not better. They were deeper than ever in debt just as IMF officials had planned. Currency devaluations followed. External debts burgeoned. Growth fell. In the prior period from 1976 to 1982, Latin American borrowing had doubled. About 70% of the new loans were needed to service old ones.

Yet Article I of the IMF's Articles of Agreement audaciously if not mendaciously says it lends:

> to give confidence to members by making the general resources of the Fund temporarily available to them under adequate safeguards, thus providing them with opportunity to correct maladjustments in their balance of payments without resorting to measures destructive of national or international prosperity.The IMF's web site states it provides loans to reduce poverty and increase economic development. It adds that "[i]n difficult economic times, [it] helps countries to protect the most vulnerable in a crisis."

In fact, it does precisely the opposite. It maliciously entraps countries in debt, poverty and deprivation. It operates as the loan shark of last resort. It demands not a pound of flesh but all of it, no matter the pain and suffering caused. Once shock therapy entrapped Chile under Pinochet, unemployment rose from 9.1 to 18.7% between 1974 and 1975. At the same time, output fell 12.9% as cheap imports flooded the country. As a result, local businesses closed, hunger grew, and so did mass disenchantment with economic austerity followed by repressive crackdowns against challenges to regime control. A decade later, GDP growth resumed, but only after conditions for most of the population worsened. About 45% of Chileans were impoverished while the nation's richest 10% saw their incomes rise by 83%.

It works the same way everywhere under IMF mandates. They cause mass impoverishment, public wealth transfer to private hands, out-of-control corruption and cronyism, leaving nations transformed into backwaters to benefit the domestic and foreign super-richelites. In 1980s in Bolivia under Victor Paz Estenssoro, austerity included wage freezes, ending food subsidies, lifting price controls, hiking oil prices by 300%, imposing deep social spending cuts, permitting unrestricted imports, downsizing state enterprises before privatizing them, and letting unemployment rise sharply.

The decade through the early 1990s saw Latin American debt rise from $110 billion in 1980 to $473 in 1992. It was accompanied by interest payments growing from $6.4 billion to $18.3 billion. As a result, worker livelihoods, health and welfare suffered.

Globally, in fact, many millions lucky enough to have work endure sub-poverty wages to let foreign predators profit enormously on human misery. It's the IMF's dirty game. It spreads pain, not prosperity by lifting all boats as it proclaims. This scenario was replicated from sub-Saharan Africa to Latin America to Russia and Asian Tiger countries in 1997/98. They were looted one at a time or in combination. The IMF invasion turned Asia's economic miracle into disaster.

The International Labor Organization estimated 24 million jobs were lost as a result of selling state enterprises at fire sale prices. Western brands replaced local ones, western ownership replaced local ownership, and foreign predators benefitted from what *The New York Times* called "the world's biggest going-out-of-business sale." At the same time, Asian workers became human wreckage. IMF policy statements never explain what actually happens. Instead, they perpetuate the myth about offering help as a lender of last resort when, in fact, their mandate is to plunder for profit, no matter the damage caused.

Expect more of the same under its new managing director, Christine Lagarde. She was Washington's top choice. Treasury Secretary Tim Geithner endorsed her over Mexico's central bank governor Agustin Carstens, her only competitor after IMF's board of directors excluded Israeli central bank governor Stanley Fischer, allegedly because of age. In fact, he lacked support outside Israel, and US officials stuck with traditional IMF policy of putting a European in charge.

An American always heads the World Bank, yet Washington dominates all international lending agencies. It picks officials heading them, public rhetoric notwithstanding. On June 28, 2011 a brief IMF statement announced Lagarde's appointment, saying"The executive board of the International Monetary Fund today selected Christine Lagarde to serve as IMF managing director and madame chairman of the executive board for a five-year term starting July 2011." China, Russia and Brazil also supported her besides America and most European nations. Britain's Chancellor of the Exchequer George Osborne called it "good news for the global economy and for Britain." Then French President, Nicolas Sarkozy, said about his departing finance minister's appointment: it's a "victory for France." French banks are heavily exposed to the Greek (and other troubled nations') debt Lagarde is mandated to protect. However, more on that, below.

Lagarde's first move was to back Western banks' tough austerity demands. As she said:"If there is one message I have to send tonight, it is to say the Greek opposition must join a national entente with the party that is in power." The primary objective of IMF loans is debt service; it tops other obligations. The IMF cannot help but know—as is empirically demonstrated time after time—that austerity doesn't work to rekindle weak economies; but then, that was never the intent. Rather, austerity policies assure that bankers get paid, no matter the hardships imposed on working households through no fault of their own. It doesn't matter that bailing out European banks violates IMF charter provisions.

In his June 29, 2011 article headlined, "A World Overwhelmed by Western Hypocrisy,"[1] economist and former Reagan administration Assistant Treasury Secretary Paul Craig Roberts said the IMF "is only empowered to make balance of payments loans, but is lending to the Greek government for prohibited budgetary reasons [so it] can pay the banks." The European Central Bank (ECB) is also "prohibited from bailing out member countr[ies]," but it's doing it for the same reason. In other words, banker bottom line priorities supersede institutional rules and legal standards. It makes a mockery of both the rule of law and of governments of, by and for people—about whom they don't give a damn and show it.

On June 29, 2011, the *Wall Street Journal* said Lagarde has unsettled legal questions at home, explaining that:

> [A] French criminal court [will] decide on July 8 whether to launch a probe into accusations that [she] overstepped her authority as finance minister in 2007 when dealing with a controversy pitting tycoon Bernard Tapie against the French state, or to dismiss the case."

The case remains unresolved and may drag on for years, according to legal experts. Given broad consensus backing her, expect eventual resolution in her favor or at least nothing worse than wrist slap fines or reprimands. At issue was her 403 million euro arbitration order benefitting Tapie over France. As a result, French Court of Cassation (its highest court of appeal) Attorney General Jean-Louis Nadal ordered the Tapie dossier made public. Included in it are allegations that "Lagarde had indeed acted in a way to defeat the law... to help Tapie gain a favourable decision, against an earlier" appeals court judgment favoring the state.

Perhaps Lagarde replacing former IMF head Dominique Strauss-Kahn is old news, but it's still germane to any understanding about the organization. He was forced out over now discredited attempted rape allegations. Even at the time, it was an implausible accusation. What is more plausible is that he was targeted for backing more responsible IMF policies that were an anathema to bankers. He endorsed employment and equity as building blocks of economic stability and prosperity, political stability and peace, counter to IMF core principles, if not its public face. . As a result, he had to go.

Wall Street and other financial giants focus solely on extracting maximum wealth at the expense of working households and nations. Lagarde's expected to assure it. Expertise aside, her background shows ready willingness to comply. In 2009, the *Financial Times* called her the best Eurozone finance manager even though her background is law, not economics. The same year, *Forbes* ranked her the world's 17th most powerful woman; by 2012 she had risen to number 8.[2]

Lagarde's official/unpublicized credentials are broad and extensive. She spent her early years in America, initially in the 1970s, as an intern of Rep. William Cohen. She later served Cohen as he became Senator and then Defense Secretary under Clinton. In 1981, she joined Baker & McKenzie (B & K) in Chicago—a major international law firm practicing antitrust and labor law—and made a career in the United States.[3] In 1995, she was elevated to its Executive Committee then in October 1999, she was appointed chairman of B & K's Global Executive Committee. From 1995-1998, she chaired B & K's European Regional Council and Professional Development Committee. In 2004 and 2005, she was an ING Groep NV Supervisory Group member, and in 2004, she became president of its Strategy Committee. She spent over two decades at B & K before returning to France as de Villepin's trade minister. She also served as Board of Governors chairman for the European Bank for Reconstruction and Development, as well as a Board of Governors member at the European Investment Bank and Inter-American Development Bank.

Other information excluded from her official resume includes her membership in America's Center for Strategic & International Studies (CSIS)—an influential organization emphasizing national security and "advancing [US] global interests." Specializing in crisis management, it's also connected to the highest government and Pentagon levels. There and later, Lagarde put their interests above those of France, including while heading (with Zbigniew Brzezinski from 1995-2002) the USA-Poland Defense Industries working group.At B & K, she noticeably favored US corporate interests over French ones, including Boeing and Lockheed-Martin at the expense of Airbus and Dassault. In 2003, she became a member of the Commission for the Expansion of the Euro-Atlantic Community, in charge of potential Poland, Latvia, Romania, Czech Republic and Hungary investments.

For many years, Lagarde was a walking conflict of interests. When the political positions of groups she represented are considered, it's impossible to ignore how completely opposite they are from the French positions defended by her former boss, de Villepin. Lagarde promoted US business interests, not those of France. In his May 30, 2011 *CounterPunch* article, titled "The IMF After Strauss-Kahn," Philippe Marliere, a University of London Professor of French and European politics, noted that while she may have served as Sarkozy's finance minister, it was "hard to find one single decision, debate or policy that she has initiated or imposed her mark on. At home, her voice has hardly been heard in economic debates, let alone in political debates in general."

No matter, she's a player, a club member in good standing, a neoliberal hardliner. As a result, she was chosen to enforce structural adjustment austerity, starting with Greece.

On July 5, 2012, Lagarde began her mandate to keep democracy's birthplace in debt bondage, assure bankers are paid, lower Greece's standard of living, impoverish its citizens, sell off all valued state assets cheap, strip mine the country of everything of worth, then replicate the process elsewhere. In other words, her job is to head the IMF's financial coup d'état against debt-entrapped sovereign states, wrecking them to pay the bankers.

Beneath Lagarde's bourgeois charm lies a financial predator chosen to pillage economies, not save them. Throughout its history, IMF policies perpetuated debt bondage, entrapping nations to service money master oligarchs, stripping sovereign nations of their independence in the process. Their peoples end up impoverished in neoserfdom if they are lucky enough to retain jobs. Lagarde's in charge to force feed austerity. She'll be well rewarded to inflict pain and suffering she'll cause, but don't expect Western media scoundrels to explain all of that.

Mandated Austerity in Greece

In his June 7, 2011 article titled, "Will Greece let EU Central Bankers Destroy Democracy,"[4] Michael Hudson discussed the proposed bailout terms. He called them "an opportunity for privatization grabs." It wasn't what local voters had bargained for with 2000 Eurozone membership. They didn't understand its unintended consequences. It included agreeing to foreign-controlled central bank authority, permitting the ECB to run Greece like a colony, substituting its will for Greek national sovereignty.

According to Professor William Black (former senior bank regulator and Savings and Loan prosecutor), Eurozone membership has strings. These include foregoing:

- the right to devalue a domestic currencies to make exports more competitive;

- sovereignty over members' own money or (for "periphery nations") influence over European Central Bank (ECB) policies;

- the right to implement expansive fiscal policies to stimulate growth.

In fact, mandated bondage "is a double oxymoron. [It prevents] effective counter-cyclical fiscal policies harm[ing] growth and stability throughout the Eurozone." Weak members hurt stronger ones. All countries lose out by spending billions on bailouts. They increase their debt and require greater amounts to service it until eventually the entire house of cards collapses.

Moreover, like all debt-entrapped countries, Greece's bailout price required structural adjustment austerity which make a bad situation worse,heaping on new penalties during hard times. Rising indebtedness results—the familiar IMF-imposed death spiral. No responsible leader should accept it.

Last year, however, in return for a $150 billion loan, Greek Prime Minister Georgios Papandreou imposed earlier cuts, including:

- large public worker layoffs;

- public sector 10% wage cuts, including a 30% reduction in salary entitlements;

- 20% cuts to civil service bonuses;

- frozen pensions;

- raising the average retirement age two years;

- higher fuel, alcohol, tobacco, and luxury goods taxes with much more to come given Greece's worsening debt problem.

Euroland officials demand multiple rounds more in return for further bailout help. Eurogroup President Jean-Claude Juncker expects nations needing help to agree, saying"In the case of countries with difficulties, it would be wise for the principal political forces of those countries to agree on the path to follow. That's what happened in Ireland, and that's what we would like to happen between the political parties in Greece," no matter the economic wreckage or human cost.

Accordingly on June 8, 2012 former Prime Minister Papandreou announced new tax increases and over $9 billion in spending cuts. Earlier he had divulged plans to raise nearly $75 billion by privatizing state enterprises, including water companies, the Piraeus and Thessalonika port facilities, the Athens racecourse, Greece's Postbank, a casino, the OPAP lottery company, and the state rail system.

He was succeeded by Lucas Papademos, a former ECB vice president, with others to follow, as the political uncertainty continues. Will the Parthenon and other national treasures be next, including the nation's soul? At year end 2011, Greek public assets were worth an estimated $440 billion. Brussels wanted at least the best of them sold, as well as assurances about debt repayment in return for continued bailout help.

However, given Greece's rising debt burden, no amount's enough. Greater austerity impedes economic growth and recovery, and deepening crisis conditions are compounded. Since 2007, Greece's economy shrank over 20% en route to exceeding 30% and total collapse. Its real debt burden exceeds $650 billion, around double the reported amount. The latest bailout deal is for about $170 billion. Its current debt exceeds what Greece can repay. Increasing it elevates crisis conditions.

Forced austerity assures harder than ever hard times. Rising unemployment exceeds 20%. Youth unemployment approaches 50%. Only a third without work get unemployment benefits. They're being slashed another 20%. There are plans for laying off another 150,000 state workers by 2015. Private sector wage cuts exceeded 20%, public sector ones around 50%. Poverty in Greece is afflicting millions. Its GDP is collapsing. So are pensions, Greece's life force, and the ability of most people to survive.

Democracy's birthplace took its last breath and died when banker-appointed prime minister Lucas Papademos (a former ECB vice president) and finance minister Evangelous Venizelos (a former Bank of Greece official) took over, exercising virtual carte blanche discretion on cuts. Parliamentarians opposing cuts are sacked. New Democracy's Antonis Samaras expelled 21 MPs, including the party's whip and shadow defense and interior ministers. PASOK's George Papandreou removed 23 opposition MPs, including former government ministers. MPs defying banker diktats don't survive.

No one's sure what's coming next. Perhaps it's tyranny under martial law, followed by new rounds of austerity cuts until Greece is bled dry and collapses. It's at the epicenter of global pillage, a symbol of how destructive money power in private hands ruthlessly pursues its interests at the public's expense. Economist Charles Wyplosz calls the austerity madness "pseudo-science," forecasting that debt default awaits Greece, Portugal, Italy and perhaps other troubled Eurozone economies. The longer they wait, the deeper the hole and greater pain.

The Argentina Solution

In December 2001, Argentina halted all debt payments to domestic and foreign creditors. Months earlier, IMF loan help had deepened the country's burden. Finally, by 2005, $100 billion in debt restructuring was completed on a take it or leave it basis. Stiff haircuts of around 65% were imposed on creditors. Most decided something was better than nothing. In 2010, the holdouts eventually capitulated, accepting similar terms. Sustained economic growth followed from 2003 through 2007. Vital debt restructuring and a devalued currency assured it.

Greece and other troubled Eurozone countries can relieve their burdens the same way, reclaiming sovereign rights by reinstating their pre-euro currencies. They never should have sacrificed them in the first place. So far, Greece's banker-controlled parliamentarians disagree. On February 12, 2012, they passed sweeping austerity measures on top of multiple previous rounds. New measures included:

- sacking 15,000 public workers in 2012 and 150,000 by 2015,
- slashing private sector wages by 20%;
- lowering monthly minimum wages from 750 to 600 euros;
- cutting fast disappearing monthly unemployment benefits from 460 to 360 euros; and
- reducing pensions many Greeks need to survive by 15%.

Another 130 billion euro bailout was secured. The more financial aid Greece gets, the greater its debt, the harder it is to repay, the more future aid is needed, and the deeper the country's economic abyss.

No matter. Troika power kleptocrats—the IMF, EU and European Central Bank (ECB)—demanded deep cuts Money power dictates that the bankers get paid first. Under crisis conditions, Greece's economy is dying. In December 2011, manufacturing plunged 15.5% year-over-year. Industrial output sank 11.3%. Unemployment topped 20%. Youth joblessness approaches 50%, and suicides doubled since economic decline began.

As a result, capital flight's increasing. People are voting with their feet and leaving. Those remaining face hospitals short of medicines, unprecedented homelessness and hunger, schools without basic supplies, and imagine what's coming when new cuts are implemented.

Moreover, bankers demand more. So far, mandated wealth confiscation alone is their only excluded diktat, but it's happening incrementally. Under systematic sacking, Greece's life force is dying in meltdown. No wonder economist Michael Hudson calls predatory finance "a form of warfare." Standing armies pale by comparison. Financial oligarchs wage war by other means and take no prisoners. They seize land, infrastructure, other tangible assets, and all material wealth. In the process, countries and ordinary people are devastated.

Greece is effectively bankrupt. Only its obituary's not written. Its people have three choices—starve, leave or rebel. Street protests and strikes produce nothing. Banker controlled parliamentarians don't care. Replacing them is crucial, by whatever means necessary. Nothing else can work, and delay only exacerbates intolerable conditions.

An Historical Analogue

Current banker-imposed policies are similar to the crushing Treaty of Versailles reparations imposed on Germany. Fascism under Hitler emerged. WW II followed. The Versailles terms were outrageous. In May 1921, Germany got an ultimatum—accept the terms within six days or face industrial Ruhr Valley military occupation. Left with no choice, it accepted. Germany's colonial possessions and raw material resources were seized.

In the end, both sides lost out. By 1929, unmanageable debt had overwhelmed world finance and monetary policy. Wall Street's crash followed. An unsustainable pyramid was built on punitive war debts. Wall Street and other major banks enforced paymentsthat exceeded America's annual 1920s foreign trade. Rebuilding and modernizing war-torn Europe was sacrificed to pay bankers.

Germany got the worst of it. Its Reichsbank had to print enormous amounts of money to survive. Catastrophic hyperinflation followed. In January 1923, the mark dropped to 18,000 to the dollar. By July, it was 353,000, in August 4,620,000, and by November an astonishing 4,200,000,000,000. It became worthless. German savings were destroyed, and calamitous events became inevitable.

Lost assets compounded economic misery. Germany's colonies became League of Nations Mandates, as Alsace-Lorraine, West Prussia, Upper Silesia and other territories were ceded to Britain, France, Belgium, Czechoslovakia, and Poland. Germany's agricultural resources were lost, along with 75% of its iron ore, 68% of zinc ore, 26% of coal, as well as Alsatian textile industries and potash mines. In addition, Germany's entire merchant fleet was taken, as well as a portion of its transport and fishing fleet, plus locomotives, railroad cars and trucks to pay war debts.

Impossible terms were imposed; 132 billion gold marks were demanded at 6% annual interest. As a result, inflation soared and German industrial activity plunged. Reichsbank and other German bank assets were seized. German marks became worthless. Public anger grew, leading to communism and fascism vying for power. In 1923, the so-called Dawes Plan (named for US banker Charles Dawes) was adopted, prioritizing the payment of the bankers. Effectively, looting was enforced which continued until 1929 when the debt pyramid collapsed.

A banking crisis followed. So did capital flight. Germany's economy crashed. The Great Depression emerged, empowering radical political elements.

The rest is history. WW II left 40 million dead and Europe in ruins. In other words, when public pain exceeds thresholds of no return, all bets are off. Often the unthinkable happens. It did before and may again now.

Don't bet against it.

ENDNOTES

1 < http://www.informationclearinghouse.info/article28431.htm>

2 < http://www.forbes.com/power-women/>

3 < http://www.globalresearch.ca/imf-regime-change-with-christine-lagarde-us-corporations-enter-the-french-government/>

4 < http://www.globalresearch.ca/will-greece-let-eu-central-bankers-destroy-democracy>

7

JPMORGAN CHASE ON CAPITOL HILL

On June 13, 2012, JPMorgan Chase CEO Jamie Dimon testified before the Senate Banking Committee. He discussed his firm's recent trading loss and industry practices. It was more of a homecoming than grilling, since Washington is Wall Street occupied territory. Foxes guard the hen house. Regulators don't regulate. There's no oversight. Investigations rarely happen but even those conducted are whitewashed. Criminal fraud is encouraged, not curbed. You could say, it's institutionalized. Congress, the administration, the SEC, and credit rating agencies are incestuously involved with giant banks and other major financial institutions. Whatever the latter want, they get. Wall Street never had it so good. Senators didn't lay a glove on Dimon. His grand theft business model wasn't explained. Why would anybody ask him about that?

Former bank regulator/financial fraud expert Bill Black's book titled *The Best Way to Rob A Bank Is To Own One*[1] told all. He coined the term "control fraud." It lets corporate officials commit grand theft. Trillions of dollars are stolen and nothing intervenes to stop it.

On May 10, 2012 Dimon announced a $2 billion trading loss. Some estimates place it multiples higher. "Trading" is now a euphemism for speculation, with the stakes high enough to cause crises. JPMorgan is only the tip of the iceberg. Other banks are similarly deeply troubled. We'll hear about that in future announcements. Only cursory explanations will be provided. Even what Morgan bet on and lost wasn't identified.

European securities speculation looks likely. The big trader in this is called the London Whale due to the size of the credit derivatives bets he took, one of which may be as large as $100 billion. Scoundrel media reports said little about it.[2] Troubled Eurozone economies face deepening depressions. Bank problems accompany them. Investing in their sovereign and/or private debt entails great risks. Dimon attributed the loss to credit default swaps derivatives trading. They're the most widely traded derivative. They're unregulated insurance bets between two parties on whether or not a company's bonds may default.

Ellen Brown, author of *The Web of Debt*,[3] once asked: What if "the smartest guys in the room designed their credit default swaps [but] forgot to ask one thing—what if the parties on the other side of the bet don't have the money to pay up?" When crises erupt, they don't. Turmoil hits markets. Lack of oversight makes it inevitable. Bankers get bailouts. Who said crime doesn't pay? Ordinary people are hardest hit.

JP Morgan's loss relates directly to the European finance capital's crisis. It also shows how Europe's banks and America's are interconnected. Trouble on one side of the Atlantic assures it on the other. Contagion then spreads globally. In 2008, speculative excess brought down investment and commercial banks, insurers, and shadow banks. They're still troubled..

JP Morgan was considered America's most stable bank but its troubles reveal an entirely different picture. Bill Black thinks it may be "the new Fannie Mae." In 2008, Fannie Mae's subprime portfolio blew up, unraveling piece by piece. It was nationalized so taxpayers pay the tab. It remains sick on life support.

Earlier problems within the banking system remain unresolved. Nothing's been done yet to fix things. The Dodd-Frank financial reform bill, which includes the much-touted Volker rule, was signed into law in 2010 and supposed to come into force in 2012. But it left the actual provisions of the bill to be defined by the central bank and other regulators, who are hoping to finish work on the actual provisions by the end of 2012, and then will give the banks until 2014 to "make a good faith effort to comply".[4] As a result, speculative excesses continue. Some analysts think it's worse than ever. Massive balance sheet losses remain and the bailouts only conceal them. Trillions of dollars given to the banks have bought them time, nothing else.

Phony stress tests conceal the gravity of today's crisis. Mark-to-market accounting was suspended. False reporting of the actual value of bank assets followed. JPMorgan's loss was inevitable and signals much more to come.

Senators didn't hold Dimon's feet to the fire. The nationally televised hearing was more love fest than grilling. Why not, when 16 of the committee's 22 members get JPMorgan campaign cash? Anti-foreclosure protesters delayed Dimon's testimony. One shouted "Stop foreclosures." Another said "Jamie Dimon's a crook." Dimon looked unperturbed. They were hustled out of the Senate chamber handcuffed. Expect charges to follow. At the same time, Dimon's free to keep stealing and let taxpayers pay the tab if the mounting losses turn out to be too great to cover.

On June 12, 2012, Bloomberg headlined "House of Dimon Marred by CEO Complacency Over Unit's Risk,"[5] saying that Dimon treated the chief investment office (CIO) differently from other JPM departments. Rigorous scrutiny and transparency were absent. Though concerns were raised, Dimon ignored them. Why worry when big money is being made? What Dimon knew and when, he didn't say. But bear in mind: he's known as a hands-on boss. He overseas a vast financial empire. With over $2.3 trillion in assets, JPM became the largest US bank last year.

According to former Federal Reserve Bank of Minneapolis CEO Gary Stern,institutions like JPM "are too big to manage because even the bank that was considered to be the best-managed turns out to have had a significant glitch." Bloomberg called risk management at JPM's CIO a "world of its own", noting:

> This year its traders valued some of their positions at prices that differed from the investment bank, people familiar with the situation have said.
>
> One trader built up positions in credit derivatives so large and market-moving he became known as the London Whale.
>
> It was those bets on credit-default swaps known as the Markit CDX North America Investment Grade Series 9 that backfired and forced JPMorgan to disclose the trading loss.When risks got out of hand, board members lacked the experience to police them. No one on JPM's risk policy committee worked as a banker. At issue is how could Wall Street's "best run bank" operate this way? Answers weren't forthcoming.

In 2005, Bloomberg reported on JPM's risk model after it acquired Bank One. When Dimon became CEO, he created the CIO, which speculates on high-risk assets like credit default swaps and similar investments. Dimon encouraged it. Again, why worry when things go well?

Former North America CIO head David Olsen said he was told when hired: "We want to ramp up the ability to generate profits for the firm. This is Jamie's new vision for the company." Until things cratered, profits and assets surged. High-risk bets paid off. Subprime ones did handsomely.

> In addition to making speculative bets, the CIO took on a bigger role after the financial crisis, hedging JPMorgan's potential losses on loans and corporate

> bonds by taking positions in credit derivatives.[6]Insiders said transparency was sorely lacking. According to "Black Swan"[7] author Nassim Taleb, JPM's "risk management is as amateurish as you can get on Wall Street." The firm "is vastly more fragile today than it was five years ago, and the system is more fragile today with more too-big-to-fail banks with proven incompetence at their management level."[8]

When Dimon announced $2 billion in trading losses last month, the CIO unit had over $100 billion in asset-backed "structured vehicles," as well as another $100 billion in credit default swaps. These types of bets contributed heavily to plunging markets in 2008. Accounting manipulation conceals the severity of the impact when they fail. The worst is yet to come out. JPM's CIO operates like a high-risk hedge fund. Taleb believes it incurs 10-15 times more risk. Losing a big bet assures trouble. Lose several or more and company solvency is threatened. Other Wall Street giants are tarnished by the same brush.

Systemically destructive strategies work as planned when things go well. Otherwise taxpayers get the bill. It's a win-win scheme. Senate banking committee members did nothing to expose it. The June 13, 2012 Senate Hearings looked more like a coronation than a crucifixion.

ENDNOTES

1 Bill Black, *The Best Way to Rob a Bank is To Own One*, University of Texas Press, 2005.

2 For a taste of how little, check out Reuters here <http://news.yahoo.com/jpmorgan-ceo-says-caught-london-whale-trades-172438058--finance.html> and Wall Street Journal here <http://blogs.wsj.com/deals/2012/10/12/london-whale-becomes-immaterial-to-j-p-morgan/>

3 <http://www.webofdebt.com/>

4 <http://www.bloomberg.com/news/2012-09-14/volcker-rule-needs-narrow-hedge-exemption-cftc-s-chilton-says.html>

5 <http://www.bloomberg.com/news/2012-09-14/volcker-rule-needs-narrow-hedge-exemption-cftc-s-chilton-says.html>

6 Ibid.

7 Nassim Taleb, The *Black Swan: The Impact of the Highly Improbable*, Random House, 2007.

8 Supra, note 5.

8

GEORGE SOROS

NEW WORLD ORDER CONFIDENCE MAN

In July 1944, 730 delegates from 44 nations met at the Mount Washington Hotel in Bretton Woods, NH for a UN Monetary and Financial Conference. Its purpose was to establish a post-war international monetary system of convertible currencies, fixed exchange rates, free trade, with the US dollar as the world's reserve currency linked to gold, and those of other nations fixed to the dollar.

It also designed an institutional framework for market-based capital accumulation to assure newly liberated colonies would pursue capitalist economic development beneficial to the victorious allies, mainly America.

In addition, the IMF and World Bank were established to integrate developing nations into the Global North-dominated world economy. Their original missions were:

- to establish stable exchange rates linked to the dollar and bridge temporary payment imbalances (the IMF); and

- to provide credit to war-torn developing countries (the World Bank).

In actuality, these institutions served as a means of debt entrapment whereby the wealth of what were then termed "emerging markets" was transferred from developing countries to powerful Western bankers. Both bodies have proved hugely exploitive, as is their purpose to this day.

The scheme obligates indebted nations to take new loans to service old ones. While many caught on to the trap, paid out their loans and sought to avoid new ones, worsening financial conditions are propelling many countries back into the maw of the IMF once again, even though this time they know better. Once again the process assures rising indebtedness and imposes structural adjustment-based austerity, including:

- privatization of state enterprises;
- mass layoffs;
- deregulation;
- deep social spending cuts;
- wage freezes or cuts;
- unrestricted free market access for western corporations;
- corporate-friendly tax cuts;
- crackdowns on or elimination of trade unionism; and
- harsh repression against those opposing a system incompatible with social democracy.

Overall, since WW II, a significant degree of what was once public wealth was shifted into powerful private hands. As the gap between super-rich elites and working households widens,the process is becoming more intensely predatory than ever, and the amounts involved are skyrocketing.

In 1971, the system unraveled when Nixon closed the gold window, ending the last link between gold, the dollar, and sound money. Thereafter, currencies floated, competing with each other in a casino-like environment. As a result, powerful insiders manipulate the process fraudulently. They include hedge funds, giant international banks, and governments, at times cooperatively with others in their own mutual self-interest. George Soros is a player, very much a major one. More on that, below.

In his book *Super Imperialism: The Economic Strategy of American Empire* and other writings, Michael Hudson explained: :

- how the dollar glut finances US imperialism and corporate interests by circulating surplus dollars globally to further financial speculation and corporate takeovers;

- how global central banks "recyle these dollar inflows (into) US Treasury bonds to finance the federal US budget deficit; and most important the military character of the US payments deficit and the domestic federal budget deficit."

In other words, the central bank's printing dollars finances US corporate takeovers and speculative excesses. These, in turn, create bubbles and global economic crises, as well as facilitate America's reckless spending, militarism, and imperial wars, enabling the establishment of hundreds of bases worldwide, and American projection overall of belligerence and exploitation at the expense of democratic values and social justice.

Sooner or later, however, excesses erode confidence and produce change. It's especially so today with the Federal Reserve sacrificing the dollar's dwindling strength to bail out Wall Street at the expense of productive economic growth and stability.

The more dollar strength and safety erode, the less likely foreign investors will tolerate buying bad dollar-denominated assets whose value is likely to decline further over time. For decades, the sale of US Treasuries has given America a free lunch to finance counterproductive policy.

Hudson sees international tensions growing for the next generation because of America's reckless monetarism, perpetual wars, and extreme wealth gap between super-rich elites and ordinary people.

For decades, US companies had a competitive advantage stemming from the Washington Consensus policy prescriptions and the Bretton Woods institutions the US controls.

They've afforded America a free lunch to rule by forcing other countries into debt bondage, and threatening to bring down the global monetary system if enough of them balk. Where financial warfare fails to intimidate, the military is sent in to do the job. So far financial domination mostly succeeds because Europe and Asia lack the political will to establish a new international economic order. They let America reap their wealth to reinforce its "new kind of centralized global planning" based on financialization and a US Treasury securities standard.

In WTO terms, this system transfers foreign trade gains from other economies back to America by way of dollar deposits in Treasuries. It drains their resources overall, and promotes their dependency, locking them in to the lower end of production chains, rather than promoting self-sufficiency. It's backed up with hard line militarism and threats of systemic monetary collapse.

Eventually, exploited countries balk when faced with "taxation without representation," a "quid without quo," and the free lunch enjoyed by "the world's payments-surplus nations."

The longer America demands this tribute by glutting the world's economies with dollars, the more likely disadvantaged nations will object, and eventually perhaps withdraw from the IMF, World Bank and WTO altogether.

Globalists like George Soros aim to exploit that possibility, among other ways through Bretton Woods 2.0 to develop ideas and policies for a new financial world order that elitists like himself will control.

George Soros—Predatory Billionaire Investor

Soros' rogue investing is notorious. For example, in 1992, he made a billion dollars sabotaging European monetary policy by attacking the European Rate Mechanism (ERM) through a highly leveraged speculative assault on the British pound. As a result, he forced its devaluation and the ERM breakup.

In June 2003, Neil Clark wrote a *New Statesman* article explaining Soros' machinations as a rogue predator—how he "made billions out of the Far Eastern currency crash of 1997," and was fined in 2002 "for insider trading by a court in France."[1] When asked about the turmoil his speculation caused, Soros dismissively said: "As a market participant, I don't need to be concerned with the consequences of my actions."

While earning billions from rogue investing, he's caused havoc for millions globally. More still by his International Crisis Group and Open Society (open meaning for him to plunder) collaboration with Zbigniew Brzezinski, Al Gore, General Wesley Clark, Richard Perle, Paul Wolfowitz, and many other notorious scoundrels and organizations.

For decades, Soros operated roguishly for a buck. For example, in 1998, he wrote an outrageous letter to Bill Clinton, calling for a "comprehensive political and military strategy for bringing down Saddam Hussein and his regime" for reasons that the Bush administration would subsequently endorse. He's also connected to the Carlyle Group that profits handsomely from defense contracts related to militarism and imperial wars.

There his partners and associates include G.H.W. Bush, James Baker, Colin Powell, former UK Prime Minister John Major, Frank Carlucci, Richard Darman, at one time bin Laden family members, and many other well-connected figures.

Clark explained that Soros "may not, as sometimes suggested, be a fully paid-up CIA agent. But that his corporations and NGOs are closely wrapped up in US expansionism cannot seriously be doubted."

He turned on Bush II over tactics, not ideology—for committing the cardinal sin of giving away the game through overzealously endorsing belligerence.

In fact, Soros strongly supports financial and military warfare for greater profits globally, to gain control over money, resources and markets. But he wants it done skillfully with little notice. It's his quiet way. Accordingly, he uses wealth and influence to oust "bad for business" regimes. For example, Clark said, he was instrumental in the Soviet collapse by:

> distribut(ing) $3 million a year to dissidents including Poland's solidarity movement, Charter 77 in Czechoslovakia, and Andrei Sakharov in the Soviet Union. In 1984, he founded his first Open Society Institute in Hungary and pumped millions of dollars into opposition movements and independent media. Ostensibly aimed at building up a 'civil society,' these initiatives were designed to weaken the existing political structures and pave the way for eastern Europe's eventual exploitation by global capital.Soros now takes credit for the "Americanization of eastern Europe" by exploiting its wealth and people for profit.
>
> In Yugoslavia, Clark said:
>
> The Yugoslavs remained stubbornly resistant and repeatedly returned Slobodan Milosevic's reformed Socialist Party to government. Soros was equal to the challenge.
>
> From 1991, his Open Society Institute channeled more than $100 million to [anti-Milosevic elements] funding political parties, publishing houses and 'independent' media [like Radio B92].

When Washington ousted Milosevic in 2000, "all that was left was to cart [him] to the Hague tribunal, co-financed by Soros" and other so-called human rights custodians. Today, Yugoslavia is balkanized, its people exploited, and Kosovar-governed by Prime Minister Hashim Thaci, a Washington-supported unindicted drug trafficker with known organized crimes ties.

Soros, however, profited hugely. He's done so, in fact, in each country he targeted at the expense of freedom, democratic values, and public welfare.

> In Kosovo, for example, he invested $50 million in an attempt to gain control of the Trepca mine complex, where there are vast reserves of gold, silver, lead and

> other minerals estimated to be worth [about] $5 billion. He thus copied a pattern he [used] to great effect over the whole of eastern Europe [through] 'shock therapy' and 'economic reform,' then swooping in with his associates to buy valuable state assets at knock-down prices.In fact, his Pax Americana strategy differs only from Bush II in subtlety. "But it is just as ambitious and just as deadly," whether forwarded by military or financial warfare for maximum profits.

Soros' Institute for New Economic Thinking (INET) Bretton Woods Conference

From April 8-11, 2011 INET's second annual conference addressed global economic crisis aftershocks, as part of a wide-ranging effort to "engage the larger European Union, as well as emerging economies of Eastern Europe, Latin America and Asia" to accept Soros' New World Order ideas.

Directed to "inspir[e] and provok[e] new economic thinking," over 200 academics, business and government leaders (many with direct ties to him) attended.

They included INET's Soros and Robert Johnson, former UK Prime Minister Gordon Brown, Paul Volker, Larry Summers, Joseph Stiglitz, Kenneth Rogoff, Jeffrey Sachs (whose shock therapy poison wrecked post-Soviet Russia and Eastern Europe), Carmen Reinhart from the [Pete] Peterson Institute for International Economics, the Bank of England's Andy Haldane, Henry Kaufman, and other New World Order elites.

They came to plot new ways for global financial control, plunder and profits. Topics discussed included:

- The emerging economic and political order: what lies ahead?
- Bretton Woods: what can we learn from the past in designing the future?
- Getting back on track: macroeconomic management after a financial crisis.
- Sovereignty and institutional design in the global age: the global market and the nation states.

- Can sovereignty and effective international supervision be reconciled: the challenge of large complex financial institutions.
- Exploring complexity in economic theory.
- The political economy of structural adjustment: understanding the obstacles to cooperation.
- The market or the state: can market forces deliver innovation, education, and infrastructure?
- Sustainable economic systems.
- Optimal currency areas and governance: the challenge of Europe.
- The architecture of Asia: financial structure and an emerging economic system, and
- Rising to the challenge: equity, adjustment and balance in the world economy.

A Final Comment

Globalist Soros believes the American empire should be replaced by world government with a global currency under UN rule. In other words, he wants national sovereignty replaced by centralized control over money, populations, resources and markets. If established, it would be an undemocratic ruler-serf society unfit to live in except for leaders and profiteers.

On January 25, 2010, *New York Times* writer Andrew Sorkin headlined, "Still Needed: A Sheriff of Finance," quoting Soros as saying ahead of the 2008 World Economic Forum in Davos, Switzerland: "We need a global sheriff"

Perhaps he has himself in mind.

ENDNOTES

1 <http://www.mindfully.org/WTO/2003/George-Soros Statesman 2jun 03.htm>

9

GOLDMAN SACHS

MAKING MONEY BY STEALING IT

Money power in private hands and democracy can't co-exist. Wall Street crooks have transformed America into an unprecedented money making racket.

Goldman Sachs symbolizes Master of the Universe manipulative fraud. It's been involved in nearly all financial scandals since the 19th century. It makes money the old-fashioned way. It steals it through fraud, grand theft, market front-running and manipulation, scamming investors, bribing political Washington, installing its executives in top administration posts, and getting open-ended low or no interest bailouts when needed. Its business model and culture assure billions of bonus dollars for company officials, complicit traders, and others on the take. It's more like a crime family than a bank. It's part of a coterie of others like it on Wall Street that includes corrupt politicians.

Compared to Goldman, Bernie Madoff was small-time. So are most other swindlers. Those who matter sit in Wall Street board rooms, plotting other scams. Bill Black, former bank regulator expert on white-collar crime, public finance, economics, and related law, explained Goldman shenanigans pertaining to earlier SEC charges this way:

> Goldman designed a rigged trifecta. It turned a massive loss into a material profit by selling deeply underwater, toxic CDOs it owned. It helped make John Paulson (CEO of a huge hedge fund that Goldman would love to have as an ally) a massive profit—in a 'profession' where reciprocal favors are key, and blew up its customers that purchased the CDOs.[1]

An SEC civil suit charged Goldman with defrauding customers. Goldman had made billions, and the suit was settled for $550 million—pocket change, the equivalent of four 2009 revenue days. It hardly mattered. No executive was fined or imprisoned.

Grand theft continues unabated. It includes fraudulent pump-and-dump schemes. Major media scoundrels don't explain what is going on to the public. Only the scammed customers and the insiders complicit in the dirty game understand.

On March 4, 2012, Bill Black used James Q. Wilson's "broken windows" metaphor pertaining to blue collar crime, applying it to far more serious elite white-collar offenses. But none rise to the level of financial crimes. The amounts involved and the degree of destruction are staggering. Broken lives, communities, and economies result. The landscape's littered with them.

No firm is more adept at amassing fraudulent fortunes than Goldman. With stupefying arrogance, its CEO, Lloyd Blankfein, calls what he does "doing God's work." But what's worse is to see the Supreme Court rulings make banks and other financial entities immune from charges of securities fraud by those they have harmed. Only Washington may sue for redress.

It's also appalling that Murdoch's *Wall Street Journal* "serve[s] as cheerleader and apologist for those" who amass wealth by stealing it, said Black.

Goldman Executive Resigns

Broken clocks are right twice a day. On March 14, so was *The New York Times*. It gave rare op-ed space to high level Goldman executive Greg Smith for views worth sharing. He served as executive director and head of the firm's domestic equity derivatives business in Europe, the Middle East and Africa. Headlining, "Why I Am Leaving Goldman Sachs,"[2] Smith wrote that after almost 12 years with the firm, today was his last day. He had worked there "long enough to understand the trajectory of its culture, its people and its identity. And I can honestly say that the environment now is as toxic and destructive as I have ever seen it."

In "simplest terms," he said client interests are sidelined. Goldman thinks only about making money. "The firm has veered so far from the place I joined right out of college that I can no longer in good conscience say that I identify with what it stands for."

In less blunt terms than Black, this writer, and other critics, Smithe stopped short of labeling its grand theft model as such, but comments he made suggested it. An earlier Goldman culture contributed to its success, he said. "It revolved around teamwork, integrity, a spirit of humility, and always doing right by our clients."

Exaggerated? According to Smith, "virtually no trace" of what he admired remains. Whatever pride he once had is now gone. It was time to leave when he no longer could look aspiring students wanting Goldman jobs "in the eye and tell them what a great place this was to work."

How can Goldman be operating like a crime family? Simple. Its business model involves grand theft. Customers are defrauded, not helped. Politicians are bought like toothpaste. Laws are subverted and ignored. Others are discarded or rewritten at its behest. Entire economies are wrecked for profit.

When future Goldman histories are written, Smith said, honest ones will say Blankfein, president Gary Cohn, and other top executives "lost hold of the firm's culture on their watch. I truly believe that this decline in the firm's moral fiber represents the single most serious threat to its long-run survival."

Smith said his career involved advising two of the largest global hedge funds, five of America's largest asset managers, and three of the Middle East's most prominent sovereign wealth funds. His clients manage over a trillion dollars in assets.

He took pride in advising them "to do what I believe is right for them, even if it means less money for the firm. This view is becoming increasingly unpopular at Goldman Sachs." He knew it was time to leave. "Leadership used to be about ideas, setting an example and doing the right thing. Today, if you make enough money for the firm (and are not currently an ax murderer), you will be promoted into a position of influence."

Three key ways to make that money:

(1) Advise clients to invest in assets Goldman wants to dump, including toxic ones.

(2) Get clients to buy what makes Goldman most money.

(3) Trade "any illiquid, opaque product with a three-letter acronym," no matter how toxic or without merit.

Smith attended sales meetings devoid of seeking ways to help Goldman clients. Instead the focus was on maximizing Goldman's profit, no matter how illegally. "It makes me ill," he said, "how callously people talk about ripping their clients off. Over the last 12 months, I have seen five different managing directors refer to their own clients as 'muppets.'"

The firm's own clients are marks to be manipulated and scammed for profit. Smith can't explain why senior managers don't understand that losing client trust means forfeiting their business, no matter if you're the smartest guys in the room. They'll know you're smart enough to scam them without having to hear back room insults about "muppets," "ripping eballs out," and "getting paid" at their expense. He hopes his article :an be a wake-up call " to Goldman's board. "Make the client the focal oint of your business again. Without clients you will not make money. ın fact, you will not exist."

"Weed out the morally bankrupt people, no matter how much money they make for the firm." Make "people want to work here for the right reasons. People who care only about making money will not sustain this firm—or the trust of its clients—for very much longer."

A Final Comment

Goldman's entire history, or at least most of it, reflects predation. Its scams pre-date Smith's birth. In the 1920s, its Ponzi scheme investment trusts defrauded investors. Goldman profited. They lost out, and when Wall Street crashed, they were left high, dry, and broke.

One trust sold to investors reflected standard Goldman practice in relation to others. Its offering price was $104 a share. It soon became virtually worthless at $1.75, losing over 98% of its value. Unwary buyers then and now lose out. Only the stakes keep on getting bigger.

Today the stakes are enormous. Getting in bed with Goldman is like swimming with sharks. You're prey. They're predators. Those burned understand Goldman's culture enough to know it's toxic and corrupted.

In 2002, Goldman was largely responsible for Greece's debt problems, assisting government borrowers in circumventing Eurozone rules in return for mortgaging assets.

Using creative accounting, the debt was hidden through off-balance sheet shenanigans. Derivatives called cross-currency swaps were used. Government debt was issued in dollars and yen was swapped for euros, then later exchanged back to the original currencies.

Debt entrapment followed. Greece was held hostage to repay it, leaving the country raped and pillaged. Paying bankers comes first. Doing it has left Greeks impoverished, high and dry. Goldman profited enormously by scamming an entire country and its innocent millions who had nothing to do with that first dirty deal. Its business model thrives on re-enacting similar schemes globally. It's about profits, no matter the huge cost to others. Expecting this leopard to change spots is like imagining reformers will transform Washington.

Former alderman Paddy Bauler once said "Chicago ain't ready for reform." It's still not ready and may never be.

Neither is political Washington, Goldman, other Wall Street crooks, or their counterparts throughout corporate America. They connive, cheat, profiteer from wars, drain trillions from households and